LONGMANS, GREEN AND CO.
55 FIFTH AVENUE, NEW YORK
221 EAST 20TH STREET, CHICAGO
88 TREMONT STREET, BOSTON
128 UNIVERSITY AVENUE, TORONTO

LONGMANS, GREEN AND CO. Ltd.
39 PATERNOSTER ROW, E C 4, LONDON
6 OLD COURT HOUSE STREET, CALCUTTA
53 NICOL ROAD, BOMBAY
36A MOUNT ROAD, MADRAS

E. F. BENSON

AS WE WERE

A VICTORIAN PEEP SHOW

By

E. F. BENSON

AUTHOR OF "DODO," "SIR FRANCIS DRAKE," ETC.

LONGMANS, GREEN AND CO.

LONDON · NEW YORK · TORONTO

MDCCCCXXXI

CONTENTS

NOTE

I HAVE to thank the Fellows of Trinity College, Cambridge, for their great courtesy in giving me the fullest possible access to the diary and private papers of my father which are the property of the College Library.

E. F. BENSON

LIST OF ILLUSTRATIONS

AS WE WERE
A Victorian Peep Show

AS WE WERE

A VICTORIAN PEEP SHOW

CHAPTER I

THE PINCUSHION

PERHAPS the pincushion will make as good a beginning as anything, that peerless object of the period, dated beyond dispute or discussion or suspicion, for which I have dived so sedulously and so fruitlessly into drawers full of Victorian relics, seeking it like a pearl in depths long undisturbed by any questing hand. But though I cannot find it, the search was richly rewarded in other respects, for it brought to light treasures long forgotten, but instantly and intimately familiar when seen again: there was a dog-eared book of manuscript music, containing among other ditties the famous tear-compelling song "Willy, we have missed you," there was a pair of goblets incredible even when actually beheld and handled, chalice-shaped, of cloudy pink glass outlined in gilt: there was a globular glass paper-weight, in which were embedded, like a layer of flies in amber, small gaudy objects, vastly magnified and resembling sections of jam-roll and sea-anemones: and there were oval cards with pictures of flowers on them, which once certainly belonged to the apparatus of the round game called "Floral Lotto" so justly popular in the seventies. But the pearl of great price, the pincushion, did not discover itself to my divings, and its disappearance is a matter of deep regret to me, for it must have been very rare and marvellous even when it was quite

1

new, and if it was in my possession today I would confidently challenge the world to produce a similar specimen. But when I force myself to think dispassionately of it, I realize that it would be now sixty-six years old, so that even if I could put my hand on all of it that is mortal, I should but find there shreds of disintegrated red velvet and scattered beads, of which the thread had long perished. Yet since it was (though not new when I first saw it) one of the earliest objects to which I gave my unstinted admiration, I can describe the sumptuous manner of it with a very minute fidelity, for it is one of those memories of early childhood, photographed on my mind in colours as bright as itself.

Picture then (with an effort) a domed and elliptical oblong, the sides of which below the dome were perpendicular. Its scale, shape and size were those of a blancmange for not less than eight people: such was the pincushion. It was covered, dome and sides alike, with rich crimson velvet, and round the lower edge of the dome ran a floral pattern, worked in white glass beads, slightly opalescent. Down the perpendicular sides it was draped with many tassels of these, swinging free, and on the top of the dome was worked a Royal Crown, also of beads. So majestic and unusual an object, though strictly in the finest taste of the period, must have been made to order, or, at the very least, the Royal Crown must have been added to it, in order that the pincushion should worthily fill the very special part for which it was cast in the year 1864. Its one official appearance, the scene in which, behind closed doors, it stood on a certain dressing-table ready to perform the function which was the cause of its sumptuous existence was only brief: indeed we shall never know whether it actually ever functioned at all. But it was there, it was ready, it was worthy, and in order to make clear the full situation, it is necessary lightly to sketch the previous act of the drama in which it may have played (though I repeat that we shall never know whether it did) its dumb but distinguished rôle. For the moment the pincushion vanishes waiting for the cue of its first appearance.

Wellington College, founded in memory of the great Duke, was opened in 1859, and my father not yet thirty years of age, was appointed first head-master. It was intended to provide a good education on special terms for the sons of officers in the army whose widows were in needy circumstances, but other boys were to be admitted as well, and its charter was that of a public school. The Prince Consort was Chairman of the governing body and, for the very short remainder of his life, its welfare was a constant interest to him, and the subject of innumerable memoranda. At his desire, my father had spent the summer of 1858 in Germany and Prussia, in order to study the methods of education in the academies of the Fatherland: the Prince Consort hoped that he would pick up some useful hints as to the general lines on which Wellington College should be conducted. This hope was not realized, for he came back with a profound conviction that English methods were vastly superior to those which he had gone abroad to study, and that there were no hints whatever to be gained from Germany.

A few months after the school was opened, he married my mother, then just eighteen years of age, and they lived in a house that was part of the College building. The numbers were not large at first, and every evening after prayers, which the whole school attended, she shook hands with every individual boy and wished him good night; she was universally known as "Mother Benjy," being at the most two or three years older than the senior boys.

The boys at first wore a uniform approved and partly designed by the Prince Consort, and it remarkably resembled that of the porters and ticket-collectors of the South Eastern railway on which Wellington College was situated. This gave rise to little confusions. Lord Derby, for instance, when paying a visit to the College on the annual Speech-day, presented the outward half of his return ticket to a

boy who had come down to the station to meet his mother,
and the boy was not as respectful as he should have been to
a member of the governing body and permitted himself to
say something unbecoming to a well-behaved ticket-collector.
It was better therefore to modify the uniform than risk the
recurrence of such incidents. The Prince Consort was still
inclined to think that German academical methods were in
many points more desirable than the freer and more self-
governing notions of the English public school in which
senior boys have a hand in discipline: he did not approve of
the fagging system, he did not like compulsory games, and
he objected to masters (other than the head-master) having
the power to cane their pupils, for one master (so he pointed
out in a memorandum) would almost certainly be stronger
than another and a more savage disciplinarian, and thus
certain boys would suffer more than others for similar faults,
which was obviously unfair. Then there was the question of
the school chapel: he thought (with a great deal of reason)
that contemporary English architecture was in a very poor
way, and proposed that the new chapel should be an exact
model of the chapel at Eton, one third of the size and built
of brick. This diabolical design was not carried out. But
with that sound wisdom which always characterized him, he
very soon saw that the English were not as the Germans and
that German methods were incompatible with English ideas,
and to the time of his most lamentable death in 1861, he
backed up the head-master, who indeed was a very forcible
man, with the utmost zeal and good-will, and Wellington
developed on native lines.

Swiftly those lines shot out, the head-master was personally astride of each of them; great and small they all were
directly under his indefatigable eye. There were stone-
masons at work on the capitals of the columns in the gateway
to the chapel about to execute conventional volutes and
sprays of a nameless foliage. He insisted that instead they
should carve the images of the flora and fauna indigenous

to the district. Squirrels must peer out of tassels of fir-leaves and pine-cones, and rabbits from fronds of hart's-tongue fern and heather and osmunda. There had been much ado about the chapel, when the Eton design was turned down: at first the Governors would only vote £2500 for its building, and so he started a private subscription in order to raise a chapel worthy of the memory of the great Duke and not merely "a frightful and indestructible meeting-house." He made his staff of masters feel that they were helping to construct a noble institution and they must give their whole time and energies to its accomplishment.

Certainly he gave his own: one evening there arrived for him the printed agenda of the business to be put before the meeting of the Governors next day in London, and he felt that the facts of a case on which their votes would be taken had not been adequately presented to them. So down he went after dinner to the book-shop where printing could be done, and there wrote out a long exposition of what he thought it was needful they should know before making their decision. Page after page as he wrote it, he handed to the printer to be put into type at once, and then all this had to be corrected and revised and fresh pulls must be made of it. It was finished and ready as morning broke after an all-night sitting, and he sent off a number of the little pamphlets to the members of the governing body, so that all might read a clear printed statement of his views before the business in hand came before them. . . There was a hard frost one week in winter, continuing for several nights and the whole school was eager to go skating and sliding on the lake. But no boy was permitted to set foot on the ice, till the head-master himself had traversed it and stamped upon it and assured himself that it was safe. But there was no skating for the school that day for the ice gave way under him and he fell in. The college porter wrote a remarkable and sympathetic poem on this disaster.

Then he set to work to compile a hymn-book for use in his new chapel, and this must contain renderings, the best available, of the great Latin hymns. They would often, he knew, be of rather doggerel sort, but they would wake the boys' interest in such great songs as "Vexilla Regis" and "Aurora nunc." He contributed several himself, and among them was "O throned, O crowned with all renown," one of the stateliest poems in the whole English hymnology. Then there must be a book of tunes to which they should be sung, and the compilation of this was indeed a feat of daring. Well-known tunes, not in copyright, like "Adeste Fideles" and Haydn's "Austrian anthem" would be included, but these would not supply sufficient melodies. So a lady called Miss Moultrie, whom he held to have high musical gifts, was called in, and by request she composed a quantity of hymn-tunes herself for this book, and when her own invention failed, she took such airs as the opening lines of one of Beethoven's Violin Sonatas, and Spohr's "How blessed are the departed," and chiselled them with ruthless carpentry into hymn-tunes of the required length and rhythm, cutting out a bar here and a half-bar there, and, where necessary, writing in extra parts. It is pleasant to picture the meetings of this musical committee; at which my father who knew nothing whatever about music of any sort, listened to Miss Moultrie playing original or adapted airs on the piano. If they were orginal and passed his audition they appeared in the hymn-book as Miss Moultrie's own: if she had utilized the ideas of other composers, the fact was duly acknowledged, and they were "from" Beethoven or Spohr. My mother assisted, and, I think, the chapel organist who kept a bookshop, but they were not of much account. Miss Moultrie was the Muse and, like Polyhymnia, her hymns were many. The Prince Consort contributed a Chorale.

AFTER the Prince Consort's death, Queen Victoria who had paid several visits to Wellington with him did not come down again (the pincushion moves nearer) till 1864, though in the interval she had sent for the head-master to come to see her at Windsor and tell her of the welfare of the school in which her husband had taken so keen an interest. She hoped it prospered: she would always take an interest in it herself and intended that her son Prince Arthur, now Duke of Connaught, who was a godson of the Duke of Wellington, should do the same. Before long she would come and see for herself how it had developed; she had meant to do so before, but she was overwhelmed with work and responsibilities. "While the Prince Consort lived," she said, "he thought for me, now I have to think for myself." On the table in the ante-room to the chamber where the interview took place there were laid out his gloves and his white wide-awake hat as on the day when he had last used them.

The visit was arranged: the Queen still in the very deepest mourning drove down from Windsor, in a landau with four horses and postilions, and was received by the staff at the gate of the College. She walked about the place full of sentiment and homeliness and dignity, showing a shrewd interest in all that concerned domestic arrangements for the boys. She wept a little over the foundation stone of the chapel, which had been laid by the Prince Consort and above which now rose a very seemly building though not of the same design as Eton College chapel: she insisted on visiting one of the dormitories, where she found that the maids had not yet finished their makings of beds and emptying of slops, and told them to carry on: she went into the class-rooms of the fifth and sixth forms, shook hands with every boy there, and asked him his name: she looked with doubtful approval on the tuck-shop, and said that in her opinion the young gentlemen would get on quite as well without so many sweets, and then she came across to the newly built Master's Lodge, where my mother, a mature matron now of twenty-three years of age, and dressed in the latest and most stupendous fashion of the day, was at the door

to receive her.   Then the Queen must see the nursery where
she found two small boys, Martin and Arthur, aged four
and two, and a baby girl not yet a year old.   She kissed
them and hoped they were good boys, and Martin who had
been regarding her with grave wide eyes, could stand it no
longer, and with a burst of laughter told her that she had
a very funny bonnet, which was probably the case.   After
that my mother conducted her to the best spare bedroom
to make herself tidy for lunch, and there were smart bows
on the supports of the looking-glass, and a cascade of ornamental paper shavings in the grate, like the skirt of a smart
lady whose body and head were up the chimney, and a can
of hot water with a woolwork cosy over it, and on the mantel
piece the pink glass goblets and a malachite clock, and on
the dressing-table that wondrous pincushion, then quite new,
which I have not been able to find.   There the Queen was
left to make herself tidy for lunch, and, as I have said, we
shall never know whether the pincushion was used or whether
it had to be content to be beautiful.   After lunch she planted
a tree in the garden and asked for an extra week of summer
holiday for the school "if it is quite approved."   These were
all great doings, but they seem to radiate like beams of light
from that effulgent centre, the pincushion.

IT WAS not till early in the next decade that I was in a position to take any definite, personal notice of the world of
Wellington, but then some very engaging film pictures begin
to flicker and fix themselves on the square of illumination.
There was a most agreeable clergyman (though from his
Norfolk jacket and knickerbockers you could not have been
expected to guess his sacred calling) who used to come over
from the neighbouring parish of Eversley, where he was rector, to see his son who was a boy in the school.   My parents
were great friends of his.   He smoked his pipe while he
walked with my father in the garden (and this was a very
daring thing to do, for tobacco was an abomination to him)

and he stammered in an attractive manner, because, so I supposed, he preferred to talk like that, and he lay on his face in the heather and peered about among the wiry stems of it to observe beetles and caterpillars. With him came his wife, and her visits were very welcome, for she never forgot her duties as godmother to myself, and she gave me an enthralling book called the "Water-babies," which her husband had written, and several of Edward Lear's books of nonsense rhymes. At the back of my mind there is a belief, though it is dim and hazy, that Edward Lear himself came over with her one day, and I think he had a beard. But I have no sort of real recollection of him: his appearance and general habit (if he came at all) must have been eclipsed by his distinction in knowing so many remarkable and amusing people, for there was no doubt at all that he numbered among his actual friends the man on the Humber, who dined on a cake of burnt umber, and the old person of Looe who said "What on earth shall I do?" and him who made tea in his hat, and him in whose beard such an embarrassing variety of birds habitually nested. All these were real people, and Mr Lear was fortunate enough to know them and make pictures of them. He impressed himself on my memory less vividly than they, for the man's friends were greater than he, and he realized that and very properly recorded them in immortal rhyme. That he himself was an exquisite artist in landscape was, of course, a piece of later knowledge: later also emerged the fact that he had taught drawing to Queen Victoria in the early days of her reign. One day, when she had finished her lesson, she asked him whether he would care to see her collection of miniatures, and they went into the room at Windsor Castle where were the cases containing that unique series. But Mr Lear did not think very much of them; perhaps miniatures seemed rather simpering and lifeless to one who was accustomed to render the faces of his friends in the grip of such various and powerful emotions. He sniffed and shook his head over them, he gave them only the cursory glances of indifference, and doubtfully asked the Queen where she had "got" them (as if she had picked them up at some second-hand dealers). She very courteously replied "I inherited them, Mr Lear." So there was not very much more to be said about that.

Then there was Aunt Emmeline, my father's sister: she is a static and semi-recumbent figure in these moving pictures of mine because all that I knew of her was that she lay in bed, and "had" bronchitis (just as she might have had a dog or a canary). Quite unconnected in my mind with bronchitis was the fact that a kettle stood by her bedside over a spirit-lamp with steam puffing from a tube attached to the spout of it, and Aunt Emmeline amused herself by holding it near her mouth and inhaling it. This was an odd diversion but not interesting for long, as it did not lead to anything. Far more vivid and highly enviable was Grandmamma Sidgwick, behind whom, when she went to attend service in the school chapel, there walked a servant carrying her Bible, her prayer-book, her Wellington College hymn-book, and the book of tunes compiled and largely composed by Miss Moultrie. She herself carried a beadbag containing her handkerchief and a vinaigrette, inside which was a tiny piece of sponge soaked in aromatic vinegar. All ladies of any refinement in those days were apt to feel faint in church, when they had to stand up without moving for so long a time: the less stout-hearted sat down, but the braver sort, like Grandmamma, continued standing with the refreshment of a tonic sniff at the pierced gold lid of their vinaigrettes, if the psalms were lengthy. Crinolines, I regret to say, were dead before my memory was alive, and she wore a maize-coloured silk dress with many flounces of lace down the front of the skirt, from underneath which, as she walked, only the tips of her toes appeared. On her head was a bonnet with purple strings, tied underneath her chin, and, according to the weather, she wore a seal-skin jacket or an Indian shawl of many colours. Am I wrong in thinking

that she held in her hand a chain with a hook or a clip at the
end of it, which prevented her skirt from trailing in the
mud ?

In the evening she was more sumptuous still. I used to
be privileged to see the final stages of her toilet when she
dressed for dinner, and to this day I cannot help believing that her jewellery, kept in a large walnut-wood box with
mother-of-pearl inlaid on the lid, was inexhaustible. Never
could I complete the examination of these treasures down to
the lowest tray. There was a necklace of garnets, consist-
ing of delicate six-rayed stars, with earrings and brooch to
match, a necklace of jet for sad anniversaries, a brooch of
diamonds with a ruby in the centre, another representing a
large bunch of white grapes, of which each several berry was
a pearl, encompassed by gold vine-leaves, another of mosaic
work in minute coloured tesseræ showing a classical ruin,
another a cameo of my father's head in profile set in solid
sausages of gold. There was a bracelet, swarming like an
ant-heap with small turquoises; a memorial bracelet, made
entirely of the hair of some defunct relative with a clasp
of emeralds and pearls, and one of broad gold with circular
Wedgwood plaques let into it, and enamelled lockets also
containing hair. By day and for evening toilet as well she,
like every Christian lady of the time, wore a gold cross round
her neck.

She had smooth brown hair on which mystic rites were
performed, and these perhaps were the most thrilling of all.
First of all she let her hair down, and drew thick tresses of
it (as much as she required) from the centre of her forehead in curving eaves over the tops of her ears, so that the
lobes of them only remained visible, and, holding these strands
firmly in place, she applied to them a brown stick of adhesive
cosmetic called "bandoline," till the hair which formed these
eaves was glued together in one shining surface like a polished
board: then the rest was twisted up at the back of her head
in a chignon. Sometimes one of these boards cracked, and

then more bandoline was applied till it again presented an unbroken area. Then she put on her evening cap, and her stiff satin dress with arms reaching to the elbow and trimmed with lace, and her maid buckled brooches all over it, and clasped the selected necklace round her neck, and proffered a choice of bracelets for her wrists. She would perhaps be occupying the best spare room, and on her dressing-table where first I saw it, stood the famous pincushion and her ring-stand, a little china tree with bare branches on which she hung her rings, among which were always one or two which contained memorial hair. She besprinkled her handkerchief with *eau de Cologne* from a cut-glass bottle and smeared a little on her forehead to refresh her after the labours of the toilet, and with fan and scent bottle and cashmere shawl and bead-bag and crochet and vinaigrette and that album of manuscript music containing "Willie we have missed you" and little pieces for the piano, such as "Yorkshire Bells" and catches for concerted voices such as

> *A boat, a boat unto the ferry,*
> *And we'll go over and be merry,*
> *And laugh and quaff and drink brown sherry.*

Grandmamma was ready, on the stroke of seven, to descend the pitch-pine staircase in the Master's Lodge, and spend a quiet evening with her daughter and son-in-law.

I pranced downstairs with her, feeling that this dainty and aged figure was somehow my handiwork by reason of the help I had given her in dressing, to say good night to my parents before they went in to dinner, my father giving his arm to my grandmother and my mother walking behind. Or, if Grandmamma got down a little ahead of time, she sat in a green velvet chair in my mother's sitting-room, waiting for the gong to sound. On the table beside her stood two rosewood work-boxes, hers and my mother's: the latter of these, to the best of my knowledge, was very seldom used for industrial purposes, but it contained white china elephants and amber beads and other agreeable toys. But Grandmamma was a worker, and now she took out her crochet from her bead-bag, or her sewing from her work-box, to make the most of these moments of waiting. If she wanted something from the table which was out of her reach as she sat in her green velvet chair, she need not rise to get it, for she had been careful to put her "lazy-tongs" close at hand. . . How difficult is is to describe that anciently familiar weapon ! There were two looped handles to it, like those of a pair of scissors, then a crisscross of silver-plated bars, at the other end of which was a pair of metal claws. As you pressed the handles together with thumb and forefinger inserted, the criss-cross of bars elongated itself, the claws approached each other, fixed themselves on the desired object, picked it up, and brought it within reach. Sargent ought to have painted her when she was old, or made a drawing of her full of antique daintiness: as a young woman the elder Richmond made a delicious finished little sketch of her. . . Then the gong boomed, and the three went in to dinner. On warm still nights of summer the table was laid in the garden on the gravel path outside the drawing-room windows which opened down to the ground, and leaning out of the nursery window upstairs I could see this romantic banquet in progress before I was taken away for bath and bed. There was a crib in the night nursery now, and a small pink creature called Hugh slept there. At present he had no conversation.

These early memories are no doubt unwittingly supplemented with information learned afterwards, which has dripped into them, and it is not worth while even if it were possible, to strain the two apart. Certainly I could never have witnessed a dinner-party in the early seventies, but I seem to know a great deal about it, partly from having been permitted by the butler to observe the magnificent preparations for it, partly from having personally watched through the bannisters of the gallery that overhung the hall the arrival of the guests, and partly from having been told later by my mother the manner of these Garantuan feasts. But I can testify how immense was the perspective of the monstrous, round-backed mahogany chairs of the period that lined the elongated dining-room table. Upon it stood a pair of branched candlesticks and other lesser lights, and for centre piece there was a wondrous silver *épergne*. Upon the ornamented base of it reclined a camel with a turbaned Arab driver: he leaned against the trunk of a tall palm-tree that soared upwards straight and bare for a full eighteen inches. At the top of this majestic stem there spread out all round the feathery fronds of its foliage, and resting on them (though in reality firmly screwed into the top of the palm-trunk) stood a bowl of cut glass filled with moist sand. In this was planted a bower of roses and of honeysuckle which trailed over the silver leaves of the palm-tree and completed the oasis for the Arab and his camel. Against the long dining-room wall stood a great oak sideboard below a steel engraving of the "Last Supper" by Leonardo da Vinci: beside this hung another steel engraving of the Prince Consort with his wide-awake in his hand. This sideboard had two fine panels from some sixteenth-century reredos let into the back, and the artificers of Wardour Street had built up the rest round them: it was considered very handsome. On it stood a row of decanters of port, sherry, and claret, and the dessert service made by Copeland, late Spode. And now the tapestry curtains were drawn with a clash of rings over the windows, and the candles were lit, and I was haled away from this glittering cave of Aladdin and hurried upstairs on the first sound of the front-door bell, breathlessly to watch from the passage that ran round the hall, the arrival of the splendid guests. The men put down their hats and coats in the outer hall and then waited by the fireplace of the inner hall (of which through the bannisters, over them, I commanded so admirable a view), for the emergence of their ladies from my mother's sitting-room where the work-boxes and lazy-tongs had been put away and pins and brushes and look-ing-glasses provided for their titivation. They had gone in mere chrysalises, swathed in shawls and plaids; they emerged magnificent butterflies, all green and pink and purple. As each came floating forth, her husband offered her his arm and they went thus into the drawing-room. When all were assembled the gong boomed, and out they came again, hav-ing changed partners, and the galaxy passed into the glitter-ing cave of Aladdin next door. Grace was said, and they sat down to the incredible banquet.

There was thick soup and clear soup (a nimble gourmand had been known to secure both). Clear soup in those days had a good deal of sherry in it. There was a great boiled turbot with his head lolling over one end of the dish and his tail over the other: then came a short pause, while at the four corners of the table were placed four entrées. Two were brown entrées, made of beef, mutton, or venison, two were white entrées made of chicken, brains, rabbit, or sweet-breads, and these were handed round in pairs ("Brown or White, Madam?"). Then came a joint made of the brown meat which had not figured in the brown entrées, or if only beef and mutton were in season, the joint might be a boiled ham. My mother always carved this herself, instead of my father: this was rather daring, rather modern, but she carved with swift artistic skill and he did not, and she invariably refused the offer of her neighbouring gentlemen to relieve her of her task. Then came a dish of birds, duck, or game, and a choice followed between substantial puddings and more airy confections covered with blobs of cream and jewels of angelica and ornamental Gothic sugarings. A Stilton cheese succeeded and then dessert. My mother collected the ladies' eyes, and the ladies collected their fans and scent-bottles and scarves, and left the gentlemen to their wine. Smoking was not dreamed of at the after-dinner sittings of this date: the smell would assuredly hang about the dining-room, and no gentleman could possibly talk to a lady in the drawing-room after he had thus befouled himself. When he wished to smoke later on in the evening, he always changed his dinner-coat lest it should get infected ever so faintly with the odour so justly abhorred by the other sex, and put on a smoking-jacket, very smart, padded and braided and be-frogged, while for fear that his hair should be similarly tainted, he wore a sort of embroidered forage-cap. Thus attired for his secret and masculine orgy, he slipped from his bedroom after the ladies had gone upstairs and with his flat candle in hand, joined his fellow conspirators, as in a charade, in some remote pantry or gun-room, where his padded coat would keep him fairly warm.

In these festive evenings of the seventies prolonged drink-ing of port and claret had gone out, smoking had not yet come in, and so when the decanters of port and claret had gone round twice, and sherry had been offered (it was called a white-wash), the host rang the bell for coffee. The men then joined the ladies, and the ladies who had been chatter-ing together in a bunch, swiftly broke up, like scattered globules of quicksilver, so that next each of them should be a vacant chair, into which a man inserted himself, prudently avoiding those who had been his neighbours at dinner. A number of conversational duets then took place, but these did not last long, for there was certain to be a lady present who sang very sweetly, or had a lovely "touch" on the piano (indeed it was more probable that they all sang and played delightfully) and now it was her hour, and her hostess en-treated her to play one of those beautiful "Songs without Words" by Mr Mendelssohn, who had taught music to Queen Victoria, or sing a song with words. She was not sure if she had brought her music, but it always turned out that her husband had done so, and had left the portfolio with his hat and coat in the outer hall. By the time he returned with the melodious volume, another gentleman had escorted her to the piano, and had been granted the privilege of turning over for her. She explained that she was terribly out of practice, as she put down on the candle-brackets of the piano her gloves, her fan, her handkerchief, and, if she was about to play, her rings and her bracelets also, and thus stripped for the fray, she cleared her throat, and ran her fingers up and down the keys with the much-admired "butterfly touch," as a signal for the clatter of talk to cease. The audience assumed expressions of regretful melancholy if the music was sad, or of pensive gaiety if it was lively, and fixed their eyes on various points of the ceiling: the more musical instinctively beat time with their fingers or their fans. A brilliant execution was not considered very important, for music was an "elegant" accomplishment: touch and expression were more highly esteemed, a little tremolo in the voice was most affecting, and these were also easier to acquire than execution. Sentimentality was, in these little concerts, the quality most appreciated, and if a lady could induce the female portion of her audience surreptitiously to wipe a slight moisture from its eyes, and the males to clear their throats before, at the end of the performance there rose the murmur of "Oh, thank you, what a treat. Please don't get up yet !" she was stamped as an artist, the music as a masterpiece, and the audience as persons of sensibility. Such songs as "The Lost Chord" (words by my cousin Adelaide Anne Procter, music by Arthur Sullivan) were accepted as test-pieces for tears: the singer tried her strength with them, as if they were punching-machines at a fair which registered muscular force. If there was not a dry eye in the room when she had delivered her blow she was a champion. Men, on these occasions, were not asked to sing, unless they were notable comics: serious playing and singing were purely feminine accomplishments.

Or if (rarely) there was no music, there might be a game of some sort. Whist was unsociable, and demanded close attention: besides in those days, young women, it was well known, did not possess the sort of brain that could grapple

with its problems and were liable to trump their partners
best cards, or not trump their worst.   "Floral Lotto" was far
easier, both sexes could play that, and it was very exciting
to see your card covered with pictures of the common flowers
of the garden gradually filling up.   But whatever the diversions, they were all brief, for at ten o'clock in came a hissing
urn and the tea-table was spread.   The gentlemen handed
the ladies cups of tea, and little hot cakes and buns ("Might
I recommend you one of these with sugar on the top?") and
they nibbled and sipped and indulged in lively conversation,
in order to restore themselves after the harrowing emotions
caused by "The Lost Chord."   ("Beautifully sung, was it
not ?   Such expression !")   After tea, perhaps another
lady sang, or she who had made them cry or clear their
throats with the "Lost Chord" was prevailed on just as the
first carriage was announced, to give them "The Summer
Shower," and this she did in so arch and playful a manner that
everybody felt young and happy again instead of luxuri-
ously miserable, and hummed the tune as they put on their
wraps and rumbled away with smiles and compliments and
firm incredulity at the lateness of the hour.

Now such an evening as this, designed and appreciated
as an agreeable dissipation, seems to us now more socially
remote than the feasts of late Imperial Rome or the parties at
the Pavilion at Brighton during the heyday of the Regent,
and so no doubt it is.   Though we may assume that human
nature in the seventies was not *au fond* very different from
human nature fifty years before or fifty years later,
there was never surely a greater gulf than that which divides
the gaieties of this middle period from those that went before
and after.   Many of the differences no doubt between their
technique of amusement and ours are purely superficial.
There is not much to choose between the ladies and gentlemen who, without knowing or caring anything about music
listened to the "Lost Chord" and those who flock to operas
which so unspeakably bore them.   Music, then as now, was

for the majority a fashionable stunt. Nor does it much
signify whether you are offered two entrées during dinner, or
two cocktails before (probably the latter is the less deleteri-
ous in the long run) nor whether you play "Floral Lotto"
afterwards or Bridge. Again the anecdotes and small
salacities which men told each other then as they sat round
the gun-room in their wadded and befrogged smoking-
jackets did not probably differ very much in kind from those
which they occasionally retail to each other now, and we may
guess that women in their wrappers over their bedroom fires
hold much the same conferences as did their mothers. But
a real gulf, vastly sundering, lies between the two periods
in the matter of their "company manners" and in the conversation between the two sexes as they sat round the dinner-
table and the subsequent tea-urn. Certain topics, like the
weather, and the iniquities of the present Government, be it
Whig or Tory or Labour, must always have been, even as
they are now, substantial standing dishes to be lightly pecked
at. They talked of archery and croquet then, whereas we
talk of tennis and golf now, they talked of the wonders of
inventions, and the new Great Western Express which ran
its seventy-seven miles to Swindon without stop at the average
speed of fifty-three miles an hour, corresponded to the
aeroplane that winged its way across the Atlantic with its
solitary voyager: they talked of books and plays and these
topics have only varied according to the progressive achieve-
ments of the age. But when these were done, then yawns the
gulf, for men and women now discuss together everything
that they could only have spoken of before with the members
of their own sex. They laugh together over the yarns of
the smoking-room: a man recounts to his hostess the difficulties attending his wife's confinement, and she tells him
the nature of the evidence in the late divorce proceedings,
which caused the judge to clear the court. Sappho and
salversan, the culture of the lower colon and the nuptials of
Pekinese dogs are subjects of unembarrassed conversation

between the sexes, and with them they refresh their souls,
much as they refresh their untrammelled bodies with sun-baths
and mixed bathing. Whether such frankness and freedom
on topics of natural history and elimination and abnormality
is desirable or not is purely a matter of taste: nobody can
pronounce about it, and nobody should desire to do so, for
it is obviously proper that men and women should discuss
whatever they think it proper to discuss. And certainly, on
general principles, there is a great deal to be said in favour
of any besom that sweeps away the cobwebs of Victorian
conventionalism which harboured such dusty rubbish as the
axiom that no nice girl knew anything about anything till
she was married, and that if she remained a spinster she continued to believe that babies were found under the goose-
berry-bushes of the kitchen gardens of married couples, or
that the chance exposure of her calves to the lascivious gaze
of men was a shock to her modesty which could only be correctly expressed by a timely swoon. In those delicate days a
certain lady more distinguished for wealth than correct spell-
ing, wrote to the chairman of the Peninsular and Oriental
Company saying that she was going to India, and that she
hoped he could manage to secure her a comfortable "birth."
He replied that he would do his best, but that he could not
guarantee her against *mal de mère*. This was considered
witty but far from nice. Rightly or wrongly the Victorians
considered that there were certain subjects which were not
meet for inter-sexual discussion, just as they held that certain processes of the feminine toilet like the powdering of
the nose, and the application of lip-stick to the mouth were
(if done at all) better done in private. The Victorian reticences and secrecies may also have been profitable as well
as prudish: for my part I only wish to point out that the
differences between the tone of their topics and that of ours
was a real and an essential one, and not like the superficial
difference between smoking in the dining-room and smoking
only in the gun-room. Queen Victoria once imprudently

inquired from a male person of her court, on which part of the body were the rheumatic pains which had invalided one of her maids of honour, and since she had asked, he was obliged to tell her that they were in her legs. She replied, no doubt humorously, that when she came to the throne young ladies, like the memorable Queen of Spain, "did not use to have legs." But before she quitted the throne it had long leaked out that such was the indelicate fact. The seventies did not officially know it, but the eighties strongly suspected it, and the nineties considered it proved, though it was left to the young ladies of the next century to demonstrate it. In fact long before the Victorian age was over, the flare of the light-house which warned members of opposite sexes off those rocks which must always be given a wide berth in polite conversation flickered, burned low, and finally expired.

CHAPTER II

BUT WHAT was the history of this smiling oasis of bland respectability and sobriety into which the social caravans entered about the year 1840 and there so long and so decorously refreshed themselves ? The reason of their entry was reaction: they fled to it from another and far less edifying encampment, where there glittered the amazing domes and pinnacles of the Royal Pavilion at Brighton, popular with houris and harpies. For close on ten years after the death of its presiding genius they had wandered rather aimlessly, uncertain of their destination. Then Queen Victoria placed herself at their head and undeviatingly led them into this irreproachable environment. While it would be far too much to say that she caused this reaction, it is certain that she and the example set by her and the Prince Consort very strongly influenced it. Probably it would have come in any case, but without her it would scarcely have been so swift in its advance and of so overwhelming a momentum. The tide would have risen gradually instead of sweeping in with that toppling wave. She had had some rather dreadful uncles: George IV though credited, by reason of the inimitable grace of his bow and the dazzling quality of his waistcoats, with being the first gentleman in Europe was, more properly speaking, the first bounder in Europe, vain as a peacock, false to his friends and remorseless to those who had offended him, selfish, greedy, and quite devoid of decent principles. Of Hanoverian origin on her father's side, this daughter of the Duke of Kent and a princess of Saxe-Coburg had barely a drop of British blood in her veins. She married a German, she inherited the instincts of her race, but by virtue of her sense of duty and her shrewdness, she made herself the most English of sovereigns who had sat on the throne since the reign of Elizabeth, and became at once the most devoted servant of her people. These excellent gifts of hers were backed up with a will of iron, and though she may not have said, "They think I am a little girl but I will show them that I am Queen of England," it was exactly that which she did, which is more to the point. England, though she was German, was her country, and the English were her people, and she knit the monarchy, which indeed was getting very much frayed and tattered, into a most durable piece. In order to understand just what it was that so completely crashed in the eighties and the nineties, it is necessary to form some idea of the character of the woman who to so substantial an extent founded the tradition of the earlier decades of her reign. She largely helped to make it, and she fashioned herself into the mirror which reflected it.

Queen Victoria was a woman of peerless common sense; her common sense, which is a rare gift at any time, amounted to genius. She had been brought up by her mother with the utmost simplicity, and she retained it to the end, and conducted her public and private life alike by that infallible guide. She had no imagination, no flight of fancy ever bore her away, she looked very steadily with her rather prominent blue eyes on every situation that presented itself, and made up her mind as to what was the respectable and the sensible thing to do. But she had a sort of dual personality, which often supplies the key to the odd complexities and complications that she sometimes exhibited. One entity in her was that of Her Majesty the Queen of England, supreme (and determined to exercise her supremacy and to demand the due recognition of it) in all questions that concerned the welfare of her realm; the other entity was that of a very shrewd *bourgeoise*. No human being of whom we have record, with the possible exception of Shakespeare, has possessed both imagination and common sense equally developed in a very high degree, for imagination gets dulled by common sense and the bright mirror is clouded, while common sense gets dazzled by imagination. There was no such disturbing glitter in the Queen's mind: common sense poured out from her, grey and strong, like the waters of the Amazon. Her intense admirer, Lord Beaconsfield, himself highly imaginative, once said that if he wanted to forecast the effect of some Parliamentary measure on the minds of the middle-class, and distrusted his own judgment, he always consulted the Queen, and always found he had been right in accepting her opinion. But it was not because she had imagination that she could foretell with such faultless precision what the middle-class would feel. She was identical (in this piece of her personality) with the governing class of her subjects, which she saw, long before any of her ministers perceived it, was no longer the aristocracy who then were the landlords of the greater part of English soil, but the middle-class. She had that strain in herself: she needed no imagination in order to picture what they would feel, because she knew. Thus Lord Beaconsfield's dictum which has been so often and so erroneously taken to mean that she was a woman of commonplace mind had no such intention, but was in reality an expression of his highest admiration for her judgment. Her mind was not in the least commonplace, it was that of a genius of common sense who knew, as a Queen who was really a Queen should know, the mentality, political and social, of that class which would shortly be supreme in her realm.

Side by side in her mind with this invaluable instinct there functioned, with no less natural vigour, her sense of Queenship. She stood for monarchy incarnate, just as she stood for the middle-class, and all that protected and championed that sacred principle was to her sacred. Church and State were the buttresses that supported the throne, and the throne must support them, otherwise they would all come clattering down together; and so, though officially she was of no political party, she was actually a Tory of the Tories. All legisla-

VICTORIA AS A CHILD
After Denning

tion that threatened the solidity of these buttresses was intensely repugnant to her, and thus, though rigidly neutral officially with regard to the will of the people, she once told my father how exceedingly pleased she was, privately and personally, to think that the House of Lords would never pass Mr Gladstone's Bill for the disestablishment of the Welsh Church, and that there was no constitutional means of removing their veto. Anything, however small, that threatened to diminish the property and privileges of these buttresses must be sternly resisted, and she also strongly recommended my father, when there was a question of Cuddesdon being given up as the residence of the Bishop of Oxford, to oppose it. "If you begin giving up," she said, "they will go on grabbing till they get everything." In precisely the same spirit more than thirty years before, she had been unable to see why the proposed new site for the National Gallery should be "exactly on the spot where Kensington Palace stood, if not for the purpose of taking from the Crown its last available set of apartments."

There was however one point which deeply affected the welfare of her realm, where her lack of imagination led her into errors from which her common sense could not save her. She knew nothing whatever of the working classes, of the barbarous beggary, of the poverty and suffering and squalor in which they lived, and when some inarticular protest from below seethed up into hoarse murmurings and mutterings, she heard in them nothing but the threats of rioters and revolutionaries who uttered menaces against all which made for stability and ordered government. She was a firm believer in classes, but she knew of only three: first came the monarchy, then came the upper and landed class which directly buttressed the throne, thirdly there was the great middle-class which she saw was becoming the governing power. Below it there came no doubt a very large quantity of dim human beings, but of these she neither saw nor heard anything to any purpose. There were, of course, crofters round about Balmoral, and she took much interest in their affairs,

especially their funerals and their marriages, and she records
the visits she made in order to see how the "poor people"
lived. To one she gave a warm petticoat, and the old lady
"shook my hands and prayed God to bless me: it was very
touching." Then there was Kitty Kear who in her presence
"sat down and spun." She also received a warm petticoat,
and Mrs Grant "who is so tidy and clean" got a dress and
a handkerchief. But her knowledge of any class below the
middle-class was limited to such as these; of slums and over-
crowding and bestial existence she knew nothing whatever,
and being without imagination, she never formed any picture of the condition of the millions of mournful workers who
never saw the sun, and certainly she never to the end of her
life conceived it possible that their votes would put a labour
party in power at Westminster. She would have regarded
such a state of things as a situation partaking of the horror
of nightmare. If by chance she had to drive through slums
they were decorated with flags which looked very bright and
gay, or if, on one of the surprise expeditions from Balmoral,
carefully organized by the Prince Consort, she found herself in "the dirtiest poorest villages in the whole of the Highlands," the sight of dismal miserable looking houses and people and "a sad look of wretchedness about it," produced no
more than a momentary and entirely barren sense of ugliness
with which she had nothing to do. In her Irish tour, similarly, she only records that "you see more ragged and
wretched people here than I ever saw anywhere else. *En
revanche* the women are really handsome — *quite* in the lowest class." She had no imagination which could be kindled
into effective compassion for those whose needs were a disgrace
to England. The warm petticoats were reserved for the
clean and tidy poor, the poorest villages in the Highlands received none, and she got back to Balmoral "safely at half-past
nine" full of gratitude to Albert for having arranged "such
a delightful, successful expedition." The existence of a
class who were milled into money and starved and sweated

did not penetrate into her; it stained the surface for a moment
and instantly passed away, and to the end of her life she
could not see "why people make such a fuss about the slums."
In this immense endowment of common sense unlit by imagination she was the exact opposite of her grandson William II of Germany, who had a prodigious imagination but
no common sense which could be lit up by it; his imagination flared on to an empty void where he beheld only the
Brocken spectre of himself clad in shining armour.   But his
imagination was largely responsible for the war which brought
disaster on his country, while to Queen Victoria's common
sense was largely due an era of unrivalled prosperity for
hers.

Though she was of almost unmixed German blood, and
though, since her ancestor George I had come to sit on the
throne of the Stuarts and the Tudors without a word of English to his tongue but with the strongest distaste in his mind
for the country and the people over which he ruled, there
had entered into her veins not a single drop of native blood,
she was from the very first completely English, and combined
the instincts of a Queen with those of the ruling class.   She
married a German, she talked German in the bosom of her
family, she interlarded her letters to her uncle with German
words, she married her eldest daughter to a German and was
on one occasion very properly and filially reminded of the
fact.   Yet she could roundly declare that she hated the
Prussians, and though that was not literally true (for she
was very fond of them) what she meant by it was exceedingly
true: she hated Bismarck, whose pro-Prussian schemes she
rightly divined to be directed against the prestige of England
on the Continent, and anything that threatened England
made her see red.   Nobody, while she was Queen, should with
impunity attack the power and prestige of England nor the
power and prestige of the throne.   The Prince Consort,
previous to his marriage, wanted to be made an English peer:
nothing could be firmer than her refusal to allow it.   It would

never do for the husband of the Sovereign to have a seat in
her Parliament, for political bias would certainly be attributed to him, and political bias must not be suspected of
coming near the throne.   He should be Royal Highness by
all means for he was her husband, but just for that very
reason, he should not be of the lowest grade of her peers.

Again she at once determined that she would always see
her ministers alone, for her business was with them, and theirs
with her, and when her mother, probably with some German
notion of chaperonage, suggested that she should be present
at Councils, she got a snub from her daughter.   But with
that unfailing common sense of hers, she presently saw that
her husband was a man of very great sagacity; more and
more she listened to his advice and trusted the soundness of
his judgment, till, at his death, she, who twenty years before
said that nobody should teach her what were the duties of
the Queen of England towards her people, wrote to her uncle
that now, less than ever, would she be guided by the views
of others.   She knew what Albert had thought, and the
principles she had learnt from him should be her guides hereafter.   It has been somewhat the fashion to judge the
character of that eminently wise Prince by the style of the
decoration on the Albert Memorial: it would be equally sensible to form an estimate of Dr Samuel Johnson from his
monument in St Paul's Cathedral, where he appears with
athletic limbs lightly draped in a Roman toga, bare feet and
curly ephebic hair.

Queen Victoria did not regard art, letters, or music as
in any way springing from national character: they were
something quite apart, elegant decorations resembling a
scarf or a bracelet, and in no way expressive of the soul of the
country.   But a pretty taste and competent execution were
part of the education of a young lady, and as we have seen,
she had her drawing lessons from Mr Lear; she learned to
etch with considerable technical skill and Mendelssohn taught
her singing.   She was very proud of this: once, when quite

an old woman, she suddenly said to Alick Yorke who was in
waiting, that after lunch he and she would sing duets. Someone sat down at the piano to play the accompaniment, and
the Queen propped up on the table between the two vocal-
ists a copy of Gilbert and Sullivan's opera "Patience," and
found the place. She said "Now, Mr Yorke, you begin,"
and Mr Yorke obediently sang to the Queen, "Prithee, pretty
maiden, will you marry me ?" He got through his verse
fairly well, and then the Queen in a very clear soft voice sang,
"Gentle Sir, although to marry I'm inclined." She was much
pleased with herself, and stopped in the middle of her verse to
say, "You know Mr Yorke, I was taught singing by Mendelssohn."

She perfectly reflected in matters of art the ordinary educated ideas of her time, as held by those who had no artistic
perception. She liked landscape painters to show her what
she herself saw, and had a strong preference for the scenes
which Mr Landseer so skilfully painted : heather and bracken
and stags and dogs with sticks in their mouths, and brown
Scotch streams (so like the "originals"), and often on her
exploring tours from Balmoral she wished she had his pencil
and could do justice to the lovely braes and glens. Mr
Turner's imaginative landscapes on the other hand, particularly those of his later period, meant nothing to her. She
thought them "most extraordinary" and there was the end of
that. A portrait, in the same way, was to be estimated by
its resemblance to the sitter, and if the sitter was herself, it
was highly important that the riband of the Garter should
be of the correct colour. If a disturbing light fell upon it,
altering its tone, that made no difference : she knew (no-one
better) what the colour of the Garter riband was, and that
was the colour she wanted in her picture. Moonlight, sunlight, firelight did not alter the colour, because the dye was
excellent, and she told the artist so. Then when all such
crucial points of true fidelity had been settled, there was the
face and the expression of the sitter. About these there

should be nothing troubling: any suggestion of the soul and its maladies and of the history that the soul had engraved on the eyes and the mouth was very objectionable. It was like exposing a piece of her leg. You did not want the artist to show what the sitter *was*, but what she looked like: the spirit within was no concern of the artist and it must be properly veiled, even as her body must be properly dressed. So she much approved the Prince Consort's happy idea of hanging the Rembrandts and the Vandycks at Windsor higher on the walls, for this enabled everybody to see the family Winterhalters so much better. Probably her artistic views were quite her own, the result of personal predilections, and they faithfully reflected the artistic feeling of the day, but certainly the Prince Consort confirmed and strengthened them, and in such matters she considered that his taste was quite flawless. It was he who converted the old Scottish Castle of Balmoral into the far more splendid German Schloss, who papered its walls with tartan, and himself designed the carpets of Balmoral tartan. "All," she wrote, "is his own creation, own work, own building, and his great taste and the impress of his dear hand, have been stamped everywhere." To all his views on "scenery" she listened with reverence: when they saw Edinburgh together for the first time, he said of Arthur's Seat, that he was sure the Acropolis could not be finer. That he had never seen the Acropolis did not matter: *ipse dixit*. In music similarly he was her infallible guide: he was quite a voluminous composer, and his "Te Deum," as I well remember, was performed in the Abbey at the Jubilee service in 1887, and his Chorale "Gotha" was incorporated into the anthem written by Sir Frederick Bridge, the Abbey organist, for the occasion. These compositions are technically quite correct, and if carefully played on the organ with a copious use of the swell, they seem, somehow, to cast a light on the Prince Consort's preference for the portraits of Winterhalter over those of Rembrandt. But it must be remembered that very few people, even among those who feel themselves to be well equipped music critics, could compose any sort of a "Te Deum," still less one that adhered to the strictest rules of harmony, and sounded, when performed, as it was meant to. It is not amateur work, but that of a trained though not imaginative musician, who praised God very sincerely in the key of C Major, without any passionate Hosannas or difficult modulations.

Their life was conducted on the same straightforward and wholesome principle as those on which his "Te Deum" was composed. As Sovereign the Queen was a slave to her duties, and no-one ever worked harder or more conscientiously at her job. This admirable devotion never left her, and up to the last years of her life when she suffered much from such fatiguing disabilities as rheumatic joints and failing eye-sight, she used often to sit up till one or two o'clock in the morning, even when on holiday at the Villa Palmieri or the Villa Fabricotti at Florence, to get her work finished. Nothing was ever allowed to interfere with her work, and in those early years, when her royal tasks were fully done, she found all her pleasure and relaxation in family life, sketching with her children, playing round games, escaping from her Queenship into the quiet of sheer domesticity, with her husband for her constant and adored companion. She cared nothing for state and splendour in themselves, and though in the performance of her royal functions she was of a superb and wholly native dignity, thus showing that she was indeed Queen of England and knew it, it was the sense of duty that inspired her, and when her duty was done, she wanted only to get back to the freedom of privacy. "We leave dear Claremont," she wrote to her uncle, the King of the Belgians, "with the greatest regret. . . Windsor is beautiful and comfortable, but it is a palace, and God knows how willingly I would always live with my beloved Albert and our children in the quiet and retirement of private life."

She was entirely sincere when she wrote that, but it was quite untrue, for she could no more have lived without her

Queenship and remained alive in the very vivid sense in which she was alive, than she could have lived without her lungs: being Queen was part of the air she breathed. It was a great lark sometimes to pretend not to be the Queen, and to set forth on an expedition from Balmoral, christening the Prince Consort and herself Lord and Lady Churchill (Mr and Mrs Churchill would have been too great a violence) but the real lark lay in the fact that she was Queen all the time, and when the guileless Highlanders guessed the majestic truth, they were "ready to die of fright." She was the Queen, and whatever her inclination, her will would never have allowed her to remain in retirement and see another than herself at "comfortable Windsor." But both as Queen and as housewife she conducted her life on broad simple principles, hating anything flamboyant or "extraordinary," quite uninterested in problems of human nature and in the dim mysterious yearnings which inspire art and music, simple and sincere in her religion, troubled neither by ecstasy nor theological complexities, bringing up her children with affection and firmness in the fear of God and of herself. As such she both set a fashion and conformed to the type which she had been largely instrumental in making. Her private life was rational, respectable and unimaginative, and she made it public to her subjects when she wrote the Journal of her Life in the Highlands. Then in 1861 came the death of the Prince Consort.

The whole fabric of her life was shattered, and as she wrote to her uncle, not only she "but England, my unhappy country has lost *all* in losing him." For many years now she had trusted and leaned upon his judgment in matters concerning the State, and not only the home life of which he was the adored centre was broken, but the prop on which she as Queen had leaned was gone, and all that was left for her was to follow out in every particular without interference from any, the wisdom and policy that had been his. She was convinced she could not live long without him, and the only thing that could make tolerable her waiting for the reunion that would never be sundered, was to walk in his steps. For many years she retired into a complete seclusion, and made no public appearances of any sort. Though for a time she would not even see her ministers, her devotion to her duty reasserted itself and she worked as hard as ever, but her labours were as secret and invisible as those of the queen-bee in the central darkness of the hive. Never had she had any taste for the pageantry of the throne, now she said it was "absolutely impossible" to face it, and it was in vain that six years after the Prince Consort's death, Lord Derby begged her to receive the Sultan who was then in England. He had been accorded an enthusiastic reception in France, and it was really a matter of national importance that the Queen should see him if only for a ten-minutes' interview at Windsor. But she still could not steel herself to the ordeal of receiving a ruling monarch alone, without the support of the Prince Consort. She was not equal to it, and again it was "absolutely necessary" that Lord Derby should see Dr Jenner, who would no doubt tell him of the "real state of her nerves." We may presume that Lord Derby did see Dr Jenner, and we can guess what his verdict was, for the interview duly took place. Her subjects never saw her at all in any official capacity, for years she hardly set foot in London at all, and the effect of this neurasthenic seclusion was that she became very unpopular. Even staunch loyalists found it difficult to answer the question as to what was the use of a Sovereign whose existence was almost mythical.

But those twenty years of duty and domestic life had done their work, and though she ceased from 1861 onwards to exercise any direct social influence, the sixties and in part the seventies were still fed by the reaction from the days of the Brighton Pavilion and the revels of Carlton House. These waters were now diminishing in volume, the reaction like a reservoir in the hills was rapidly declining, and the stream-bed once bright with its water was getting overgrown with a tangle of vivid vegetation that was soon so to obscure it that it was only by diligent search the pools could be found, still and dwindled beneath the gaudy growth. During all this period the Queen remained socially cataleptic, and we can no longer refer to her as typical of what was going on. The decline and fall of Victorianism took place while she, busy and as industrious as ever, was out of touch with everything. We may indeed compare her to the Sleeping Beauty, waiting the advent of the fairy Prince to hew his way through the thickets and overgrown avenues of Osborne.

MY FATHER came of an exceedingly long line of ascertained persons, all entirely undistinguished. In the fourteenth century his forefathers were settled in the West Riding of Yorkshire, and were leaseholders of Fountains Abbey, first as tenant-farmers and subsequently acquiring by purchase acres of their own. By means of the Register of the Abbey and certain ancient wills, the whole pedigree from that time onwards happens to be known, both the names of these undistinguished people, of the places they lived in, and in most cases of their wives, and from then onwards, for the space of five centuries, my father was the first of that long line to attain any sort of eminence. There are a few collateral minor lights, such as a Chancellor of the Exchequer in the reign of Queen Anne, raised to the peerage as Lord Bingley, who built Bramham, and a few of the women made interesting marriages, but in the direct male line there is no name at all, until my father's, which is even faintly notable. They prospered in a comfortable rural tranquillity, they lived on their freehold farms in small rather dignified manor-houses, they raised and educated large families, they went to York or Ripon for a little gaiety in the winter, and are only remarkable for having gone on so long and having done so little. By the last half of the eighteenth century they were very substantial people, and, as always happens sooner or later, had begun to drift from their country houses into York, where a couple of brothers, Christopher, and my great-great-grandfather Edward Benson owned considerable property. The fortune of the latter had been increased by

35

the fact that a solitary old bachelor, named Francis White,
left all his property in equal shares to three friends of his
(of whom Edward Benson was one) who played whist with
him once a week. . . Then after these careful centuries of
solid respectability there came the black sheep of this
monotonous line, my great-grandfather Captain White
Benson.   Perhaps black is too pronounced a hue for this mild
monster who was in the main only a gay young spark with a
reputation for wit and gallantry.   He was in the 6th Foot
(Royal Warwickshire regiment), and a friend of Prince William, Duke of Gloucester, under whom he served in the Irish
rebellion.   He wrote and published a volume of ballads,
which are not very bad, and he had a great flirtation with the
exquisite Lady Morgan, the much admired authoress of
"The Wild Irish Girl," and "Ida in Athens."   Some of his
letters to her remain.   They are full of modish sighs and
aspirations.   Beyond his facility in writing verse, his only
real talent was that of getting through money with grace and
rapidity, and having spent most of his own fortune he eloped
with his first cousin, Eleanor Benson, then aged sixteen, who
with her sister was joint heiress to what was then called "a
pretty little fortune," and got through the greater part of
that as well.   Lady Morgan, who wrote a rather lively volume of memoirs, was in error over some points about her
lover, for she recorded that he committed suicide in 1798.
As a matter of family history, he married this young cousin
of his in that year: perhaps that represented itself to Lady
Morgan as the equivalent of suicide.   He died from a fall off
his horse eight years later, leaving one son with a much
straitened fortune.

White Benson had a very remarkable sister, Anna
Dorothea, younger than himself, who became by her second
marriage the famous Mrs Basil Montagu.   She was first the
wife of a York attorney, named Thomas Skepper, whose death
in 1805 left her an extremely attractive widow of twenty-
five years.   She came up to London with her young daugh-

ter Anne to stay with friends who no doubt had held
forth about her charms, for, as her friend Miss Frances
Kemble tells, one evening "soon after her arrival as she was
sitting, partly concealed by one of the curtains in the drawing-room, Basil Montagu came rapidly into the room, exclaiming (evidently not perceiving her), 'Come, where is
your wonderful Mrs Skepper ? I want to see her.' " He
was already twice a widower, but the wonderful Mrs Skepper
was quite too much for him. Indeed she seems to have
known that she had met her second fate, as he his third, "for
during the whole evening he engrossed her attention, and
talked to her, and the next morning at breakfast she laugh-
ingly complained to her hosts that he had not been content
with that, but had tormented her in dreams all night. 'For,'
said she, 'I dreamed that I was going to be married to him,
and the day before the wedding he came to me with a couple
of boxes, and said solemnly, "My dear Anna, I want to confide these caskets to your keeping: in this one are contained
the bones of my first dear wife, and in this those of my second
dear wife. Do me the favour to take charge of them for
me." ' " And married they were as soon as the year of her
widowhood was over.

Basil Montagu was the natural son of "Jeremy Diddler,"
Earl of Sandwich, and his mother was the actress Miss Reay,
who was shot as she came out of the stage-door by an insane
clergyman called Hackman. He was now a very successful
Chancery barrister with high literary tastes, and his house
in Bedford Square became under Anna Montagu's presidency
the nearest approach to a salon that London has ever arrived
at. Even Thomas Carlyle, eternally snapping and snarling
at those who most befriended him, and finding Basil Montagu "a bore by degrees and considerably a humbug if you
probed too strictly," confessed himself a "thankful debtor to
his wife, this noble lady, this high personage" who was mistress there. He cannot find a flaw in her perfections, her tall
figure, her penetrating face, her lips "always gently shut, as

if till the enquiry was complete and the time came for something of royal speech upon them. . . You might have printed every word, so queen-like, gentle, soothing, measured, prettily royal towards subjects whom she wished to love her." Indeed the only satirical thing he could find to say about her was that her "notable dress" which so impressed him "must have required daily the fastening of sixty or eighty pins." About that dress Miss Kemble waxes dithyrambic. Mrs Montagu was "so superior in this point to her sex generally, that having found that which was undoubtedly her own individual costume, she never changed the fashion of it . . . it seemed the proper expression in clothes of her personality, and really a part of herself. It was a long open robe, over an underskirt of the same material and colour, always moonlight silver-grey, amethyst purple or black silk or satin of the richest quality, trimmed with broad velvet facings of the same colour, the sleeves plain and tight-fitting from shoulder to wrist, and the bosom covered with a fine lace half-body, which came like the wimple of old mediæval portraits up round her throat, and seemed to belong in material and fashion to the clear chin-stay which followed the noble contour of her face, and the picturesque cap which covered without concealing her auburn hair and the beautiful proportions of her exquisite head." A majestic figure surely, with her queenly speech and her exquisite dress and manners. In a brusquer age, when manners are at a discount, we are apt to think that such a fineness of speech and of bearing denote insincerity. But that is a hasty conclusion. There are those, and Mrs Montagu was one of them, who are as truly themselves in being well-bred as others in being rude. The most finished politeness and reserve were natural to her: that was what she felt like. One day a friend came to her daughter and said, "I'm afraid your mother is ill: she has allowed herself to cough in my presence." There, at 25 Bedford Square, she held this daily court of culture and politeness, and looked after her husband's two children by his previous marriage, and had a daughter by him who married Count William de Viry. Not the least remarkable of the inmates of Basil Montagu's household, at one time, had been a young tutor who taught the children of an earlier marriage; his name was William Wordsworth and he had a great taste for poetry. Mrs Montagu's cousin, Mrs John Benson, had, some years later, an equally remarkable governess for her girls, whose name was Charlotte Brontë.

Anna Montagu's daughter by her first marriage became the wife of the poet Bryan Walter Procter, better known as "Barry Cornwall": their daughter (here linking us up with the mid-Victorian age) was Adelaide Anne Procter, whose "Lost Chord" became the tear-test of the merits of ladies who had brought their music (they believed) when they went out to dinner and sang afterwards. Mrs Procter carried on her mother's tradition of salon and beautiful speech, but her tongue could have an exceedingly sharp edge to it, which earned her the sub-title of "Our Lady of Bitterness." Thackeray, Browning, and Kinglake were of her intimate circle, but Carlyle was ignominiously hounded from it, for that bilious temperament of his prompted him to attack her mother, whose "thankful debtor" he was, and to write after her death, in epilogue of his panegyric of her, a scandalous and false statement to the effect that she had "entered Basil Montagu's house under the name of 'governness.' Had succeeded well, and better and better for some time, perhaps for years in that ticklish capacity, whereupon at length offer of marriage which she had accepted." The innuendo, more than hinted, though less than stated, was absolutely untrue, and Mrs Procter very properly printed and privately circulated some of Carlyle's letters to her mother, showing the kindly way in which he had been treated in that house, and labelled his statements as "malignant lies": to which plain speaking there was no rejoinder.

The spendthrift Captain White Benson left one son, my grandfather, who had a genius for chemistry. He made two

very valuable discoveries, the one a process for making co-
balt, the other for the manufacture of white lead, out of
which large fortunes were reaped, but not by him. He sold
what the spendthrift father had spared of the property in
York, married Miss Harriet Baker, sister of Sir Thomas
Baker of Manchester, and spent his days in the laboratory
and in writing one or two pious books: "Meditations on the
Works of God" was one of them. He died at the age of
forty-two leaving his wife to bring up a family of seven children on an inconveniently small income. My father was the
eldest and was then aged fourteen.

He spent much of his holidays with the numerous aunts
and uncles and cousins who bestrewed the West Riding of
Yorkshire, and his early diaries and letters give the oddest
glimpses into the sort of life which tranquil well-to-do folk
used to live then, but which now is utterly extinct. I draw
upon these, for such first-hand records are now few. His
grandfather's first cousin and sister-in-law had married William Sidgwick, and she lived, then a widow, in Skipton
Castle, and he describes in a letter to his mother that remote
and delectable existence. "My aunt is not at all strict except
that I am obliged to eat bread and butter with a knife and
fork, not to set my feet on the chair staves, and not to
tumble off the Castle leads." She walked in the Castle
grounds every morning, she saw personally to the washing
up of the fine china, and did nothing else in particular. She
was much horrified at the way in which people in this year,
1844, gadded about. One young lady who came to stay
with her, was only proposing to stop for a fortnight instead
of her usual month, and meant to pay two more visits before
she went home. (Indignant marks of exclamation.) Another shocking thing was the extravagance in living: people
now wanted the most elaborate dinners. "But give me," she
said, "a trout from my own stream, and a grouse from my own
moor, and an apple tart from my own orchard, and I ask
nothing more." That this utterly delicious dinner implied

the possession of a trout stream, a moor, and a garden, did not seem to detract from the spirit of Spartan simplicity which was content with it. Every day Christopher and James, her two unmarried sons, who were in the family business in Skipton, used to pay a call on their mother and when they retired from business in the early prime of life, they both came to live at the Castle with her. Christopher spent his money in building a church at Skipton and the Church Schools. He slept at the Castle, but went down to attend service in the church he had built at seven o'clock in the morning, after which he read church history in his private library at the schools and ate a slice of sponge cake which was brought in under a bell-glass as the clock struck noon. He then continued his studies till three in the afternoon, when he went back to the Castle to dine, and spend the evening there. His brother, James Sidgwick, led a less strenuous life, he walked in the Castle grounds at eight in the morning for half an hour and passed the rest of the day indoors. He was liable to catch cold and so he sat always in a porter's chair with padded wicker sides and back, and there read all day. His reading chiefly consisted of the study of Bradshaw's railway guide, which, as railways multiplied, became more voluminous and required increasing industry: with its aid he worked out the most elaborate cross-country journeys though he never took any of them himself, nor stirred out of Skipton Castle. Every year, and on the same day of the year, Messrs Lincoln and Bennett sent him a new beaver hat of precisely the same shape as its predecessor, for his morning walks.

Then when that visit to Skipton was over, my father went to stay with the eldest of these brothers, John Benson Sidgwick, who lived at the fine house his father had built at Stonegappe. His greatest claim to fame is that Charlotte Brontë had been governess to his children and that he and his family appear in "Shirley" as the "Yorkes." Their intentions towards her seem to have been of the kindliest;

if they thought she would like to take part in the family diversions out of lesson-hours, they invited her to do so; if
they thought she would like to be left to herself, they did not
worry her.   But these amiabilities sadly miscarried, for she
bitterly satirized their treatment of her in letters to Mrs
Gaskell.   For if she was asked to join the family, she complained that she was a mere slave, and that she was allowed
no leisure at all, while if she was left to herself, she wrote
that she only existed for her employers as a teacher of their
children, and that when lessons were over she ceased to be.

There were odd stories, too, of superstition and magical
beliefs still credited among educated people in those days,
when the railway had not yet reached Skipton or come near
Stonegappe: uncles and aunts and grandmother had creepy
tales to tell on the long dark winter evenings.   My father
records how he heard of his father's upbringing: he was a
delicate boy and not fit for school life and his education was
entrusted to Dr Sollitt of York, a great chemist, a notable
astrologer and framer of horoscopes, and, apparently, a
practiser of more dubious arts than these.   He had drawn
out the horoscope of Cousin Joanna Benson who about the
year 1800 was one of the young beauties of the North
country, and had found that the stars portended matrimony
for her.   This marriage, so Dr Sollitt read in the heavens,
would take place in March, and if anything came in the way
of this March marriage of hers, she would never be married
at all.   Not long after the beautiful Joanna was very happily betrothed to one Colonel Shaw, and even as the stars
had said, (or perhaps in consequence of what the stars had
said) the wedding was fixed for the month of March.   It was
to take place at her father's house in York, and the bridegroom that morning would ride in from his country house,
breakfast with the family, and so to church.   Breakfast
was waiting, but still no bridegroom came, and the time went
on, till at last a messenger on horse-back was dispatched to see
what had delayed him.   The messenger returned with the

news that Colonel Shaw had been thrown from his horse as he rode into York and had been instantly killed. His will, new-drawn, was in his pocket and he left all he was possessed of to Joanna, but his will was still unsigned by him, and therefore invalid. Joanna fell into a deep melancholy, and having missed her March marriage, she died unwedded, even as Dr Sollitt had predicted from the celestial signs.

Dr Sollitt's education of my grandfather included the arts of astrology, and his pupil made some singular predictions which were duly fulfilled. The friendship continued after my grandfather married, and the two left York one day to pay a visit to one of his relatives, and there Dr Sollitt was cured of his darker studies. Alone in his room he locked the door and made ready the spell which would raise Satan. He marked out on the floor the circle in which he would himself stand, and he fenced it with signs of the cross and with the mystic pentagram, across which the powers of hell could not operate. Then standing inside this circle he began his incantations, and had got as far as the repetition of the Lord's prayer said backwards, when he heard his name loudly called from somewhere in the house just outside his locked door, and he unbolted himself and ran out to see who called like that. There was no one on the landing nor on the stairs, but he ran down to see who this could be, and why he was wanted. But he had not yet reached the bottom step when he heard a tremendous crash from the room he had just quitted. Up he went again, and he found his bed overturned and his wardrobe lying on its face among splintered chairs and broken crockery. But the room was empty, and none could have entered it and gone again in so brief a space. At that, panic seized Dr Sollitt, he saw how potent was the power he evoked, and he made a solemn bonfire of his magical books, and practised no more. My grandfather was of the same mind, and convinced that he too by means of astrology had acquired such knowledge as was not proper for men to at-tain to, burned his books likewise and devoted himself to more legitimate investigations into white lead instead of black magic.

Now such a tale as this, though written down by my father from the mouth of the narrator, is not interesting because of its intrinsic truth (for we do not believe that Satan will manifest himself for the mishandling of the Paternoster) but because a hundred years ago there were shrewd and well-educated and sensible folk, living in remote places, where not so long before, old women had been burned as witches, who did so believe. My father's grandmother (the eloping heiress of sixteen) was at this time not more than of middle age, and she too had a wonderful story-box for the long evenings. . . A friend of hers, belonging to the Protestant religion, had been staying near the town of Waterford in Ireland, and his host was a Roman Catholic. One evening this host of his begged him to come to church with him, for it was expected that a great miracle would be performed, and the sight of it might turn his heretic heart into the way of salvation. He asked what this miracle would be, and was told that the Priest would show to the congregation certain souls who were now in Purgatory in visible form, for God would give them remittance for a little while, suffering them to appear before the eyes of those still on earth, thereby quickening their faith and encouraging them to have masses said on behalf of the departed for their speedier release.

Accordingly the two went to church, and they were bidden to kneel at the chancel rails in front of the altar, where they would get a very good view of the miracle. The church was not more than dimly lit, and presently as the prayers for the souls of the departed were being said, the Englishmen saw that there were creeping out from under the altar small black, mysterious shapes which moved about on the floor of the chancel. The worshippers who knelt beside him, showed great emotion at this sign of the souls from beneath the altar being thus made manifest and he himself was much perturbed for this was indeed a miracle. But he took hold on himself, and observed more closely: there were several of these souls, and they seemed to be wrapped about in some black stuff like crape.   Then one of them as it crawled slowly about, came very near to where he knelt, and a sudden impulse prompted him to catch hold of it and pick it up, and in the dim light, he did so unobserved.   He was much comforted to find that it could be no disembodied thing, for it was of sensible weight, and he put it away in the pocket of his great-coat. So all gave thanks to God for this miracle, and when the service was over, the two friends left the church, and when they reached home, the Englishman said to his host:

"I've got a soul in my pocket, and here it is."

He took it out and laid it on the table.   It was, as he had observed, thickly but loosely wrapped about with crape, and he unwound it, layer after layer, not knowing what he should find.   At length the last covering came away, and there was a fine crab.   His host was much troubled.

"Now you must away for your life," he said, "and that's all about it.   The Priest is sure to have counted how many souls he put under the altar and he'll find that there's one missing.   You are known to be a heretic, and you knelt by the altar rails, and they'll soon be after you.   Take the first ship that leaves Waterford harbour, for if you stay, you're a dead man."

So WITH eyes round with pleasing terror, my father would steal up to his bed at Stonegappe or Skipton Castle, and when the holiday visits were over, returned to his mother's house at Birmingham Heath, from which every morning he walked to King Edward's school in the town, where he was now a day pupil and one who promised very well.   From the time when he was quite a small boy, anything connected with the church and priestly functions had been a passion with him; he had always loved the forms of worship as well as the faith, ritual, and cathedrals and ceremonies, and in a letter of his to one of his uncles, written when he was only

just ten years old, he asked him whether he thought there
was a chance that he might become a clergyman when he
grew up. He was of that way of thinking still, for his
mother had given him a big empty room in her house, for
his own purposes, and to use as he pleased, and he made an
oratory of it. He draped a table for an altar, he got a
fald-stool to kneel at, he hung its walls with sacred prints
and here, all by himself, every morning and evening he made
his devotions. He had forbidden his sisters to enter it at
all; it was his oratory, and nobody else should pray there.
But now, when he was away at school all day, he suspected
that the perfidious creatures trespassed there in spite of all
their promises, and he set to work to ascertain that. So one
morning before he started off for school, he put the door of
his oratory enticingly ajar, and perched a crafty booby-
trap on the top of it. And Emmeline, incautiously entering the precinct, loosed a clatter of books and other hard objects on her head, which cured her of her piety.

THROUGHOUT his school days this fire of ecclesiastical zeal
burned ever higher, and in the holidays he corresponded with
Lightfoot and Westcott, school-fellows then and life-long
friends ever after, and each in turn Bishop of Durham, about
these matters. . . They carried on by letter the conversations they had held about Purgatory: they hurled at each
others' heads Gregory the Great, the Council of Trent, Romans iii. 23, 24; they discussed the validity of lay-baptism,
they kept (or intended to) Canonical Hours, they hatched
a scheme for a Brotherhood of Holy Living, "to bring the
kingdom of God to the poor, to promote the spiritual unity
of the Church and to practise the precepts of the Sermon
on the Mount." During another vacation Lightfoot en-
treated my father not to go to hear Newman preach, but he
did, and came away, so he wrote to his friend, enormously
struck by "the sweet flowing unlaboured language, the frail
emaciated appearance," the thought that "this timid-look-

ing, little, weak-voiced man had so moved England. . .
Surely if there is a man whom God has raised up in this
generation with more than common power to glorify His
name, this man is he." Lightfoot must have been perturbed
at these high impressions, until he read, "But never turn
Romanist if you are to have such a face as that: it was awful,
the terrible lines deeply ploughed all over it, and the craft
that sat upon his retreating forehead and sunken eyes !"
But in all this correspondence, strange as it seems now in
more tepid days, between boys of sixteen to nineteen, there
is never the slightest touch of priggishness. They wrote
with just such eagerness concerning baptism and canonical
hours and heresies, as other boys might use when they wrote
of cricket or golf. These were the subjects that interested
them most.

His mother found that she could manage to send him to
Cambridge, but to help the family finances he spent some
weeks in the summer of 1848 before he went up to Trinity,
as tutor to two boys whose father had taken Abergeldie
Castle from the impoverished Gordons who owned it. The
Queen came over to see Abergeldie while he was there with a
view to acquiring a lease of it, as she did not long after, when
it became the Highland residence of the Prince of Wales,
who, with the Prince Consort accompanied her on this occasion. My father records this visit in a letter to his mother,
and gives an odd account of the Highland games at Inver-
cauld, which the Queen attended with her family; the Dukes
of Atholl and Leeds who were to receive her, were late. She
was the most plainly dressed woman there, was his opinion;
Prince Albert was "horribly padded and belted," the Prince
of Wales, "a fair little lad, rather of slender make," the
Princess Royal "a plain child with a will and temper of her
own, I should think." It would have surprised them all to
know that the rather shy, handsome young tutor of nineteen from Abergeldie, would in ten years time be stoutly
opposing Prince Albert's scheme for the introduction of Ger-

man methods of education into England, that not twenty-
five years later "the most plainly dressed woman there" would
be "ever his affectionately," and that "the slim little lad of
slender make" would be hearing what this same tutor thought
about baccarat.

During his first year at Cambridge, his mother wrote to
him of a project which filled him with horror. She was the
owner of her husband's patent for the manufacture of co-
balt, and she proposed, with the utmost good sense, as we
should now think, to start a business for its exploitation.
The expenses of a growing family with the eldest son at
Cambridge were heavier than she had anticipated, and being
an exceedingly able woman, she would very likely have made
a success of it. But the idea that his mother should embark
in "trade" was to his notion too dreadful to contemplate.
"I do hope and trust you will keep out of it," he wrote. "It
will do me so much harm here, and my sisters so much harm
for ever ! I trust that the scheme may be abandoned once
and for all."

Today it seems almost incredible that a boy should have
considered it an indelible disgrace that his mother should
supplement her income by running a business, or that a
mother should have given up her scheme because of such fas-
tidiousness in her son. But so earnest was this supplica-
tion, that she abandoned her idea, and presently we find
him taking pupils and sending her the half of what he
earned. He was elected a sizar, and then a scholar of Trinity, and his sister wrote to him prophesying that if he went
on like that he would soon be Archbishop of Canterbury.
The great Dr Sollitt, before he burned his books, could not
have read the face of the heavens with surer skill.

Then there descended on this young family and their
mother a tempest of woes. She invested a large portion of
her not too abundant capital in some freshly floated railway company; railway companies were booming now, and
also breaking, and she lost it all. Then two of her daugh-

ters fell ill with some virulent fever, subsequently declared
to be typhus. She wrote to my father not to come back
from Cambridge for fear of infection, and the next news he
got was of the death of his eldest sister Harriet. He instantly started to go home, but before he got there a further
tragedy had befallen.

His mother had refused to look again on the face of the
dead, but that night, yearning to see it once more, she got
up from her bed where another daughter was sleeping with
her and told her she was going to the room where Harriet lay.
Soon she came back, lay down and went quietly to sleep.
When morning came she was lying very still and the child
could not waken her. She got frightened and ran to fetch
somebody, and then it was found that her mother had died
as she slept at her side without a sigh or a movement. After
the double funeral her money affairs were looked into, and it
appeared that all she had left was the last payment but one
of the annual sum for which she had sold the patent which
she had once thought of exploiting herself. Beyond that
there was nothing. She had given no hint to any of her relations of the state of her finances.

The family of six children, the youngest of whom was a
boy of only eight years, had to disperse, for it was impossible
to keep the home together. A grandmother took two of
them; the rest went to various cousins. An uncle, Sir
Thomas Baker, a wealthy business man and a bachelor, offered to take the youngest brother, adopt him, and make him
his heir, but my father, just of age and *in loco parentis*,
absolutely refused to allow this, for his uncle was a Unitarian, and whatever worldly prospects the boy might thereby
forfeit, all such considerations were dross compared with that
pearl of great price, the Christian faith which, so he held,
would be imperilled if Charlie was brought up in such
guardianship. Nothing was further from his uncle's intention than to attempt to influence the child with regard to
religion and my father was solemnly assured of that, but he

still saw danger in committing his brother to a Unitarian household, and remained firm. A heated and painful correspondence took place between uncle and nephew, and my father's final word on the subject in which he undertook full responsibility for the boy's education and start in life is an extraordinary document, written as it was by a young man of twenty-one. It burns with the uncompromising faith out of which, in days of persecution, martyrs were made.

"My religious principle is not a thing of tender feelings, warm comforting notions, unproved prejudices, but it consists of full and perfect conviction, absolute belief, rules to regulate my life, and tests by which I believe myself bound to try every question the greatest and the least. . . I shall constantly hereafter as a Priest in the English Church, if God will, several times in every service proclaim 'Glory be to the Father and to the Son, and to the Holy Ghost': I shall offer humble prayer on my own behalf and on behalf of the Church at large to my Redeemer, — with what conscience or with what countenance if ever memory should suggest that in one person's case, and his the dearest that could be, I had robbed those Divine persons of the worship and the praise that should have proceeded from his heart, his mind, his lips, his whole life ? Whom could you more rightly brand as Hypocrite than him whose professions should be so loud, whose actions so discrepant ?

"This is a very serious matter, and I hope you will not think bitterly either of the young man's presumption, or the young churchman's bigotry. Bigot, thus far, a conscientious Christian must be."

IN ADDITION to these relations there came forward a man who had no connexion with the family but who instantly begged to be allowed to take upon himself the whole of my father's expenses at Cambridge, and all future maintenance till he was earning an adequate income for himself and for the sup-

port of his brothers and sisters. This was a middle-aged
bachelor don and bursar of Trinity College, Mr Francis
Martin, who had a romantic and devoted affection for him:
had Francis Martin been a poet we should surely have had
some sonnets. He furnished new rooms for my father in
College, cheques were ready for all his reasonable needs and
small luxuries, he took him on tours and expeditions in the
vacations, and reading parties in the Lakes, he nursed him if
he was ill, humorously lamenting that he was not worse and
would need more ministrations, he treated him with a half
lover-like, half paternal adoration, assuring him that it was
a privilege of which he felt himself unworthy, to be allowed
to do anything for him. Not content with these present
personal services he put by £500 for each of his sisters as a
dowry for their marriages, or to be used in any way that
seemed useful. All he wanted in return was the boy's companionship and confidence. And indeed that companionship
must have been to such a man a very delightful thing, for the
boy who could write so uncompromising a letter to his uncle,
was one of gay and sky-scraping spirits, exceedingly handsome, loving long walks and bathes in high tarns, and study
of noble books and silly jokes and all the beauty of the visible
world, crazy with the joy of life on a summer morning, and
with a mind alert and sensitive. One day he had twisted
an ankle jumping down from the top of a coach, and his
"misery-leg" only allowed him to hobble down to the edge
of Grasmere, where at sunset he watched the herons coming
in to roost in the fir-trees, and so he scribbled a little poem
about them for his friend:

> *One floating o'er the gorge, and one*
> *Down dropping o'er the scar,*
> *And one, wide-oaring o'er the wood,*
> *The Herons come from far,*
> *From lonely glens where they had plied*
> *All day their feasts and war.*

Ah, goodly lords of a goodly land,
How calm they fold the wing:
How lordly, beak on bosom couch'd,
To their pine-hung eyrie swing,
And stand to see the sun go down
Each like a lonely king.

He read it to him that evening and Mr Martin stroked his
hair, and said he was a poet; then they had a great discussion
as to whether it was ever justifiable to kill a moth that flut-
tered about the lamp and on to your book when you wanted
to work, and then they talked of the future. My father
said he would marry when he was thirty, the other told him
it must be much sooner than that.

AFTER two more years at Cambridge with this fine friend
always constant, my father took a brilliant degree and won
the Classical blue riband of the year, the Chancellor's gold
medal, given by the Prince Consort. In his holidays now
he often spent weeks with his widowed cousin, Mrs William
Sidgwick, sister-in-law to James and Christopher of Skipton
Castle, and it was to her house at Clifton that Mr Martin
came flying down from Cambridge to carry the magnificent
news of the Chancellor's medal. Mrs Sidgwick was the
mother of William, Henry, and Arthur Sidgwick, and of
one daughter. This daughter Mary was my mother, and
this is what my father wrote in his diary about her in the
year 1852, he being now twenty-three ears of age, an earnest,
young Victorian wooer.

"Mrs Sidgwick's little daughter Mary is this year eleven
years old. From a very young child great parts and pecul-
iarly strong affection have been discernible in her, with a great
delicacy of feeling. She is remarkably persevering and
though (naturally) lacking the taste for dry sorts of knowledge, which her brother Henry, whom she most resembles, had
from an infant, she has much fondness for histories, above all

the ancient, and a most striking love for poetry, and taste in fine poetry, and has a wonderful deal of it committed (always of her own inclination) to memory. As I have always been very fond of her and she of me with the love of a little sister, and as I have heard of her fondness for me commented on by many persons, and have been told that I was the only person at whose departure she ever cried, as a child, and how diligent she has always been in reading books which I have mentioned to her, and in learning pieces of poetry which I have admired, it is not strange that I, who from the circumstances of my family am not likely to marry for many years to come, and who find in myself a growing distaste for forming friendships (fit to be so called) among new acquaintances, and who am fond indeed (if not too fond) of little endearments, and who also know my weakness for falling suddenly in love, in the common sense of the word, and have already gone too far more than once in these things and have therefore reason to fear that I might on some sudden occasion be led . . . (here the manuscript takes refuge in cipher) it is not strange that I should have thought first of the possibility that some day dear little Minnie might become my wife."

Now we must remember that this very able and masterful young man, who here perhaps rather chills us by the painstaking quality of his emotions, had lately, as we shall see, been reading Tennyson's "Princess" with Minnie, and his communings with his diary are clearly inspired by certain very elevated and properly expressed passages in that typically Victorian poem, and in especial on the homily which the Prince there reads his young lady on the nature of love. He could not endure to "keep his winged affections clipt through crime": he reminds her that the nature of a woman has to grow in sweetness and strength,

> *Till at the end she set herself to man,*
> *Like perfect music unto noble words.*

That sounds remote enough from modern notions of mating: not one girl out of a hundred but would have a fit at the thought of fitting herself like music to the noble words of her suitor, but that was emphatically the Victorian ideal of marriage; man was superior and supreme, and the more thoroughly that women recognized that fact, the happier would marriage be. And if this passage from his diary sounds a little too enumerative of Minnie's promising points, it must also be remembered that she was only eleven years old, and that he was not in the least in love with her, nor professed to be, but only confiding to his diary in very proper language what he thought might someday happen. But immediately after this there follows a passage that makes us suspect that there was some pleasing agitation already at work below the correctness. The edifying discourse of Tennyson's "Princess" did not cover the whole ground. He goes on:

"Whether such an idea ever struck the guileless little thing herself I cannot tell. I should think it most unlikely. Yet I could not help being surprised one night when she was half lying on the sofa on which I sat, by the following conversation:

MINNIE: 'Edward, how long will it be before I am as tall as if I was standing on that stool ?'

EDWARD: 'I don't know very well, Minnie, five years perhaps . . .'

MINNIE: 'When I am twenty shall I be taller than that ?'

EDWARD: 'Yes.'

MINNIE: 'When I am twenty, how old shall you be ?'

EDWARD: 'Thirty-two.'

MINNIE: 'Thirty-two ! Edward, I shan't look so little compared to you, shall I, when I'm twenty and you're thirty-two, as I do now that I'm eleven and you're twenty-three ?'

EDWARD: 'No, no, you won't, Minnie.'

"This unexpected close made me blush indeed, and the palms of my hands grew very hot."

Somehow one feels that Minnie has got in behind the edifying sentiments recorded in the diary, though after this surprise he tries, not quite successfully, to entrench himself in them again. "The 'Princess' we read through, and she introduced me to the 'Lord of the Isles,' who was a mighty favourite with her. I had on many occasions reason to be struck with the keenness and depth of her thought: how her eye would flash at a fine expression, and the really striking voice and gestures with which she would read through a fine passage. Whatever she grows up to be, she is a fine and beautiful bud now. Whatever she may be in countenance hereafter, I think that the fineness of her expression in these cases will remain. She is remarkable for great beauty and changefulness of expression: one of the sweetest things I ever saw is her look of affection or of tenderness."

Though still holding on to the Tennyson ideal, he could not keep the growing perturbation to himself, and one night, talking to her mother he told her that "if Minnie grew up the same sweet clever girl she was, she would make such a wife as I had often said I should most pray for myself." Mrs Sidgwick not unnaturally was a good deal startled at this sort of option which he claimed on a child of eleven, and with much tact told him that no doubt he would constantly come across maturer incarnations of what Minnie might become: he mustn't attempt to make up his mind yet, and Minnie, he must remember, had not yet got a mind at all in these matters. But this good sense and prudence did not serve to stop his feeling, and the very next year he persuaded her mother to allow him to speak to Minnie on "The Subject." "In our rides," he records, "those charming rides, many little things occurred which made me believe that she saw something of my thoughts, and so at last the day came and I spoke to her. Let me try to recall each circumstance:

the arm-chair in which I sat, how she sat as usual on my knee, a little fair girl of twelve with her earnest look, and how I said that I wanted to speak to her of something serious, and then got quietly to the thing, and asked her if she thought it would ever come to pass that we should be married. Instantly, without a word, a rush of tears fell down her cheeks, and I really for the moment was afraid. I told her that it was often in my thoughts, and that I believed that I should never love anyone so much as I should love her if she grew up as it seemed likely. But that I thought her too young to make any promise, only I wished to say so much to her, and if she felt the same, she might promise years hence, but not now. She made no attempt to promise, and said nothing silly or childish, but affected me very much by quietly laying the ends of my handkerchief together and tying them in a knot, and quietly putting them into my hand. I asked her whether the thought had never struck her when she read the 'Princess' to me so constantly. 'Never,' she said. She would then turn the pages backward and forward and say again she wondered she had never thought of it, and again she would exclaim she never understood this passage and that till today. She could say it almost by heart: she repeated the words 'Love, children, happiness.' 'Two of those are mine now,' she said."

This same year my father was elected a Fellow of Trinity, Cambridge, and became a master at Rugby School. Mrs Sidgwick had now gone to live there, for her boys were being educated at the school, and my father became part of the family and made his home with her. And then this little authentic Victorian love story so precise and fabulous with its readings out of Tennyson's "Princess" and its adorable heroine of twelve years old, tenderly and exquisitely plighting herself, and striving to "set herself to man," without as yet the slightest notion what it all meant, becomes a very real affair (though indeed it was that already but somehow disguised to our thinking by its mode) full of hesitations and misgivings. My mother wrote down a little inner history of those years soon after her marriage, and it is a unique revelation of the mind of a child, sensitive and affectionate, and filled with the notion of the responsibility she has undertaken. From the moment that she had pledged herself with that true lover's knot which she had placed in his hand, she regarded herself as his: her destiny was sealed and signed, and she must fit herself for it. She must certainly grow taller, she must get to be as high as when she stood on that footstool, and she must cultivate her mind and be much more diligent at the reading and the lessons which he now daily set her, as lover but as tutor also, so as to be worthy of him. She must study architecture because he was so fond of churches, and be able to recognize without any mistake whether this arch was Perpendicular and that window Early English. And she must be more painstaking with her arithmetic, for before long she would be keeping house for him and adding up the weekly bills. She was "more volatile," so her mother wrote of her, than her brilliant brothers, and that volatility must be sobered (*laus Deo*, it never was !) and she must become more serious, or else Edward, who in this wondrous way had chosen her and to whom she now utterly dedicated herself would be disappointed with her. She admired him, she revered him, she was not ever the least afraid of him, as many others were, but was she at all in love with him ? She was happiest, she confessed, when she knew he was happy, but not necessarily when she was with him. She confessed too, that though her mother had forbidden any private endearments, she had allowed him to kiss her in the garden and that weighed heavy on her, for it must somehow have been her fault. . . And his ways were different from hers: if people had done wrong, he was stern with them. No doubt that was quite right, for he was anxious for their sakes that they should not err again, and if they were well scolded, that would help them to keep straight. But her plan was otherwise: if anyone was suffering even for their own fault, her instinct was first of all to make them happy again at once, and after that it was time to see about being good. "And though he was right," she wrote, "I was right too," and to the end of her life she continued to be right, and to be that well-spring of comfort and love and humour to all who dipped therein.

And so a few years slipped by; my father was providing now out of his own purse for that big family of brothers and sisters, for this he considered was the first charge on him, and his income did not yet warrant a wife and family of his own. Then, when my mother was just seventeen, there came his appointment to be first head-master of Wellington College, and it was settled that as soon as he was established there his marriage should take place, and so the little girl whom he had chosen at the age of eleven, if she grew up as she promised, was his. From that time onwards she was the staff on which he leaned, and the wings that gave him flight.

CHAPTER IV

LINCOLN AND TRURO

EARLY impressions are like glimpses seen through the window by night when lightning is about. The flash leaps out without visible cause or warning, and the blackness lifts for a second revealing the scene, the criss-cross of the rods of rain, the trees shining with moisture, the colours in the flower-beds, and then darkness like a lid snapped down hides all till the next flash flickers. So it is with memory, my early blinks are exceedingly vivid, but they are sundered, and though the passage of time does not dim them, as it dims the more fading impressions of later life, they do not form part of a continuous picture. Grandmamma and her bando-line, the table laid for a dinner-party, my mother playing croquet and with poised mallet sending her opponent's ball on to the gravel path, my father's figure in rustling silk gown, the gardener killing an adder with a pair of shears, Charles Kingsley lighting his pipe, the agitating but inter-esting moment when on biting a piece of toffee something gave way inside my mouth, and I found a front tooth em-bedded in the sweetmeat, and must detach it before con-suming the rest, the mystical and remunerative visits at Christmas and on birthdays of the fairy Abracadabra, dur-ing which for some reason gradually conjectured, my mother was always invisible: all these are blinks, each separate. By degrees the blank spaces of darkness between such flashes grew shorter, until they became more like a film of moving pictures, still misty in places and jerkily exhibited, but fairly continuous and connected.

My father who had hewn Wellington out of the heather, left it in 1873 a full and prosperous public school. The pioneer work was over: he had launched this ship, he had steered it safely past innumerable shoals, he had coaxed it along through contrary cross-currents, and now it was sailing brave and free on the high seas. His boyish devotion to the Church, its organization and its place in the life of England was still a passion with him, but his exclusive view of the benefits of prayer, as shown in his oratory with the booby-trap on the door to catch trespassers had given place to the widest catholicism, and the schedule of devotional activities for the day of rest at Wellington, not forbidden to boys but compulsory on them, was really prodigious. There was chapel at nine in the morning, after which Bible verses were learned by heart and repeated to form-masters at ten. There was chapel again at a quarter to twelve, and after dinner, at half-past one, there was more Bible-study, followed by a Bible-class in school at half-past three. A third Chapel service was held at half-past six, and there were prayers in the dormitories at nine. No secular books could be taken out of school library that day, but a special section of it, furnished with devotional and religious volumes, was open for those who wanted them. It was not indeed to be wondered at that the Prince Consort had asked my father to consider "Whether there may not be too much excessive employment in Religious Exercise in the present system of the College." But he did not think so: a day spent like that was festival to him.

But now his work at Wellington was done, and with the desire to devote himself more directly to the service of the English Church, he accepted a Canonry and the Chancellorship of Lincoln, and swept everyone along with him in his ecclesiastical fervour. He instantly established a theological College for young men studying for Orders, where he lectured twice a week, he opened night schools for working men and boys and taught there regularly, and he and my mother blew like a spring wind through the calm autumnal Close. For her part, she started, under the auspices of John Farmer,

E. W. BENSON

organist at Harrow, a musical society which met weekly not only to sing the consecrated Victorian glees like "Oh, who will o'er the down with me ?" and "Since first I saw your face" but Chorales of Bach with interspersed gavottes and sarabands on the piano. She sang alto and beat a rigid time with a paper-knife. This, for mid-Victorian ladies and local musical societies was distinctly advanced. She was also very daring (for a clergyman's wife) in her open advocacy of George Eliot's novels, in spite of all that was known about her life. She read "The Mill on the Floss" aloud to her children and she thrust "Adam Bede," which had some very shocking passages in it, into the hands of Canons' wives and told them not to mind. I think indeed that she must have read "Adam Bede" to us as well for an acquaintanceship with Mrs Poyser seems to date from then, and she would certainly have been ready with some adroit answer if any inquisitive creature had asked why Hetty and Arthur Donnithorne should not meet and talk in the wood. She was equally up to the mark when one of her children publicly demanded to know the difference between a bull and an ox, for she at once said that the bull was the father and the ox the uncle.

At Riseholme three miles from the city lived Bishop Charles Wordsworth, who was recognized to be kind at heart, but was felt to be formidable. At the same time he was enviable, because he could skate on one foot, holding the other completely off the ice. Riseholme was an earthly Paradise: it had a scagliola hall, a housekeeper with ringlets and an inexhaustible mine of Osborne biscuits. Then there were two lakes of infinite acreage and depth which held monstrous pike of which Arthur caught one, a prodigious thing of over two pounds, and we had it for nursery tea, since which day I have never cared much for pike at table. Upon these waters were swans as befitted the home of the successor of St Hugh of Lincoln, and I was presented with one of their eggs. I essayed to blow it for my collection, but it was addled,

and since that day I have left the blowing of swans' eggs to
those who do not mind the risk; such are the simplifications
of life which experience teaches.   Bishop Wordsworth (to
descend to lesser matters) was the nephew of the late Laureate,
and he talked about Uncle William, whose poetical aptitude
he had inherited, for he wrote a complete hymn-book entirely
out of his own head, called "The Holy Year," and in my
father's oratory at the Chancery (unguarded by booby-traps
and open to all) we often sang those hymns at family prayers,
accompanied by my mother on a minute harmonium with a
tremolo stop, which occasionally collapsed with a polyphonic
groan and pinched her feet as they plied the bellows.   Some
of these hymns were fine poetry: "Hark the sound of holy
voices" was among them, and "Gracious Spirit, Holy Ghost,"
but Bishop Wordsworth also inherited his uncle's tendency
to lapse into meaner strains.   One hymn, for instance, contained a stanza which few could call felicitous:

> *What the Holy Prophets meant*
> *In the Ancient Testament,*
> *Thou revealest to our view,*
> *Lord, for ever, in the New.*

Emotional appeal is somehow lacking in such a lyric: there
seems no particular reason why it should be sung, and presently there was a very particular reason why some of these
hymns should not be sung at family prayers in the Chancery.
One of them for instance, an ode in honour of the day of
St Philip and St James, was better avoided, It began:

> *Let us emulate the names*
> *Of St Philip and St James,*

and it became known that some of the children had composed
a somewhat similar opening for another apostolic feast, and
were heard chanting,

Let us try and be as good
As St Simon and St Jude.

It was wiser therefore to sing something else on the day of St
Philip and St James, for fear of giving rise to deplorable
levity.

But the Lincoln days were brief; hardly had my father got
his Theological School working, when Lord Salisbury privately inquired of him whether he would accept the Bishopric
of Calcutta if he was offered it.   He declined that: there was
a young family of six children ranging from the age of
sixteen to five, who would have to spend the formative years in
England without their parents, and also his heart was in
the Church at home.   But it was certain that Episcopacy
somewhere was imminent for him, and next year Lord Beaconsfield at the suggestion of the Queen and with her expressed wish that he should accept it, offered him the newly
created See of Cornwall.   That was a very different matter;
there was pioneer work to be done there as at Wellington
and after an interview with the Prime Minister, he accepted
it.   Lord Beaconsfield's comment was "Well, we *have* got
a Bishop !"

He had hardly set foot in Cornwall when he began raising
funds for the building of a cathedral, the first that had been
erected in England since the Reformation.   There was a
church situated in the centre of Truro, mostly empty, for
the place was a stronghold of Methodism, and just as, forty
years before, he turned the empty room in his mother's house
into an oratory, so he made this empty church into the nucleus
of his cathedral.   £100,000, he estimated, would be needed
for the completion of this new oratory, and Cornwall with the
decline of its tin-mining industry was a very poor county,
but he never had a moment's doubt that this big sum would
be raised.   Old Lady Rolle of Bicton, daughter of a Cornish
clergyman, and born in 1793, instantly lost her heart to him;

she called him "my bishop" and supported her claim to him by sending a cheque of £40,000 for the purposes of the See. She was an ancient and picturesque figure, she drove out in a chariot with four horses and postilions, she ruled her local kingdom with a rod of iron, and was herself terribly afraid of being left alone for a moment either by day or night. There must always be someone in the room with her to scare away the thought of the solitary journey she must soon take without companion. She had been present as a peeress at the homage following on Queen Victoria's Coronation, and her husband, Lord Rolle, vastly older than herself and very infirm, had tripped in his robes as he ascended the steps of the dais where the young Queen sat, and had *rolled* down to the bottom of them as if he was acting a dumb-crambo. So the Queen rose and went down the steps herself to receive his salutation there: perhaps she whispered in his ear that she had guessed. . .

As at Wellington, there was nothing concerning the new See which my father found too great to be tackled, nothing too small to claim his absorbed attention. The first meeting of the Committee for the building of the cathedral produced £15,000 raised in the room, the work began within a year and he lived to see the dedication and opening of his last oratory though not its completion. He appointed a Chapter for the cathedral not yet built (they could do without a Dean at present, and also without any income since there were no available funds), he made his friend A. J. Mason whom he subsequently appointed to a Canonry at Canterbury, chief Missioner of the Diocese to war against Methodism and that "confusion of sensual excitement with religious passion," so characteristic of "revivals"; he selected figures of Cornish saints, Petroc and Piran and Probus and Austell and Neot and the rest to fill the windows (when there should be any) of his Cathedral: he applied to the Heralds' College for a design for the arms of the See quartered with his own, and when they sent him a sketch he pointed out the errors of the blazonry, and sent a friend a message to be conveyed to the Heralds that he would not accept such stuff and that "he would sooner have

THIS
IS THE SEAL OF
E. W.
BISHOP
OF
TRURO

than submit for an instant to the rubbish which Heralds' College calls a 'Design.' It is not fit for the sign of a public house." He was up at six in the morning for his hour of private devotion before work began, and with a couple of hours out of doors on horseback or on foot was at his tasks again till two the next morning, thriving on labours that would have driven most men into a rest-cure.

Railway communication was non-existent except just down the spine of the county from Saltash to Penzance, and he drove over the whole of his diocese to visit and confirm, dictating letters to his chaplain on the way, and receiving from the warm-hearted folk such a welcome as was rarely accorded to "a foreigner from England." There was not a parish in the remotest coasts and fastnesses of the county which he did not periodically visit. Perhaps the church was in such disorder of repair that the sky showed through its gaping roof and the ivy penetrated through the walls of its aisles, and then he gave squires and landowners no peace till they had taken the necessary restoration in hand. There were queer pastors in many of these isolated hamlets; he arrived one morning, for instance, to preach and celebrate the Sacrament at one of these, and while he was talking to the vicar before church-time, the parlour-maid came in to ask for the cellar key that she might take a bottle of wine to the vestry for the Communion. "We'll have a bottle of white wine today," said the vicar, "just for a change." . . Another incumbent candidly acknowledged that he had little time for visiting his flock as his garden gave him so much pleasant occupation, but the most remarkable of all was a vicar who never set foot in his church at all, far less held any kind of service there. Occasionally some neighbouring parson came over to minister to his unshepherded parishioners, but their rightful parson would not even then consent to attend church as a member of his own congregation. It was quite in vain that the patron of his living pleaded with him. "I don't ask you to do anything,"he said, "but for the sake of example couldn't you just go to church yourself sometimes ?" But it was no use: he preferred to stroll down to the garden gate of the vicarage which adjoined the church clad in a flowered dressing-gown and smoking a hookah, and when his parishioners came out he chatted with them very amiably. There he was, living in the vicarage, a beneficed priest performing no duties of any sort, and there was no ecclesiastical process by which he could possibly be deprived of his house and his income. Many of the livings were miserably endowed, and their occupants had a hard struggle against poverty and Dissent. From one of these my father rented his vicarage for a month, so that the incumbent might get a holiday, and took the duty himself, by way of enjoying his own. The vicar's wife there played the organ, so my father deputed one of his sons to take her place in her absence. On a certain Sunday morning it was announced that the offertory would be devoted to the "organist and choir fund," and that son still labours under the sense of injustice that was his when he found that not one penny of the congregation's subscriptions was allotted to him. . . Then one winter's day my father had a nasty accident when riding, straining his knee very badly, but next day there was a confirmation to be held ten miles away, so, strapped and bandaged, he was hoisted into his landau and on arrival lifted onto a sofa and wheeled into church, where he took the service. There had been a fall of snow the night before: this had half melted during the morning, but in the afternoon a great frost such as had not been known for years in Cornwall set in, and turned the roads to ice. The Bishop's carriage came slewing and skidding down the steep street into Truro with him perfectly helpless inside, looking out of the window straight down the road, and wondering in what fashion he would arrive at the bottom.

On these diocesan travels church people and Wesleyan ministers alike gave him the warmest welcome. They found him personally irresistible, so intensely jolly, so full of enjoyment and keenness and humour, and even when they considered that he was frankly an enemy, that he had the bitterest hostility to Methodism and was come to blow the trumpets of the Church of England till (as he hoped) the walls of their conventicles would fall flat down like those of Jericho, they quite appreciated that he was doing his duty. And when he went back to his cathedral town they did their duty too, and made the most violent attacks on him and his work, exhorting their congregations to stand firm against the intruder. He knew all about that, and he loved his enemies, vowing that of all mankind the Cornish were the most God-fearing and the best-hearted. The walls of his cathedral were now rising apace, and that would be a fort in the enemies' country whose guns would carry far. For relaxation he worked at the "Life of Cyprian," which once, in those days of comparative leisure at Wellington, he had promised his patient publishers should be ready in six months for certain, but which was to occupy him for twenty-two more years instead, and still lacked at his death its final revision. It was no wonder that he wrote this impressionistic comment to a friend, "You have no idea what life is becoming to me, a humming top is the only thing that resembles it: perpetual motion, very dizzy, hollow within, keeping up a continuous angry buzz." But Christmas was approaching and, buzzing or not, he must send a card of greeting to all his great family of godchildren not with a word just scribbled on the back, but with a letter to show that the spinning top in spite of its dizziness, was not so hollow within, but was really thinking about them with a strangely wistful tenderness.   This is one of those Christmas letters accompanying a picture of a river with an empty boat drawn up on its bank.

Decr. 24, 1881

My dear little boy,

I wish you and your Papa and Mamma and everyone you love a very happy Christmas, and may the love of Jesus Christ make it happy.

The picture of the river which I send you is very like the river near to us.   And that is why I liked to choose it for you.   I hope it will be like your life.   It is all covered with bright reflections of earth and heaven.

And I should like you and life to reflect calmly the beautiful things that are in heaven and that are in earth, and not to be soiled and not to be rough.

Do you understand that ?   You will if you think a little. Again there is the boat waiting with her masts ready, but no sails set.   That is the boys', waiting till they go to school.

I wish you a happy voyage whenever it begins.

I thought your first letter was very well written, and I hope the sums and the Bible lessons and all else are going on well.   I suppose you are thinking about Latin too.

God bless you and keep you.   Give my love to your papa and mamma.

Your affectionate friend,
E. W. Truron.

But there fell over his life at Truro, within a year of his appointment there, a shadow out of which he never wholly emerged.   It was the one event in a life of ceaseless work and success, of keen and vivid interests and energies and of unquestioning faith in the decrees of God, which remained enigma to him and stood apart, just a little apart, from all other experience. This was the death of my eldest brother Martin, so called after that friend of Cambridge days, at the age of seventeen. Mentally he was a boy of extraordinary brillance. He had a gay passion for sheer learning which made its acquisition more of a pastime than a task: in a few weeks for instance, merely for amusement, he taught himself as a mere recreation enough Italian to be able to read it with perfect ease. The bent of his mind, its character and attitude, was wholly that of my father's, intensely serious, intensely religious, and without the smallest touch of priggishness. In him my father saw one who would carry on the work of the Church militant here on earth. He would be a great scholar refuting the skeptical conclusions of the higher criticism by a more exalted learning; perhaps he would heal the breach now rapidly widening between the revelations of science and those of religion: perhaps, apart from the world, he would live in that mediæval air of saintliness and scholarship which sometimes seemed to my father the highest call of all, and indeed the boy's mind from its intellectual grip and from that gay holiness of his, seemed capable of a unique maturity. Then one morning there came from Winchester, where he was at school, a telegram that took my father there without delay. Martin, without any warning of approaching illness, had been stricken with aphasia. But in a day or two that passed off: it went as causelessly as it had come, and though he was weak, he appeared to be perfectly well again. Had it not been for the length of the journey he would have come home, so instead, the head-master, Dr Ridding, suggested that he should come to stay in his house for his convalescence. Martin was very fond of him, but whimsically alarmed at the prospect. "It would be dreadful afterwards," he said, "to break down in scholarship. A false quantity would seem like a breach in

hospitality." My father went back to Truro, for all cause
for anxiety seemed over. The seizure of speechlessness had
been alarming and its origin mysterious, but it had completely passed, and Martin was quite cheerful and normal.
Then, after three days he had a relapse, he lost all power
of speech again, and it was evident that there was grave
mischief somewhere. My father and mother were sent for,
and his diary written fifty-two years ago records the rest.

"He looked from one to the other, and took our hands
for a moment, then dropped them again, and folded his own
together and placed one of mine against the other that I
might pray.

"Soon after we began thus to pray I worked into my prayer
the clauses from the Communion service that the Body and
Blood of Christ given and shed for us might preserve his
soul unto Everlasting Life, and placed my finger upon his
lips, saying 'you receive this in the spirit.'

"But he would not let me then proceed, but looked very
anxious and imploring and rather tearful. He was restless,
and moved his hands and his fingers until at last I saw, and
said to the nurse, 'He wants to speak on his fingers.' Then
he quickly formed the letter B, and I said 'Bread and wine'
and he was happy again instantly. A little bread was
brought and we all received when I had consecrated it, and
wine in a glass. The matron put a little wine in a spoon for
me to give him, but he would not take it so, and most reverently grasped the glass, and he received the Lord's Blood
with the happiest look.

"His breathing was loud and difficult, and his mother began to say gently in his ear 'When I survey the wondrous
Cross' and his very soul went with it. But when she came to
the second verse,

'See from His head, His hands, His feet
Sorrow and love flow mingling down,'

he with a sudden momentary look of inquiry, which instantly
changed into an expression of both awe and pleasure, the
most perfect look I ever beheld of satisfied adoration, gazed
at something, Someone; tried with his eyes to make me look
at the same, and then pointed to it with his fingers.

"Presently I went on, 'Thou who art in the midst of the
throne amid Thy angels and Thy holy ones,' and at that I
wish it were possible to describe the gentle and strong and
distinct sweep with which stretching out his left arm, he
gently waved it along a quarter circle from a point just above
him.

"He beheld ἄρρητα — things which it is not lawful for men
to utter, and perhaps it was for this that he was silenced,
that he might see such things and not utter them. So passed
on silent hours, yet so much faster than we imagined. Every
now and then at shorter and shorter intervals a flush passed
over his face, and his breathing changed. There was a
sigh like weariness, and again the heavy breathing.

"A few minutes before ten the heavy breathing quite
passed away to become quite soft. His lips gathered themselves nearly together: it looked like a baby's mouth, so soft
and sweet and small. The nurse placed her hand gently
across his eyes. He breathed in soft little gentle sobs and
these ceased to come, and our Martin was gone to God.

"My dearest wife understood it all more quickly, better,
more sweetly than I. At once she knew that she had never
cared for anything but his happiness and that it was come.

"On that Saturday night we were indeed broken. But
his dear mother was even then Christ's, and felt Christ to be
God. The moment after he had gone, her exclamation was
'Oh, my Martin, how happy you are now, my darling.'

"His mother's bearing of all seems to me as perfect as
anything can be. A few hours after she knelt in our
room and prayed aloud 'It is Thy will only that we will.
He is Thine, Thou hast a right to him,' I cannot reach to
this.

"To him, we know, going is gain, pure gain, and I am learning from my wife to subdue the longing for his sweetness back again. She has never faltered."

THE work in Cornwall went on in a stream of ceaseless activities, and now the stream was spreading outside the diocese. He had rooms in the Lollards Tower of Lambeth Palace, he preached as Chaplain to the Queen at Windsor, he preached also in Westminster Abbey on three not very auspicious occasions, for he recorded that:

"(i) The first time I preached in the Abbey I lost my voice, so nobody could hear me.

"(ii) The second time there were six inches of slush and violent rain after snow so there *was* nobody to hear me.

"(iii) The third time, tomorrow, owing to the fog I believe there will be no light in the sky, and so there will be no-one to see me."

In London he had interviews with General Booth about the work of the Salvation Army: these were of an ambassadorial nature, and altogether it looked as if some force was beginning to exert its pull from somewhere outside the orbit of his Cornish activities. Archbishop Tait of Canterbury came to stay with him at Truro and in the autumn of 1882 he was sent for to Addington where the Archbishop, then in his last illness, spoke directly to him, expressing the hope that he would succeed him at Canterbury. On Archbishop Tait's death just before the end of the year, Gladstone, who was Prime Minister at the time, went to see the Queen about the new appointment and this was one of the not very common occasions on which he and the Sovereign were entirely of one mind. They agreed that Bishop Harold Brown of Winchester was too old for the post, and that there was only one man, and he among the junior bishops at present without a seat in the House of Lords, who could adequately fill it.

Gladstone instantly wrote to my father, offering him the Archbishopric in these terms:

> Downing Street
> Dec. 16, 1882

My dear Bishop of Truro,

I have to propose to your lordship with the sanction of Her Majesty that you should accept the succession to the Archbishopric of Canterbury now vacant through the lamented death of Archbishop Tait.

This proposal is a grave one. But it is, I can assure you, made with a sense of its gravity, and in some degree proportioned to it, and it comes to you, not as an offer of personal advancement but as a request that, whereas you have heretofore been employing your talents in the service of the Church and Realm, you will hereafter employ then with the same devotion in the same good and great cause. I have the honour to be,

> my dear Lord Bishop,
> with cordial respect,
> Sincerely yours,
> W. E. GLADSTONE

The same day there came a telegram from the Queen saying that she was writing. Her letter arrived just before Christmas. She spoke of the high esteem in which she and the Prince Consort had always held my father during his years at Wellington College, and expressed the earnest hope, both on Ecclesiastical and personal grounds that he would accept the appointment.

A week had already elapsed since the Prime Minister had offered him the Archbishopric and he had not yet made up his mind whether to accept it or not, for he knew himself that his genius lay in personal, pioneering work, such as had been his in the creation of Wellington College, and in the

new diocese of Cornwall, and the Primacy was mainly an
administrative post, much concerned with political legislation, and, though large in scope, fettered by tradition. All
his life, supremely sincere in purpose, and of a masterful
will and energy that carried all before it, he had occupied
positions where, having made up his mind, he got his own
way. But now, though entrusted with a far larger responsibility, he knew that his freedom would be far more curtailed.
As a small boy he had informed his mother that he intended to
be Archbishop of Canterbury, and his sister had chaffingly
told him that, even at Cambridge, the fulfillment of his ambition was growing appreciably nearer. And now it was given
him. But he saw that there would be no more of that militant
liberty through which he had driven to accomplishment his
own policy on his own responsibility: whatever he did now
as head, under the Sovereign, of the Church, was a matter
of State. His measures would be bills for which the Government of the day must find a place on their programme, and
of which Parliament must approve. But now with the personal appeal from the Queen, he hesitated no longer, and
he wrote to Mr Gladstone accepting the Primacy.

"God give grace. God give all that I only can know to
be so fearfully wanting. I will give all that He gives to
the service of the Queen and people and Church."

"That Her Majesty herself approves it, knowing almost
better than anyone my earlier work, is a thought full of
strength."

CHAPTER V

TWO SISTERS

THE RETICENCES and reserves which were practised in the intercourse between men and women in the seventies, seem now to our minds as remote and outlandish as whiskers or crinolines, and there is nothing easier than to make fun of them, for the habits of one generation are always a legitimate source of amusement to the next. But they were founded on a tradition that was wholly worthy of respect, the principle of which was that when the two sexes met together for social enjoyment they should preserve a certain outward form of dignity and politeness. Of course there was as much scandal then as now, women had their lovers and men their mistresses, but there was not general gabble on these and kindred subjects. To many of the women of that time, this dignity and reserve were perfectly natural, and, just then, that tradition prevailed and governed the speech of mixed intercourse. Men did what they thought good, and saw what they chose, and said what they liked to each other, but women according to the same code only saw what it was fit for them to see, and however vividly a domestic scandal or outrage was thrust in front of their eyes, the traditions of a certain class enjoined on them to assume in public a bland blindness to it; fine breeding demanded that a woman should be unconscious of it. Any public recognition of it was unthinkable, and even more unthinkable was it that she should talk about it, or seek to protect herself against a domestic situation even if it threatened to ruin her life or render it intolerable. It was correct to be blind and dumb, and to see or speak was an offence against the laws that governed the behaviour of her class. Tragic could be the consequences, if she took steps to

75

defend herself.   The life of one of the finest women I have
ever known was thus temporarily wrecked, but out of the
wreck her courage constructed an ark for others.   The story
is full of typical figures, of which the central one though
grimly Victorian by upbringing and marriage, was at heart
the most amazing mixture of modernity, saintliness, humour,
and humanity.   She was also one of the pioneers who have
won for their sex liberty and the right to work.

To realize the different strains of character which determined the situation in which this very noble woman was
entangled and from which she triumphantly extricated herself, it is necessary to begin rather far back.   Her grandfather on her mother's side was a certain Mr Pattle, merchant
in Indian tradings, who had made a very considerable fortune.   He married the daughter of one of Marie Antoinette's
pages of honour, and that strain of French blood was des-
tined to play a part in a wholly English drama.   Mr Pattle
was the father of five extremely attractive and handsome
daughters, and was himself remarkable for his reputation
of being the greatest liar in India; somehow we feel inclined
at the outset to like Mr Pattle, though we shall see nothing
of him except that which was not meant to be seen.   But
to have such a reputation is endearing; it connotes a gar-
rulous and clubbable fellow.   He died out in India, and since
he had expressed his wish to be buried in England, his widow
procured a large barrel into which the deceased was folded,
and the barrel was then filled up to the top with some reliable
preservative, rum or Pondicherry liquor, something with
body in it, in two senses of the word.   The widow then
travelled back to England where her daughters awaited her,
on the ship which conveyed the remains.   Steam in those
days was unknown as a propulsion, the shorter route through
the Suez canal not yet made, and off the Cape of Good Hope
the vessel encountered so violent a buffeting from a storm,
that Mr Pattle's barrel broke from its moorings and rolled
about with a very dreadful liveliness.   Before it could be

bridled again, a violent collison with the ship's side broached
it, smashing off the top and spilling such contents as were
liquid: what was solid peered starkly over the battered staves.
There was not enough liquor on the ship nor a large enough
barrel to make possible any further homing of the contents,
and after the widow had formally identified them, they were
buried at sea.   Before the ship reached England Mr Pattle's
widow also died and his large fortune descended to his daughters.

The youngest and far the most beautiful of them all was
Miss Virginia.   From her mother she inherited an exquisite
French patrician charm and a strong strain of melodrama.
In 1850 she married Lord Eastnor, eldest son and heir of Earl
Somers, to whose title and estate he presently succeeded.
Two years after her marriage was born a daughter Isabel,
and later another daughter Adeline, but there the family
stayed.   The two were brought up by their mother according to the strictest Victorian standards as set up by the
Prince Consort for the education of the Royal children, with
this difference that she did not give much personal super-
vision to it.   Backboards and scales on the piano, French
exercises and the use of the globes, lodgings at the seaside
for the sake of its healthful and tonic airs, rugs for the
knees and scarves for the neck, prohibition to read anything
amusing, particularly novels, charitable expeditions to the
village with jellies and knitted articles for the deserving
poor, restricted pocket money and cloistered ignorance of
all that was likely to be met with in later life, were the principles of it and a governess the administrator, while their
exquisite mother entranced the fashionable and artistic world
of London and made romantic journeys to Italy, constantly
writing to her two girls the most affectionate letters, but not
really seeing very much of them until they were of ripe years
to be shown to men and under her deft guiding hand to make
brilliant marriages.   The system of their education in fact
had a strong French flavouring mixed with its English mode.

The first to appear was, of course, Isabel, and it looked as if
almost immediately a very suitable young man, with a dukedom waiting for him, would carry off this lively heiress to
Eastnor Castle and a very ample property. But another
mother had her eye on the Marquis of Lorne who shortly became the husband of Princess Louise, and Lady Somers must
look elsewhere. The sooner Isabel was suitably married the
better, for her mother had ideas already for the younger Adeline, and the correct use was that the elder of two daughters
must be married first: anything else was irregular. Then
Lord Henry Somerset came on the scene; he was not quite as
good, for he had an elder brother, unmarried at present, who
stood between him and the Dukedom of Beaufort, but the
Somersets were a very great family and he would do. He was
a very attractive man, of artistic tastes, he composed songs
which made the Victorians dissolve into copious tears, and
Isabel would be reigning daughter-in-law of the magnificent
Badminton. So the marriage took place, and quickly she
captured the hearts of her father- and mother-in-law. She
had not got Lady Somers's beauty, but this girl of twenty
must have been an enchanting creature, deliciously pretty,
auburn-haired, and full of grace and gaiety and wit.

She told me once of a scene that took place at Badminton
shortly after her marriage, which admirably illustrates the
high-bred reserve of great Victorian dames. The Duke of
Beaufort was away, but there was a party in the house, and
one day the butler told the Duchess as they went in to
lunch that a package had arrived for His Grace, which he
had unpacked: it contained a picture and he wanted to know
where he was to hang it. So the whole party went into
the corridor, when lunch was over, to see the picture, and
they found the portrait of a very pretty young lady whom
everybody knew to be the Duke's mistress. Was that an
awkward situation? Not in the least. The Duchess with
complete self-possession looked admiringly at it, and said,
"Is it not charming? A fancy portrait I suppose," and

without a grin or a wink or a whisper, they all looked at the
fancy portrait and liked it immensely. It would do very
well, thought the Duchess, just where it was, hung on the
wall there. Then as they moved quietly on, she changed
her mind. "His Grace might like it in his own room perhaps," she said to her butler. "You had better hang it
there." That was all; reticence and dignity had perfectly
solved the method of dealing with this awkwardness, and
when the Duke came home there was the fancy portrait hanging in his room as a pleasant surprise for him.

But there was an unpleasant surprise for him not long
afterwards, for the lady determined to transfer her charms
to another admirer and wrote to tell him so. Victorian reserve
was not binding on men, and with tears he bewailed to his
sons and daughter-in-law his cruel fate. Being a thoroughly
religious man, he sought spiritual consolation in his trial, so
the order went forth that next Sunday every groom and
coachman and helper in the Badminton stables should attend
church and receive the Sacrament with their master. This
was quite characteristic of the time: a man could be a sincere and devout Christian and yet be keeping a mistress:
besides his mistress had left him, so he no longer had one.
In just the same manner, a certain notable Oxford professor
of strict tractarian views, who kept a mistress in the town,
learned casually from her that she had never been confirmed.
He was very much upset by this, and persuaded her to receive instruction and repair this shocking omission. That
made him quite happy, and their relationship was resumed
with no cloud to mar its brightness. . . Lady Henry Somerset, devoted to her father-in-law, full of humour, and intensely comprehending shook with kindly laughter that must
not betray itself and delighted in him.

Then tragedy developed. Lady Henry became aware of
things in her husband's life that made it impossible for her
to go on living with him. For a long while she bore them
in silence and then could bear them no more, and said she

must be separated from him. Possibly the affair might have
been managed without public scandal, but at the moment
when careful thought and wisdom were most demanded Lady
Somers descended on the situation, in a whirlwind of French
horror and dramatic tableau, and persuaded her daughter
not to spend another night in her husband's house, but to
take refuge with her baby at Eastnor. A more unwise handling of the situation cannot be conceived, for instantly it
flamed into a public scandal of the most atrocious kind. Lady
Somers had not in the least understood what would be the
result of that flamboyant gesture, and it was perhaps lucky
for her sense of maternal duty that she had already married
her second daughter to the next holder of the dukedom of
Bedford.

Lady Henry sought for and obtained her separation,
stating her grounds. She did not ask for a divorce because
her religious principles forbade that, for she believed that
marriage was an indissoluble tie: God had joined together
and no sundering was possible. Nor indeed could she have
obtained the divorce for which she never sought, for there
had been neither desertion nor technical cruelty. But by
making public the reason for her separation, she had outraged the sacred principle of womanly reticence, and dire
was the wrath of the silent ones. The code of Victorian
"Reticence for women" had been violated, and it showed,
when defied, of what savagery it was capable. For it was
not, as it now proved itself, a mere matter of mere convenient blindness that affected not to see what was disagreeable, nor a matter of acquiescing dumbness, which considered
it just a piece of good taste not to talk about subjects which
were better passed over in silence, but a rooted and sacred
principle that a woman in Their class, must, whatever her
domestic trouble, hold her tongue. They would have nothing
more to do with the offender, and "Society" cut her.

So fire and brimstone rained down on Lady Henry, and
she retired from the world of her upbringing and marriage,

which would no longer receive her. She had delighted in its glitter and splendour, she had revelled in its gaiety, its operas, its jewels, but she never, in the middle-class manner of Byron, shook off the dust of it from her feet, nor pretended to think that the world in which she had lived was all dross and malice and corruption; it remained, though she was no longer of it, a most delightful place, full of agreeable and congenial and amusing people. She lived for a while at the Priory, Reigate, a beautiful house belonging to her father, and at his death she established herself at the Norman Castle (rather late Norman, since it was built at the end of the eighteenth century) at Eastnor, where she had been brought up. Her mother, half French by blood, and wholly French by instinct, retired to Aix-les-Bains where, still a marvel of distinguished charm and beauty, she made a centre for the more notable sections of the shifting population who came there for cures. For that particular sort of supremacy she had a real genius, and taking the house of Dr Brachet, a leading physician there, she exercised a gracious and queen-like and slightly theatrical hospitality.

Lady Henry at her father's death was only thirty-three years old, of rich and radium-like energy, for which there seemed no outlet. She could not marry again, she was cut off from the world which she knew, and there seemed nothing for it but just to live at Eastnor unoccupied and chiefly alone; and that, to one overflowing with life and with the strongest need for bringing herself into human relationships, was absolutely impossible. She looked after her estates, she visited her tenants, and from that developed her work among women, which she continued to the end of her life. She interested herself especially with those who had come to ruin through drink. Drunkenness she never thought of as sinful, it was just a consoling habit, leading to wretched results, which was the natural effect of living in beastly houses, and in sordid and depressing conditions. So she began rebuilding, regardless of expense, the insanitary cottages on her estate, in order to give women of intemperate habits a chance of regaining the self-respect which would break the curse, and she exhorted them, of course, to take the pledge of total abstinence, instead of messing about with compromises of the harmlessness of an occasional indulgence. Then it seemed to her humorous and candid mind that it really was not fair to expect others to practice an abstinence which she did not observe, and most regretfully she decided that she must become a teetotaler herself. She wanted to make this ceremony impressive, and arranged to take the pledge publicly at Eastnor (was there a touch of her mother's dramatic quality in that?) among her assembled tenants and dependents, so that all should see that her practice was as thorough as her preaching. The rite was to take place in the hall in the Castle on her return from London, but on the way back she had to change trains at Worcester, and she recounted with peals of the most delicious laughter that ever came from human mouth what happened at Worcester. "I hurried to the refreshment room and had two glasses of rich fruity port. Just that one more drink!"

It was thus that she began the rebuilding of a life that seemed so utterly wrecked. Instead of having nothing to do, she was overwhelmed with the work she had taken up. She was a born orator, humorous, incisive, convincing, she had a voice of gold, and she travelled not only over England, but made tours to America, speaking for the cause of temperance. There was no nonsense about her; she did not say that alcohol was evil in itself, or that the Last Supper was celebrated, as the fanatical affirmed, with an unfermented juice of the grape. Alcohol, according to her, was as good a gift of God as roast chicken, and only dangerous to the vulnerable. Religion and rescue-work were the motives of her life, no saint ever devoted himself more unreservedly to the practice of his faith, and yet saintliness was the very last quality that could be attributed to her, so wholly secular was her sense of humour, and so abhorrent to her was any-

thing like asceticism or ecstasy.   She attended, for instance,
a Salvation Army meeting, and (though she hated doing it)
she felt herself obliged to stand forth and kneel at the "peni-
tence form," a thing that surely required a good deal of
courage and sincerity.   But she could not see herself in the
regulation poke-bonnet, though, as she told me, a pathetic
appeal had been made to her by an aged leader of the movement.   "Oh, Lady Somerset," she had said, "how I pray God
that before I die, I may see you in a saved 'at !"   Or again,
when about to stay with her at Eastnor, I was astonished to
receive a telegram from her reading, "Please bring a bottle
of whisky."   I obeyed, and she explained this curious request to me on my arrival with her irresistible merriment.
Her principles, she said, forbade her to supply me with alcohol in her house, but her sense of hospitality revolted at
the thought of my finding myself forced to be an abstainer.
"So I had to send you that telegram," she said, "though I
know that now I'm completely in your power.   You've only
got to tell everyone that though I preach teetotalism and
affirm that I practise it, I get my friends to bring me drink
on the sly.   My telegram proves it."   Later, she gave up
Eastnor, for she wanted all the money she could possibly
get hold of to support her settlement at Duxhurst which she
had opened to reclaim drunken and criminal women.   She
took them from their squalid surroundings and established
them in bright, cheerful little abodes, she gave them outdoor
work to do, she established a further colony of children whose
presence satisfied their womanly instincts.

She went entirely on the admirable lines that women take
to drink in order to put colour and a sense of enjoyment into
drab and dreary lives, and at Duxhurst she established herself as matron, and apart from rare holidays spent the rest
of her life there.   She wore a uniform of a nunnish nurse-
ish sort, and one day, having gone down from London to
visit her, I was astonished to see her abstaining from cigarettes.   In answer to my question whether there was a crusade

against smoking also, there came that laughter which was
surely the most infectious expression of amusement ever
heard: no-one could help laughing when she laughed. "I
had to give it up," she said, "I saw in the train the other
day a stout elderly woman like me in a nurse's dress smoking
a cigarette. An awful sight; I couldn't bear the idea that
I looked like that."

WHILE Lady Henry was still at Badminton, Lady Somers
had had the happiness of seeing her second daughter Adeline
married to Lord Tavistock, the eldest son of the Duke of
Bedford, and installed as daughter-in-law at Woburn Abbey
in the midst of such high traditions of antique aristocracy
as are now scarcely credible. Her father-in-law had just
such an outlook on life as David attributed to Jehovah: "all
the beasts of the forest are mine, and so are the cattle upon a
thousand hills." He was prodigiously wealthy — how
should he not be, being Duke of Bedford ? — and had an
immense property in London, for all the streets and squares
of Bedford and Russell and Woburn and Endsleigh and
Tavistock were his. "If one hadn't a few acres in London
in these times of agricultural depression," he said, "I don't
know what one would do." So as he had a nice acreage
there, he did nothing. Covent Garden with its filthy slums
belonged to him, and it was a disgrace to any civilized town,
but where was the use of being a landlord if you had to ex-
pend vast sums on your property ? Indeed it required full-
page cartoons in *Punch*, in which he appeared in his coronet
holding up his Garter-robes for fear they should trail in the
stinking puddles of Mud-Salad Market, before he could be
induced to remedy its monstrous dirt and squalor. As well
as his wealth, he inherited the brains of one of the cleverest
families in Europe, and he devoted their keenest edge to the
nirvanic enjoyment of being what he was. It was better,
too, that his eldest son should leave the House of Commons
for he in turn would be Duke of Bedford, and that gave

anybody enough to think about. It was time also that he should marry, for it was a proper thing that a future Duke of Bedford should have a wife, even if her whole duty was confined to looking graceful and reserved and well-bred. But it was not fit that the future Duchess, when at Woburn, should drive about in an open carriage where anybody on the roads could stare at her, and his wishes were conveyed to her, that when she went out into the country roads round Woburn, where neither she nor her equipage could be *incognita*, a brougham would be more suitable. As regards her unfortunate sister she was not forbidden to see her, but neither the Duchess nor he would meet her.

Duchess Adeline (as she duly became) had neither the irrepressible vitality of her sister nor her unfailing sense of humour, and while the lack of the former made her suffer less under this stifling tyranny and emptiness, the lack of the latter did not enable her to see the ludicrous side of these rich pomposities. Lady Henry would have found in this arid existence bright spots of the ridiculous, but though Duchess Adeline found none, she had inherited from her mother (which her sister had not) a perception that after all it was something to be a Duchess; it supplied a palliative to the aching joylessness. Like Lady Henry she had a strong devotional and religious sense, and on the appointment of my father to the Archbishopric, she formed the two closest friendships of her life with him and my mother. She was often at Lambeth and Addington, she went abroad with us on Swiss High-Alp holidays, where, with a Parisian sense, derived from her mother, of what was suitable, she walked about on the paths through the meadows with an elegant stick fitted with a chamois-horn as a handle, and a spike on its ferule. From then onwards she kept up a most intimate and constant correspondence with them both, and there was nothing in her own life which she did not confide to one or other of them. My father delighted to consult her on points connected with Church policy and organization: if

he had to write a charge to his clergy, he talked to her about
it, taking long straying strolls with her, deep in discussion.
It was a very shrewd and intelligent sympathy from outside that Duchess Adeline gave him, he wanted to know just
what she could tell him, namely the "lay view" of movements
in the Church. On his side he brought to her whole regions
of interests outside herself.

This bond between the three of them which grew ever
stronger as the years went by, was first really woven when in
the early days of their friendship she, while still Lady Tavistock, asked if she might bring to Lambeth a deputation of
personal friends of hers who wanted his help and counsel in
a matter which they all had very much at heart. He consented to receive them, and among them were the Duchess of
Leeds, Marchionesses Tavistock, Bristol, Ailsa, Countesses
Aberdeen, Zetland, Haddington, Stanhope, Ladies Mount-
Temple, Muncaster, Harriet Ashley, Welby-Gregory, Mrs
Lowther (the late Speaker's mother) and Mrs Reginald Talbot. They were, in fact, very fairly representative of the
influential and serious women of the day, and the deputation was significant in two ways; it was concerned with the
break-down of the conventional proprieties of the seventies,
and with that of the Victorian tradition that the first duty of
women was to be blind and dumb. Women like these, ten
years before, could never have taken part in a concerted
movement of which the object was to disclose scandalous matter. But the ice of convention which before had frozen them
in, was now swiftly melting, and they broke through it. The
whole story of the deputation not a word of which ever became
public, now violates no reasonable discretion, but to place
it in its right setting, a few words of explanation are necessary.

The Queen, it may be remembered, had completely retired
after the Prince Consort's death; almost her only public appearance had been when she attended the service of thanks-
giving for the recovery of the Prince of Wales from typhoid,

she attended no State functions and her influence on the social life of the upper classes was non-existent. She saw her ministers, she visited her crofters, but she was otherwise invisible, and socially she was represented by the Prince of Wales. But while she remained thus utterly withdrawn, she kept in her own hands every atom of the more solid functions of the Crown, and neither consulted the Prince of Wales on affairs of State or diplomatic relations with foreign countries, nor paid the smallest attention to his views. Twenty-three years ago she had declared to her uncle, the King of the Belgians, that nobody, now that the Prince Consort was no longer there with his help and counsel, should be her adviser; she knew precisely what his views were on every matter that concerned the realm, and she would undeviatingly follow them, and not allow anybody to come between her and her people. She still adhered to that disastrous resolution, and instead of consulting her singularly intelligent son, and committing to him those diplomacies and administrations, which he, vividly in touch with the times, was so competent to conduct, and which he so sagaciously conducted as soon as he had the chance of doing so, she withheld from him everything of the kind. She refused to let him be Governor General of Canada or Viceroy of Ireland, and to open a few docks and bazaars and lay a few foundation-stones was not employment for a mentally energetic man, now in the very prime of life, who would have been of inestimable service in imperial concerns; she even saw in his visit to Ireland reasons for regret that it coincided with the Punchestown races. It was therefore not only natural but laudable that, denied the work to which he longed to devote himself, he used his energies in enjoying himself, for which also he had a very enviable aptitude. He was handsome, he was popular, he had tearing spirits, and if he was not allowed to fill the proper office of a Prince of Wales whose mother was in complete retirement, but was shut out of all the State business of the country he would someday rule, he must occupy himself by making the most of a Prince's pleasures. He had had a most repressed and depressing youth, saddled and bridled with tutors, and cut off by the well-meaning unwisdom of his father from any free intercourse with his contemporaries: he had been to no public school, and at Oxford and at Cambridge, to both of which Universities he went up as an undergraduate, he had been made to live with his tutor in a private house, instead of having rooms in college like everybody else. It had been a regime to which no young man could adapt himself without asserting his own rights to youth. No doubt it was intended to rouse in him a due sense of the responsibilities that would one day be his, but now, when he was grown up and eminently capable of assuming some of them, he was denied all exercise of them, and being debarred from being *bon ouvrier*, there was really nothing for him to do, except to be *bon vivant*. To him more than to anyone was due the break up of the mid-Victorian social tradition of frozen pompous dignity, and all its repressions and reticences. He toppled over that futile, forbidding old idol, he broke down the staid hedges that surrounded society, and beckoned in a quantity of lively and gay young persons with whom, as he was forbidden to work, he could play, and just as, towards the close of the fifteenth century, Columbus discovered America, so now Columbia discovered England, and came over in fleets of Mayflowers to receive the welcome of genial John Bull. And though into those exclusive coteries of New York no Jew was ever allowed to penetrate, they found that they must not be so particular in England, for Jews were always among the closest of the Prince's friends.

And now for the business of this deputation of ladies for which these reactions were responsible. With the best and highest of motives they had come to ask my father if he could do nothing to stop the moral rot which, they affirmed, was ruining London. Girls newly "come out," they said, of high tone and upright intentions were speedily corrupted by it, and what they had been brought up to regard as evil they soon regarded as natural and inevitable; young married women had no standard of morality at all, and the centre of the mischief was the Marlborough House set. They wanted my father to start a sort of moral mission for women of their class and to hold devotional meetings for them at Lambeth, thus creating a powerful and influential nucleus of those who aimed at high ideals and would not tolerate the looseness of life which was becoming general. They thought it would give a great impetus to the movement if the Princess of Wales would come to these meetings: it was no use trying to get the sympathy of the Queen, for that would have no effect as "she was not smart enough." Finally they all agreed that my father should talk to the Prince about the harm that was going on "for he would listen to no-one else."

It was a situation which required thinking about before he could make up his mind exactly what to do. Many of these ladies were friends of his, and he had nothing but the warmest sympathy with the object of their deputation, namely the setting of a higher moral tone in society. He was quite at their service there, and since their desire was that he should hold devotional meetings at Lambeth he at once instituted them, and from that year, the first of his Archiepiscopate, he annually held a series of these, till the time of his death; there was a short service followed by an address, and the attendance filled Lambeth Chapel to overflowing. But as regards telling the Prince of Wales that he and his friends were setting a bad example, that was a very different affair. He was a friend of the Prince's, all he had heard was of the nature of vague gossip, and to go to the Prince of Wales and tell him he must mend his ways, seemed to him an unwarrantable intrusion into his private affairs, though when a few years later a certain scandal became public, he had not the smallest hesitation in telling the Prince what he thought about it. Besides this was not, to his mind, the right way to set about raising the tone of London life, and he suggested a better one at the first of these meetings which took place within a week or two. He addressed his ladies on the subject of sincerity, and the pith of his advice, as recorded in his diary was, "Don't meddle, or try to improve anyone, but lead your life well yourself."

Then there was the question of whether the Princess of Wales would attend their meetings, and she was asked if she would. Before she could give an answer to this, she felt she must consult the Queen, for devotional meetings were outside the general routine of royal engagements. The Queen did not like the idea; for in spite of her own firm religious convictions and the faith of which she was the Defender, religion was not a thing to be mixed up with life. Nor could she, by any possible elasticity of terms, be called devotional. To go to church or chapel on Sunday morning with unfailing regularity, to ask God's blessing on launched ships, docks, regimental colours and foundation-stones, to attend all family christenings, marriages, funerals, and anniversary services, comprised the sum of public religious observances. She indicated her attitude to one in whom she much confided with some vexation. "I can't understand," she said, "why princesses should want to go to Lambeth meetings. It's all sacerdotal. I can't think what it's all about." She was impatient of such notions. To want to go on a weekday to Lambeth chapel for purposes of prayer and devotion was "most extraordinary." We may guess that she regarded my father as the leader in some sacerdotal conspiracy, and for quite a long period she ceased to write to him in the second person, and sign herself, "ever yours affectionately," but became "The Queen." Or had she somehow got to know that the conspiring ladies did not think her smart enough to be of any use?

CHAPTER VI

THREE MONUMENTAL FIGURES

THE EXPERIENCE of going back to a house familiar in childhood, but not seen since, and finding it strangely dwindled in size, is a common one, but one that is easily accounted for. It took more steps for a child to traverse a passage, the door handle was on a level with the face, the bed of seeding asparagus in the garden was a thicket in which it was possible to be completely hidden, a table suitably draped in a dust-sheet was a cave of ample proportions for the domestic comfort of several brigands. All is a question of relativity: these things were proportionately bigger to a child than they are to an adult. And when it comes to mental impressions made on youth or early manhood by eminent folk, there may be some similar reason to account for their appearing to the memory (since we cannot actually revisit those years as we can a house of childhood) of greater psychical stature than the corresponding eminent folk of the day. But the illusion, if it is one, is absolutely convincing and nothing can make me believe that a person like Mr Gladstone was not of some higher voltage of power than more recent Prime Ministers.

I once attended some political meeting addressed by him, and saw there, so I believe, a greater demonstration of sheer force than can be equalled today by any politician. He was being heckled by one of his audience as to the views he was then expressing, which seemed (as indeed they were) to be flatly contradictory to those which he had propounded with no less emphasis and authority a year or two before. He could not get on with his speech: the interrupter was surrounded by his friends, he was persistent, he had a loud voice, he was sitting close to the platform, and he was ready with chapter and verse to support his contention. Mr. Gladstone bore it for a little, but suddenly he had enough of him. He pointed at him thrusting out his arm as if stabbing him, with furious face and fierce imperious gesture. Three times there shot out that menacing hand and the heckler could not stand against it. He sat down and thereafter was dumb. Then Mr Gladstone in a voice quivering with indignant energy, said "It would be tedious to compare what I may have happened to say a year ago, or perhaps two, with what I have the honour to be saying to you now." He made no explanation nor attempted to prove with that incomparable ingenuity of his, that though a year ago (or perhaps two) he had seemed to say precisely the opposite, he had quite clearly meant precisely the same, for it was not worth while. It would be tedious; and so he went on with his speech without any further interruption. He was the stronger: instead of arguing he knocked the man out by a pointing finger, charged with irresistible force. Indeed one might say that the rash fellow had touched that awful dynamo and his mind was instantly electrocuted.

All that Mr Gladstone did was charged with that terrific voltage. I went more than once to Hawarden when, after taking my degree at Cambridge, I was archæologically employed in examining the north wall of the city of Chester, into which had been built a quantity of tombstones from a Roman cemetery. There I had the good fortune to discover some inscribed monuments to men who had served in the tenth legion, "Valeria Victrix," of which no record in Britain had hitherto come to light, and I took over to Hawarden to show to Mr Gladstone blotting paper "squeezes" of some of them. (The method of making these squeezes is to spread a sheet of damp blotting paper over the inscription of which you desire a facsimile and then to tap it gently with a clothes brush, until the blotting paper has moulded itself into the lettering. When dry, it thus becomes a portable cast of the stone.) Mr

Gladstone was enormously interested in the discovery of this legion having been in England, though it was only the minutest contribution to the details of the Roman occupation seventeen hundred years ago, and he got down some books of military inscriptions for reference. But equally fiery was his advice about making squeezes. The blotting paper, he said, ought certainly to be laid down dry on the face of the inscription, and then be sprinkled: otherwise it was liable to tear. For the same reason it should be left on the stone till it was dry again: otherwise damp fragments might stick to it, and the squeeze be spoilt. I felt that Mr Gladstone had devoted his whole life to making squeezes, and that he occupied his leisure only in conducting the affairs of the nation. Though Mrs Gladstone had come to remind him that lunch was ready, he would not go till he had made conjectures about a few missing letters in one of these inscriptions: the thing might have been a dispatch from Downing Street which must be deciphered and dealt with at once, otherwise some hideous European imbroglio would follow. And there was the table at which his political work was done, and close by the "Homer-table" where he found coolness and refreshment when hot with polemics.

At lunch there was a discussion about the dismal task of packing a bag, when one was leaving by an early train in the morning; the sponge was wet from the traveller's ablutions and it always oozed dampness into neighbouring linen. Then came the oracle: "You none of you know how to pack your sponge. The only way of packing a sponge is first to wrap it up in your bath towel, and then to stamp upon it." Surely he had never done anything all his life but pack sponges in bags for early morning travel ! On another occasion he had retired after some such oracle into remote regions of his own again, while the table-talk went on. Clever women was the subject now, and it was generally agreed that my mother was the cleverest woman in England. Out he came again from his meditations. "No, you're wrong," he said.

"She's the cleverest woman in Europe." Everything that he was engaged in for the moment was of supreme importance: it was the same with his backgammon with which he relaxed himself in the evening. But relaxed ? He rattled and threw the dice, as if he was playing with the devil for his own immortal soul, and was temporarily engaged in a war with the powers of darkness. One afternoon he drove me to St Deiniol's, the library of his own books which he was arranging with the purpose of bequeathing them to the clergy of the Church of Wales, which he hoped to disestablish. That was exceedingly like him: his conscience told him that the Church should be disendowed, and in anticipation of that he began to endow it personally with a magnificent library, for the clergy must have access to sources of learning. A pony-carriage came round, and I was aware that he was going to drive himself. Before getting in he went round to the pony's head and peered at him. "He's a beast," he said, "I must get a heavier whip." Out he came again with his more formidable weapon, and off we went, he the intrepid charioteer of something over eighty years. He whacked the pony over the rump, and talked about the manner in which men who had retired from active work in their profession should employ themselves. He wanted to know what I thought my father would do if ever he retired from the See of Canterbury, and chuckled when I told him he would certainly apply for the post of librarian at St Deiniol's.

Always there was this huge concentration of force; purpose at white-heat roared like a furnace in every action of his life. When once he had convinced himself on any subject, it ceased to be his opinion, and became a cosmic truth, which it was the duty of every right-minded person to uphold. Just as the only method of packing up a damp sponge was to begin by stamping on it (he being merely the exponent of this dazzling truth to an ignorant world) so he was convinced, and said so, that the will of the English people was set on giving Home Rule to Ireland, and that he was the appointed

instrument to accomplish their will for them. God gave
him his health and vitality for that.   Thus his conscience was
invariably clear of personal ambition: he was working not for
his own idea but for some great cause external to him.
Never, so Mrs Gladstone told my mother, did the estrange-
ments and execrations of those who had been his friends cause
him to say, "I wish I had never done it !"   He might regret
the bitterness he had aroused, but he never regretted those
measures which had caused it.

This remorseless inflexibility was one of the reasons why in
his official relation with the Queen he so often irritated her.
He always paid her the most profound respect, but his deference to her person did not include the slightest deference
to her statecraft, and nothing she said influenced him in the
least when his mind was made up, for he knew he was right,
whereas she, on those many occasions when their views differed, was equally certain that he was wrong.   Though she
maintained an impeccable impartiality in politics and would
never attempt to resist the will of her people, she was a thorough Tory at heart, and regarded him as an enemy to Church
and State, and thus an enemy to the throne, for he had disestablished the Irish Church and now he wanted to give Home
Rule to Ireland.   It was therefore with the most unfeigned
pleasure that she saw the fall of his last ministry in 1894, and
she commented on it privately to my father with remarkable
frankness: this was perfectly correct on her part for he officially had no politics any more than she.   "Mr Gladstone
has gone out, disappeared all in a moment," she gleefully observed.   "His last two ministries have been failures, indeed
his last three.   Mr Gladstone takes up one or two things, and
then nothing else interests him.   He cares nothing for foreign affairs which are always essential to England, knows
nothing of foreign affairs, and is exceedingly distrusted on
the Continent.   They have thought he might abandon Egypt
at any moment.   He will not attend to any suggestion but his
own mind's.   He does not care what you say, does not attend.

I have told him two or three facts of which he was quite ignorant of foreign tone and temper.   It makes no difference.
He only says 'Is that so ?   Really !' "   Indeed it must have
been most irritating, for the Queen had an unfailing fund of
first-rate common sense, and her very long experience of
foreign affairs made her a far more dispassionate observer
than Gladstone on the war-path for an idea.   Besides she
happened to be Queen· of England, and it was surely reasonable that she should expect to be listened to.

There was another reason why she disliked him, and when
that was made known to him his reception of it was characteristic of the real greatness of the man and of his uprightness.
There had been from time to time odious gossip of the falsest
sort arising from his interest in the deplorable women on the
streets.   He used to talk to them, when he walked back at
night, as he so often did, from the House, trying to persuade
them to go home.   He even brought one, with Mrs Gladstone's full knowledge and approval, into his house, for a
night's shelter.   Very possibly he behaved imprudently, but
such imprudence was due to his own consciousness of his high
motive, and no-one who knew him could fail to be aware of
his absolute moral rectitude.   The gossip had somehow
reached the Queen's ears, and she hinted at what she had
heard to Lord Beaconsfield, who, at the least, did not tell her
that there could be no truth in it, but, for whatever reason,
let her continue to suspect ugly things of him.   Mr Gladstone was speaking one day about the Queen's coldness and
unfriendliness towards him to the late Lord Stanmore, who
was an old and valued friend of his, and Lord Stanmore
thought he had better tell him that the Queen suspected him
of immoral behaviour with common women.   And Mr Gladstone's answer was one that could only have been made by a
man of truly great nature.   "If the Queen thinks that of
me," he said, "she is quite right to treat me as she does."

That was his scale: he was like that all through.   He had

in his late years to undergo an operation on his eyes, which was performed by the oculist Mr Nettleship, and after it was over the light had to be kept from him for a few days. During this time Mr Nettleship examined his eyes to see whether the result of the operation was all he hoped, and was not quite satisfied. He said nothing to Mr Gladstone, but went to his daughter Mrs Drew and told her that he was afraid the operation had not been as successful as he had hoped. They settled that Mr Gladstone had better know, and she undertook to tell him. So she went into the room where he sat in the dark, and broke it to him. At once he replied, "How dreadful for Mr Nettleship !"

Whatever entered his mind (and what did not ?) was subjected to his fiery scrutiny, and came out molten, with the heat of it. During one night at Lambeth, he discussed "George Eliot's Life," lately published, with my mother and passionately exclaimed, "It is not a Life at all. It is a Reticence, in three volumes." Presently it was time for the ladies to move, but for a while she could not stir, for Mr Gladstone was denouncing some views of a problem as presented in this Reticence. Eventually she was obliged to get up, and he sprang to his feet with her and summed it all up. "It is disgusting," he proclaimed, "and repulsive, and revolting." The more tepidly minded man of today, would have been content to say "horrid" and leave it at that, but such undocumented disapproval would not do for him. Besides, each of his epithets was deliberate, "It is disgusting because such a notion nauseates you ; it is repulsive, because you instinctively recoil from it : it is revolting because — " I forget why it was revolting, but the reason, I am sure, was logical. Whatever came within the wide circle of his interest was to be taken seriously, he pounced on it, he pronounced upon it. He even took "Robert Elsmere" seriously, and devoted to its discussion a solid article in the *Nineteenth Century*, in which he examined it as if it had been a heretical document of the Early

Church. It was believed that Mr James Knowles, the editor of the magazine, paid him £250 for this article; that seemed in those days an almost incredibly large sum for even a Prime Minister to receive for a magazine article, though to subsequent politicians who, deprived of political leadership, have devoted their talents to writing, it would seem a very paltry remuneration.

In that tremendous mind there was not much room for lightnesses. Jocular conversation perished in his presence, it was like the prattle of a brook which the torrent of molten lava streaming out from the mountain side silenced and turned into a whiff of steam before it really touched it. But occasionally there was a lull. One night, for instance, my father and mother were engaged to dine with the Gladstones, and Mrs Gladstone had written the invitation on paper stamped with the die of "Dollis Hill" (a house belonging to Lord Aberdeen, some five miles out of London, which he frequently lent to Mr Gladstone), forgetting that before the date of the dinner they would have moved up to their house in Carlton House Terrace. The evening happened to be that of Derby Day and, naturally assuming that, as the invitation came from Dollis Hill, the dinner was to be there, my father and mother drove out there on this hot June evening, much enjoying the air. But on arrival they found the house was in the hands of a caretaker and that the Gladstones had gone up to London the day before. There was nothing to be done but to get back into the carriage for another pleasant drive of three quarters of an hour (those were the days before motors existed) and go to Carlton House Terrace. Meantime the rest of the dinner-party had assembled, and had waited and had waited, but still they came not. Mrs Gladstone was sure (quite sure, for sometimes she was a little vague about such things) that she had invited them and that they had accepted. Mr Gladstone got rather fussed, and after a full hour had elapsed, they settled that they

WILLIAM EWART GLADSTONE
Reprinted with permission from Churchill's "The Marvelous Year"

must go in to dinner without them.   And as Mr Gladstone gave his arm to his lady, he turned to the room in general, "We must not forget that it is Derby Day," he said.   "His Grace has evidently been delayed by the congested traffic on his way back from Epsom."

In spite of their strong antagonisms on matters connected with the Church, he and my father had the greatest respect and liking for each other.   Though Mr Gladstone had disestablished the Irish Church, was hoping to do the same with the Welsh Church and would have liked to see the English Church disestablished also, he was a devout Churchman, and had its welfare most keenly at heart, thinking that these drastic operations were for its good.   On all such subjects as the appointment of bishops he invariably consulted my father, and adopted his nominee: a further bond between them was the study of the Classics.   It was to Hawarden that my father and mother came on the last evening of his life: he had been making a tour in Ireland, on a pastoral visit to the churches which Mr Gladstone had disestablished there, and the two sat up late together on that Saturday night, deep in classical and ecclesiastical topics.   My mother had got to bed when my father came up, and as he undressed, he came in and out between his dressing-room and the bedroom, full of the delightful talk he had had with his host.   Then a curious thing happened.   A woman in a room not far away, heard loud sounds of knocking from my father's room: it vaguely occurred to her that perhaps he had lost the key of some dispatch-box which he wanted to open, and was hammering at it. After a little the knocking ceased, and she thought no more of it.   Simultaneously a servant had heard exactly the same thing, also localizing the noise as coming from my father's room.   He started to tell my father's valet, thinking that he might be wanted, but did not rouse him, as the knocking ceased.   The matter was alluded to at breakfast next morning, but neither my father nor mother had heard anything whatever. An hour or so later, they walked across to church, he apparently in excellent health and spirits. He stood up for the exhortation, knelt for the confession, and during it sank back and died.

The next day the rest of us arrived, and I went in to see Mr Gladstone in his study. He spoke of my father warmly and weightily and soon he said, "I remember when you were here once before, you brought me some very interesting squeezes of tombstones of soldiers in the Tenth Legion." That was over four year ago, and yet that colossal memory had it all docketted and available.

DURING these years of the eighties and early nineties when so many of the stereotyped values were altering, and so much of the old coinage of social laws and customs was being called in and put back into the melting pot to be minted anew and to receive the stamp of fresh images and superscriptions, three great figures seem to stand out. They were like rocks of granite which the surge and stress of the new tides were powerless to batter or undermine. Gladstone was the first of these, the other two were Queen Victoria and Tennyson, and all three seemed antique and imperishable. Tennyson had been Laureate since 1850; he was a peak much shrouded in mist and the clouds were thick round that Parnassus. In spite of Mr Swinburne who had written some biting criticism about his "Idylls of the King," he was still, in the opinion of a large and intelligent majority, the only authentic incarnation of English poetry, and it was generally considered that when Mr Gladstone recommended the Queen to crown his laurels with a coronet, the House of Lords was more honoured by his entering it than he. He was recluse, he did not appear much in London, but a somewhat famous occasion of the sort was when he attended a garden party at Marlborough House. He was there seen by Mr Oscar Browning, a Fellow of King's College, Cambridge, who had an amiable but insatiable passion for intercourse with the eminent. So he went up and shook hands with him, and as the poet seemed not to have the slightest idea who he was, he introduced himself by saying, "I am Browning." Tennyson must have thought that he was impersonating Robert Browning, so he merely replied, "No, you're not," and seemed disinclined to listen to any explanations.

This brusqueness was rather a way of his: at another function of the sort near his country house at Aldworth, there was a young lady of the neighbourhood the dream of whose romantic soul was to be introduced to him. Her heart's desire was granted her, and they sat down side by side on a garden seat. Dead silence fell: she was far too rapt and reverent and overpowered to speak, and he had nothing to say. Suddenly he found something to say, and he pronounced these appalling words, "Your stays creak."

Nearly swooning with horror and deeply hurt at this absolutely unfounded accusation, she fled from him without a word, and recovered her composure as best she might by converse with less alarming folk. Presently she observed that he was stalking her: she tripped from one gay group to another, and always the poet followed her, like a bloodhound on her trail. The dream of her soul had turned into a nightmare: certainly he was after her, and who could tell what he would say next? She dodged and she doubled, she hid behind trees, but she could not shake him off. Then she made a dreadful tactical error, for she scurried up a long path to the kitchen-garden hoping to distance him beyond pursuit, only to find that she had entered a *cul de sac* bordered by cabbages and asparagus and closed at the far end by the potting-shed. She fumbled at the latch, intending to hide herself from the dreadful presence, but it was locked, and now he closed in on her. "I beg your pardon," he said, "it was my braces."

Again, a certain Doctor of Music had set one of his poems as a Cantata, and went down to see the author in order to play him some melodious morsels. Tennyson had no taste for music, but there was nothing he more enjoyed than reading aloud, with deep emotion in a hoarse rumble, his own verse, and so it came about that instead of the composer playing his music to the author, the author read his own poem to the composer. That was very pleasant, though it was not quite what the composer had in view. But he was very appreciative, and at a pause in the reading, he said, "That's an awfully jolly stanza." Tennyson eyed him. "Don't say 'awfully,' " he said. "What shall I say then ?" asked the composer. "Say 'bloody,' " said Tennyson.

This disconcerting brusqueness, so unlike the smooth sweetness of his work, was coupled with a theatrical avoidance of the hordes of inquisitive worshippers who, he felt sure, were for ever scheming to catch a glimpse of him, but possibly he did not really dislike the pilgrimages of the devout. For if, when walking on the cliffs at Freshwater, he observed some stranger approaching, he would pull his hat over his eyes, and cast his cloak about his mouth, but it was noticed that if the pilgrim (he was sure it was a pilgrim) paid no attention whatever to him, and went whistling on his way, instead of being rooted to the spot and reverently saluting, Tennyson seemed very little gratified at the success of his shrouding of himself, but would make some rather acid comment about great men not being recognized. Like Queen Victoria he liked being flattered, if it was done to his taste, and just as Lord Beaconsfield called her the Fairy, so Mr Alfred Austin who succeeded Tennyson in the Laureateship, used always to address him, so he told me himself, as "Bard" or "Immortal Bard." He once gave me a great discourse about his visits to Tennyson, but his memories of them entirely consisted in what he had said to Immortal Bard, and though that was rich and precious, I should have liked to have heard a little more of what Immortal Bard said to him. Perhaps he said nothing: he was able to say nothing for a long time together.

A pleasant link between the author of so much noble verse

and the lover of less exalted rhymes was his affection for the form known as the 'Limerick.' He liked its terseness, he also, it is idle to deny, took a sort of school-boy pleasure in the hectic situations which it sometimes disclosed. Little tales of the same sort pleased him: he could tell them himself with considerable gusto. In this connection I cannot forebear to recount a story which though I will not vouch for its authenticity, I give on the authority of Sir Edmund Gosse. He and my father were talking about Tennyson: they were contrasting him with Dickens; Dickens they agreed was not very markedly Puritanical in his life, whereas Tennyson was Galahad. But Dickens abhorred any sort of coarseness in conversation, whereas Tennyson had no great objection to it. Then said my father:

"Yes, that's quite true. I went out for a walk with him the last time I ever saw him, and he suddenly said to me, 'Shall I tell you a bawdy story ?' Of course I said, 'No, certainly not.' "

Their talk went on for a little till there came a pause. Gosse broke it with a touch of that impish humour of his.

"I feel sure Your Grace heard that story !" he said.

My father was a little off his guard.

"Well, it wasn't so very bad after all," he said.

Swinburne shared Tennyson's taste, but his friend Mr Watts-Dunton must be consulted first. "Shall I tell our visitor about the man of Peru ?" he once asked Mr Watts-Dunton. But no. "I think that goes a little too far, Algernon," was the reply, and so the doings of the man of Peru remained shrouded in a discreet mystery.

Throughout his life Tennyson was abnormally short-sighted, and the genesis of that sonorous line in Locksley Hall "Let the great world spin for ever down the ringing grooves of change" is an odd instance of his deficiency. In the very early days of railways he came across, for the first time, one of the newly laid lines of rails, and did not perceive that they were metals laid upon the earth, on which the wheels of the trains ran, but thought that they were parallel lines of grooves cut in it.　The mistaken image sank into his mind, and he used it in his poem.　But what did that matter ?　A fine line of poetry was worth more than the truth about the railway line.

THE third of those imperishable peaks, round which was wrapped an even denser mist than round Tennyson's Parnassus, was Queen Victoria.　Her long seclusion, as we have seen, had at one time been extremely unpopular, but, as the years went on, another effect of this invisibility asserted itself. Though so seldom seen, and never in the pomp and splendour of Monarchy, she became something august and mysterious. She began to get a hold first on the imagination and then on the hearts of her people, and it was with a sense of deep reverence and affection that the Empire awaited the year of her Jubilee in 1887, when the whole of her subjects, with delegates from the far-flung lands, would give thanks to God for the fifty years of her glorious reign, and she would once more inspire the nation with that thrill of romantic loyalty which had been hers when half a century ago the slim girl received its homage.　She was growing old now, she was stout, she was lame, and vain were the efforts to induce her to put on robes of State: the last emissary to attempt it was the Princess of Wales, who came out from her mother-in-law's presence with a humiliated mien, saying that she had never had such a snub in her life.　My father submitted to her the order of the proposed service; she "admired" the prayers, and thought that a "*short* portion of Scripture should be read, or a psalm chanted."　But the whole thing must not be too long, "for the weather will probably be hot, and the Queen feels faint if it is hot."

I had come up from school for this day, and drove to the Abbey with my father.　He had forgotten to give his coachman the carriage-pass, which would admit him within the cordon of police and troops through which, coming from Lambeth, he had to pass, and a polite but quite firm inspector refused to let his carriage proceed: nobody without a carriage-pass was allowed to penetrate. On which, with an engaging smile, he leaned out, and said, "They can't begin till I get there," so all was well. The Abbey was already filling up, and soon the tiers of seats that rose high in the transepts were crammed to the top. Then from outside came the sound of the saluting guns and a murmur that rose to a roar, as the Queen drew near with the princes on horseback for her retinue. The whole Abbey rose, and up the nave came the kings and the queens and the princes and princesses, and went to their seats on this side and on that of the throne. And after the jewels and the robes and the uniforms had flashed by, there moved up one solitary little figure in a black satin dress with a white front and a white bonnet with a band of black velvet. How right she had been to come like that, and not listen to those who would have her in robes of State. She was Queen of England and Empress of India, and she was mother and mother-in-law and grandmother of that regal company, and there she was, a little old lady coming to church to thank God for the long years in which she had ruled her people. She listened once more to her husband's "Te Deum," and the hand that held her book trembled, for she remembered how he had played it to her on the organ he had built at Windsor. Then when the service was over, her family and the kings and queens, her brothers and sisters, came to make their obeisance to her and kiss her hand, and as they rose she kissed them on the cheek. Long and affectionately did she cling to her eldest daughter, the Crown Princess Frederick of Germany, for she and her husband, the noblest figure in the Abbey, had come to England not only to attend this celebration, but to seek medical advice for a persistent hoarseness in his throat, and a fear, undefined as yet, lurked in the

shadow of his imminent throne. The first anniversary of this
day had not come round before he had become Emperor of
Germany, and his son had succeeded him.

THE Queen had looked forward to that day as a frightful ordeal, and had a fit of weeping before she could nerve herself to
set out on that triumphant drive to the Abbey, but having
faced it, she never went back again into an unbroken seclusion. She opened the Imperial Institution exhibition: the
little black figure rose in her box, she addressed the vast assembly in that clear quiet voice which penetrated into every
corner like a ray of light, and, when she had done, she made
three low curtsies to her people.   She opened the new Tower
Bridge, and the miles of streets through which she drove were
a roar of welcome to her.   My mother, I remember, attended the function, rather pleased with herself and her
smart landau with its pair of great black horses and her coachman in a wig.   But that little bubble of pride was soon pricked
for her, and she was very properly put in her place by a ribald
voice in the crowd which shouted " 'Ullo! 'Ere comes the
Queen's cook !"   And the Queen enjoyed it very much herself, recording with a delightful touch of royal vanity, that
"Bertie and Alix" never evoked half the enthusiasm that she
did.   She had kindled the imagination of her people, as no
other English monarch perhaps had ever done, and the throne
had never been held in such love and reverence.

CHAPTER VII

CAMBRIDGE

IN THIS year of the Queen's first Jubilee the horizons of school broadened out for me into those of Cambridge. I followed my elder brother to King's College which, not many years before, had been exclusively a college of Etonians: boys from the Foundation at Eton became, without competition from outside, scholars of King's, and in due course Fellows, as long as they remained unmarried, for life. Indeed from the age of twelve or thereabouts, they lived on the bounty of the pious Founder, King Henry VI, in quiet scholastic competence, most of them without duties, to the end of their days. They had their lodging provided for them, their Commons and their dinner, and a salary of several hundred pounds a year, because they got a scholarship at Eton in their early teens. The system gave them the leisure of the lilies of the field, freed them from any care concerning the necessities and moderate luxuries of life, and while they could thus devote their whole time to scholarly research, they could equally well devote it to the gentle art of doing nothing at all. If we look at the lists of the men whom King Henry's bounty enabled for centuries to give themselves up to scholarship, it must be confessed that the vast sums thus expended had not yielded any very notable dividends. Tutors who continued to hand on the torch of learning to generations of undergraduates received extra emoluments for their work, but for the rest there was no need to work at all. Young men came up yearly from Eton, and in time grew into old men in these celibate surroundings, and it was not to be wondered at that there were some very queer old men among them, not Victorian at all, but belonging to some far earlier epoch, strange mastodons and

107

plesiosauri, learned lizards in human form, with caps and gowns.   One of these for instance, not so long before my time, had lived since his earliest manhood in a set of Fellows' rooms from which he never emerged except in the evening gloaming. He then shuffled out on to the big lawn, with a stick in his hand, and he prodded with it at the worms in the grass, muttering to himself, "Ah, damn ye: ye haven't got me yet." He said with Dr Faustus, "This feeds my soul," and after this psychical refreshment, he returned to his rooms till the same hour next day.

The throwing open of King's to other schools, and the abolition of these life-fellowships caused a dwindling in the number of such, until they finally perished.   It is impossible not to regret their complete extinction, but the modernizing of the college implied that there was no longer any place for them.   Their extinction was brought about gradually: those who held life-fellowships under the old order, were not deprived of them and some odd persons still lingered, not quite like anything else ever seen, degenerate as mastodons, but bearing some of the marks of type.   One of these, till the young gentlemen of the college set to work to modernize him, according to the standards of 1887, was certainly of an older civilization.   Though he had no truck, as far as was known, with worms, he, too, seldom appeared in the open blaze of day, but at precisely three minutes to five of the afternoon, he came out from his rooms which none entered save his bed-maker, and crossed the same grass as the worm-poker, to attend chapel.   It happened that two of these young devils were looking out from the screen of their window-boxes at this moment, and one of them began, quite casually, to whistle.   Instantly Mr Mozely stopped, but on the cessation of the whistle started off again.   Then rather less casually and observing his movements the whistler whistled more piercingly, and again Mr Mozely stopped.   A definite suspicion concerning cause and effect, now entered the brains of the watchers, and they continued to whistle.   Mr Mozely could face the music no longer, and instead of going to chapel went back to his rooms.

The two proceeded to verify their theory that the sound of whistling prevented his going to chapel, and it was soon proved beyond all possible doubt, that if one whistled he went home. Any student of human nature (and where is a nobler calling?) must want to know more of so rare a type, and they left their cards in his letter-box. Mr. Mozely duly returned their formal visit, and the ice being thus broken, they asked him to tea. Other young devils happened to drop in while he was there and they were all introduced to him. Not long afterwards they all received invitations to go to tea with Mr Mozely, but only one of them could manage to go. He found a table with a white linen cloth, laid for eight persons, with knives and forks for each: at one end there were tea-pot and milk-jug and sugar-basin and eight cups and saucers, at the other was a leg of cold mutton and a pile of plates. As nobody else appeared, Mr Mozely suggested that we should sit down: he poured out tea, and I cut the cold mutton. As we talked, it was discovered that he played the violin, and there was just time for a tune before evening chapel. Thereafter there came to him an extraordinary blossoming: his stem shot up like that of the flowering aloe. There were more tea parties, there was more playing of the violin, and before long he played a solo at a College smoking concert. Then the madness of modernity got hold of him, and though well advanced in life he married a girl who played in the band of the Salvation Army and went to live in Guernsey, because there was no bother about vaccination laws in that island.

Then there was Mr J. E. Nixon: though he was of the earlier day and held a life-fellowship, he was no recluse but wildly sociable. He had realized that the old order was changing and had enthusiastically gone out to meet the new. He was Dean of the College, he was lecturer in Latin, and for sheer experimentalism he was further ahead in the van of progress than the most extravagant of modern pioneers, and

had more new notions every day than most people have in a
lifetime.   He held glee-meetings once a week after Hall, at
which he sang Victorian catches and madrigals arranged for
male voices.   Dr Ford, the present Dean of York, sat by his
elbow, and with him sang the tenor part, while Nixon beat
time (like my mother at Lincoln) with a paper-knife.
Faster and faster under the intoxication of the music rang out
our melodies, until the paper-knife flew from his hand, like
Excalibur, and crashed into the fender.   Between the songs
he handed round hot buttered buns, anchovy-toast, Borneo
cigars and Tintara wine.   In person he was small: a short
honey-coloured beard framed his chin, he had one glass eye,
and only one hand: in place of the other he had a tight black
kid glove (I think pneumatic, for it sometimes seemed to be
deflated) which was attached to his wrist, and protruded
from the sleeve of his tail-coat.   But these physical deficien-
cies were no handicap to his activity: rather, they seemed to
stimulate it, as if he was gallantly bent on showing how much
could be done with how little.   He rode a tricycle intrepidly
about the traffic-crowded streets of Cambridge, he played
lawn tennis on fine summer afternoons in the Fellows' Gardens,
taking down there a small black bag containing tennis-balls
and sealing-wax, and pieces of string (for there was no telling whether some emergency would not arise when string or
sealing wax would be urgently required) and Borneo cigars.
When he served he lodged a ball in the crook of his arm and
by some unique jerk of his body, tossed it into the air and
gave it a savage underhand blow.   Everything he did was
performed at top speed, and he generally dropped something.
His mind whirled about incessantly in a maelstrom of new
dodges for counting the attendance of the undergraduates
in chapel, for registering votes at Fellows' meetings, for in-
suring regular supplies of toilet paper in such places as the
dons needed them, or for ascertaining the speed of the train
in which he was travelling.   He was also (God knows how or
why) a Gresham lecturer in London, and I once went up from

Cambridge in order to attend one of these discourses. The subject was either "Poetry in Rhetoric" or "Rhetoric in Poetry," but the course of the lecture did not make it clear which it was, and there has been complete confusion in my mind about it ever since. On Sunday in May week at Cambridge, there was always an immense crush to get into King's Chapel for afternoon service, and in preparation for this, Nixon printed a small leaflet "On the Management of Large Crowds," which he distributed to the vergers, so that they should know what to do. The crowd this year was more unwieldy than ever, and Nixon popped out of the organ-loft where he had been observing the management of it, and cried in a lamentable voice, "If there is any more shoving, there will be no Divine Service at all." As a teacher of Latin prose he was chiefly remarkable for correcting the exercises shown up to him, partly in red and partly in purple ink. Red ink indicated grammatical errors, purple ink errors of construction, or something of the sort. But he was not very clear about it himself, and he could not always read what he had written, and sometimes he had evidently dipped his pen first in red ink and then in purple so that there was no clue to the nature of the correction, for it was of a rich lake tone, and denoted neither grammar nor construction. . . I do not pretend to reproduce these details with literal accuracy, but I will vouch for their impressionistic truth. The world, to Mr Nixon, consisted of Latin prose, lawn tennis and glee-singing, and contained besides numbers of problems to which he sought solution; how to turn envelopes inside out and use them again, how to cut pencils without blackening the forefinger, how to stop a draught from an ill-fitting window-sash. Each of these was as bright as a new pin, and he never succeeded in picking any of them up.

But the really outstanding figure of that time not among the dons of King's only, but of the whole of Cambridge was Oscar Browning: he would have been notorious and absurd and remarkable anywhere, and if he had ever succeeded in

getting into Parliament, he must have made a mark of some
unusual kind there, as surely as he made it everywhere else.
He was a tragic instance of such stupid jokes as Nature
plays when, after she has formed by means of cosmic pres-
sures and secular incandescences, some noble gem, she proceeds with a silly giggle, to plant a fatal flaw in the very
heart of it. He was a genius flawed by abysmal fatuity.
No-one had finer gifts than he, he could think on large lines,
he could strike out great ideas, he had wit, he had the power
of planning largely and constructively, he had courage and
a high scorn of ridicule, it was impossible to come into contact with him without being conscious of great intellectual
force. But it was impossible not to be aware that he was a
buffoon. As an Eton master, before he came to take up his
fellowship again and reside at King's, he had been the first
to grasp the fact that boys had minds, and that public-
school education should not merely consist of loading those
minds with irrelevant knowledge about Greek particles, but
of opening them to the reception of ideas, and of teaching
them how to think. His colleagues of that day looked with
traditional suspicion on such crazy notions, and instantly
the flaw began to manifest itself, for he always took any
opposition to his ideas as a personal attack, and instead of
defending them, defended himself. He was immensely liked
by his house and his pupils, he treated them with the warmest
friendliness, he had Sunday concerts for them, he had social
gatherings in which, without the least encouragement to
priggishness, he interested them in topics of history and
politics. But with a fatal silliness he made pets of those
who were handsome and attractive, and the head master, Dr
Hornby, who looked with the darkest suspicion on everything
he did, took advantage of a technical breach which he had
committed in the school rules concerning the number of boys
in his house, and dismissed him. He then took up residence at
King's as a life-fellow, and became a unique institution. He
was appointed a lecturer in history: probably there was no

epoch on which he was not prepared to discourse without any preparation. He was very inaccurate, for he never was a scholar, nor took the trouble to learn anything thoroughly, but he had the superlative gift as a teacher of being interesting. Then, just as at Eton he had made social gatherings for his boys, so at Cambridge he opened his rooms every Sunday evening, to anybody who cared to come. The idea was excellent, for there poured into King's, still rather a close corporation, dons and undergraduates and general intelligentsia from other colleges. There were members of that mystic and elevated society called the Apostles who were supposed in their lighter moments to chat about Determinism: there were sporting gents from the Athenæum, which, in spite of its name, had nothing whatever to do with learning, there were lights from the University Musical Society. For these there was special provision, for O. B. had four instruments of the nature of harmoniums, popularly known as Obeophones, possessed of a pleasant buzzing tone, remotely resembling that of stringed instruments, and vividly that of combs wrapped in toilet paper. They were of different compasses, one had the compass of a 'cello, another of a viola, two others, one of an inconceivable shrillness did duty for violins, and the quartettes of Mozart and Beethoven rent the air. But then that fatuous egotism came in: O. B. found the slow movement rather tedious, and said "Ha, ha, isn't it awfully jolly? Let's stop." So instead he went to the piano and bellowed "Funicula, funicula," or collected a group round him and gave them a curious pink liqueur tasting of furniture polish, and told them about the Empress of Austria's visit to Maloja, when, dressed like a Roman Emperor and attended by four youthful lictors, he went out to welcome her, and made her a speech in Latin. His snobbishness was of a really remarkable order: it was impossible not to respect a quality of such fire and purity, for, although already waddling with obesity, he took to playing hockey simply for the pleasure of being wiped over the shins by

H.R.H. Prince Edward of Wales, when he was an undergraduate at Trinity.

Whatever he did was a matter that aroused attention and
comment: that was because he was a great man.   But whatever he did also aroused opposition and ridicule, and that was
because he was such a silly ass.   His facility and his exuber-
ance in ideas made him indolent: he could not bother to work
any of them out, because it was so much easier to think of
fresh ones: besides there were so many small grudges which
he cherished against those who had belittled him, and they
must be dealt with before anything else was done.   He must
speak to the Provost about the conduct of the Classical
Tutor, and when he had spoken he would certainly have to
complain to someone else about the lack of sympathy the
Provost had shown him.   Then there were many diversions:
it was a cold winter afternoon, and he would go after lunch to
the Coffee Club in the College, always sociable, but always
wanting to shine, and there one day he imprudently asked
Jim Stephen what was the derivation of the word "microbe."
Jim instantly replied: "It's derived from the Greek word,
μικρòs, meaning small, and O. B. meaning you.   It's a little
O. B."   After that it would be pleasant to have a Turkish
bath, and he tried to persuade some member of the Coffee
Club to come with him.   "Awfully jolly: you can't be healthy
unless you sweat every day as the Greeks did.   Hesiod says
that Sweat is the threshold of many virtues."   So he went off
to the small hot closet which represented a Turkish bath, and
after sitting copiously on the threshold of many virtues, he
reclined in a small cool closet, wrapped in towels, and ate
quantities of hot buttered toast.   Or if it was summer he
found it pleasant to have a bathe at the University sheds, on
the upper river; some sort of Charley or Bobby would row
him up there, and tie his shoe-laces for him when he had
dressed again.   Then came the end of term, and he went up
to London for a month, taking lodgings as nearly as possible
opposite Marlborough House.   As he grew old he became

OSCAR BROWNING ["O. B."]
Reproduced from a Vanity Fair cartoon by
permission of the National Magazine Co., London

impossible to work with: he quarrelled with everyone who was associated with him on board or committee, accusing them of plagiarizing his ideas and organizing them. He left Cambridge and went to live at Bexhill where he played golf in cap, coat and gloves of bright red, and became a Christian Scientist. After that he settled in Rome where with incredible fluency he engaged himself in writing a history of the world. He calculated that he wrote about a million words every year, and wondered that he could not get them all published, suspecting conspiracy: in the intervals of composition he learned Polish. Never was there a man of so much originality of mind who did less with it, or one of so much genuine kindliness which was so curdled by egotism.

O. B. became a legend in his lifetime, which is always a mark of distinction. He was a model for every sort of caricature, a constant subject for the invention of the quickwitted, and many of these items, though possibly fabulous, ring so true that it really does not much matter whether they are authentic or not. Internal evidence based on a thorough knowledge of the character to whom they are attributed is the only test which is worth anything: if they are really characteristic they should be accepted, and the story of O. B. returning to Cambridge after a delirious July in London among the eminent, and remarking quite casually that William II of Germany was one of the nicest Emperors he had ever met, is, by such a test, obviously authentic. Anyone who had known O. B. in moods when he was dead drunk with the strong wine of royalty, could not hesitate about passing it, and if it was not true, so much the worse for the truth. Indeed it is a tribute to his personality that so many tales were invented about him, for nobody troubles to make up stories about every-day people, nor would anyone listen to them if they did.

Of all the Classical Fellows of King's about this time there was just one, and he of a younger generation and not of Eton, who worked conformably to the spirit of the bounty of

King Henry VI, for in return for his board and lodging and
fellowship, he devoted himself entirely to the study of Greek.
Those who lectured, those who taught, those who, like Mr
Nixon, looked over our weekly efforts in Latin prose or Greek
Iambics were not scholars at all in any real sense of the word:
their knowledge of these languages was of the same class as
that of the twenty or twenty-five undergraduates who yearly
took a first in the Classical Tripos.   They knew the principal
dates and main operations in the Peloponnesian war, they
could translate passages of Greek and Latin into grammatical English, and they could turn passages of English
prose into Greek that probably bore the same relation to
classical Greek, as written in the age of Pericles, as the best
Baboo does to plain decent English prose of the day.   Like
the Baboo clerk, who, when asked by his employer for what
reason he wanted a day's remission from office work, replied
"The hand that rocked the cradle has kicked the bucket" (the
proper English for which is "my mother is dead") so these
admirable preceptors of ours would produce the most remarkable patchwork of recondite constructions and unusual words
snipped from Thucydides and Plato and neatly stitched together, and hand them to their pupils as models for classical
composition.   Had any of them competed in the Classical
Tripos of the year, they would probably have taken quite
good degrees, but there their attainments ended, and their
years of teaching had not taught them anything that dif-
ferentiated them from their more intelligent pupils.   Their
knowledge of Greek ended just about where Walter Headlam's began: his mind was Greek, and he kept on learning
the lore of its ancestors.   The fragmentary mimes of Herondas had lately been discovered, and on this new text he poured
out a knowledge which was as far beyond that of the accred-
ited tutors of the College, as is some advanced treatise on
mathematics beyond the scope of an ordinary school-teacher
of algebra.   Though he was of a rich and boyish humanity,
he had also that queer aloof quality which develops in those

whose life is centred on research, and he passed into regions where no calls or needs of the flesh could penetrate.

One morning, for instance, his water for shaving was not hot, so after breakfast he put a small kettle to boil over his spirit lamp, and as he waited for that, he sat down in the armchair where he worked and casually looked at a note he had made the evening before. It was about a change of rhythm in a Greek chorus, or perhaps it was a word in his Herondas, which occurred in no dictionary, but which he knew he had seen before in some scholiast on Aristophanes. But where was the particular book he wanted ? His room was lined with book-shelves, books that he was using paved the floor round his chair, and the table was piled high with them. There it was underneath a heap of others on the table, and he pulled it out: those on the top of it tumbled to the ground. He put down his pipe on the edge of the table, and as he turned the leaves, he found not just that which he was looking for, but something else he had wanted yesterday. He made a note of this on a slip of paper and picked up his pipe which had gone out. There were no matches, so he folded up the paper on which he had made his note, thrust it into the flame of the spirit-lamp and lit his pipe again. Then he found the passage he had originally started to hunt up. Awfully interesting : it was a slang word, not very polite, in use among the daughters of joy in Corinth during the fifth century B. C. These intelligent ladies seemed to have an argot of of their own ; there were several other words of the sort which he had come across. He became lost in this pursuit, his pipe had to be relit several times, and presently a smell of roasting metal brought him back for a brief moment to the surface of life. His shaving-water had all boiled away, and so he put out the spirit-lamp. Later in the morning his gyp came to see if he wanted any lunch ordered for him: bread and butter and cheese would do, with a tankard of beer. These were laid and left in the next room, and he wandered there after another hour or two deep in his investi-

gation.   The sight of food aroused no association of desire,
but he had a drink out of the tankard and carrying it back
with him, put it in a nest of books on his table.   Presently
more books got piled up round the tankard; he absently laid
a folio note-book on the top of it, and so it completely vanished.   Then he wanted more books from his shelves, in one
of these excursions he stepped on his pipe and broke the
stem.   It did not matter for there were others about, but he
forgot to look for them in the heat of this diverting chase.
"I shall write a monograph on the slang current in Corin-
thian brothels," he said to himself.

It began to grow dark on this early close of the autumn
afternoon.   There was no electric light in those days, and
he fetched a couple of candles and put them on the edge of
his table.   He was hungry now, and he gobbled up his bread
and cheese, wondering what time it was, for his watch had
stopped.   Beer too: he felt sure he had ordered some beer,
but where the devil was it ?   It should have been on his
table with the bread and cheese.   He looked everywhere
for it, even in his bedroom, but it was nowhere to be seen.
Then his razor lying ready on his dressing-table reminded
him that he had not yet shaved.   It was true there was no hot
water, but cold water would do, and though it was rapidly
getting dark, he had not yet found any matches to light his
candles.   But one ought to be able to shave in the dark, he
thought, for an action, often repeated, became, as Aristotle
said, an instinctive process, and it would be interesting to
see if he could not make quite a good job of it.   He made
a fair job of it, there were a few negligible cuts, and finding
that he had a box of matches in his pocket all the time, he lit
his candles and went back to the ladies of Corinth.   Then his
gyp came in to see if he would go into Hall for dinner, or
dine in his room: he settled to have some cold meat here, but
where was the beer he had ordered for lunch ?   The gyp
felt sure he had brought it, but evidently he was mistaken

for there was no sign of it.   So he brought the cold meat
and another tankard and with this comfortless refreshment
Walter Headlam pursued the ladies of Corinth till the small
hours of the morning.   The missing tankard came to light
the next day.

He would work like this for several days on end (the details of my description are in no way composed but actually
and collectively true) and then he was drained of scholarly
energy and emerging as from deep seas with some pearls
of research, he busied himself with social concerns and diversions till he could dive again.

One day he fell in love with an intelligent young lady from
Newnham, but he soon forgot about her, because he went to
a concert where he heard Schubert's "Unfinished Symphony."
Instantly all became dross except Schubert, and though he
could not read a note of music, nor play a correct scale, he
sat hour after hour at his piano, dabbing at single notes till
out of them he had extricated a short melody of four bars,
which I wrote down for him; it was to be the air in the slow
movement of "Headlam Op. 1."   Then he immersed himself in Greek again, and again rising to the surface came
across a pseudo-medical primer.   The study of this convinced him that he had diabetes, and so sure was he of this
that he never consulted a doctor at all.   He had a tragic
collection of unmistakable insignia, headache, fitful appetite,
fatigue, and so there was no doubt about it.   He told me
very seriously that he had not long to live, and when I asked
what was the matter with him, he said in a hollow but resigned
whisper "Sugar."   So we went to a race-meeting at Newmarket, and entirely bowled over with adoration for the
splendour and the speed of the flying hooves and the rhythm
of their galloping, he felt that he must instantly learn to
ride: for the moment the whores of Corinth were pale to him.
He ordered some elegant riding breeches and hired a horse,
and we set out along the backs.   One of his feet slipped

out of its stirrup, but in these first moments of poise upon
a horse's back, he did not think it wise, in spite of advice and
proffered assistance, to imperil his balance by recovering it,
and in consequence when his horse decided to walk into the
shallow water of the Grantchester mill-pool and drink, he
slipped gently out of the saddle and fell in.   Then he thought
he would like to go for a drive, as a less hazardous method
of commerce with horses, and he asked a friend to come out
for a spin with him.   On arrival at the livery stables, a high
dog-cart was made ready for them, and Walter Headlam
asked his friend if he would do the driving.   The friend very
properly replied that he had never done such a thing in his
life, and so he said, "Nor have I," and was instructed that
the reins went in the left hand, and the whip in the right.
A little way out of Cambridge, in trying to turn a corner, he
drove up a bank at the side of the road, and the dog-cart
upset.   As he flew out of it (still with the reins in his left
hand) he was head to observe, "Damn: I shall never finish
Herondas," and alighted unharmed in a hedge.

Mr Charles Waldstein, Reader in Classical Archæology
was another of these Fellows of King's who was not quite like
other people: King's was rich in variations from type.   By
blood of birth he was German, American, and Jew, and Sir
Charles Stanford at a musical rehearsal of a Greek play,
at which he had been irritated to the verge of insanity by
Waldstein's continually interrupting the chanting of Athenian elders, in order to show them how to stand and move
in truly Pheidian attitudes, exclaimed in a highly injured
brogue, "I wish that German-American-Jew would go back
to his respective countries."   There was a coolness in consequence, or you might call it a heat.   He was one of those
fortunate folk to whom for no particular reason, ludicrous
things happen: thus he was a source of fearful joy as well
as affection to his friends.

He belonged to an earnest and exclusive Literary Society
called the "Chitchat."   Both dons and undergraduates were

among its members, and we assembled in each other's rooms
in rotation every Saturday night during term time, on terms
of equality. The host for the evening provided claret cup
and hot buns and anchovy toast, and the Society owned a
snuff-box from which, as a piece of ceremonial, we all took
pinches. When the sneezing had died down, the secretary
called upon the host to read a paper which he had written
on some literary or ethical subject, and during the reading
the claret cup went quietly round. On one memorable evening when Waldstein entertained the Society, he told us
that he had not had time to write down his lecture, and so he
addressed his fellow-members instead, on the subject of
"Manners." He stood in front of the fire in cap and gown,
and was full of glorious gestures. He lit a cigarette and
put it down on the chimney piece, he lit another and another
and put them down on table-edge or chair-back. An eloquence of sentences, faintly Teutonic sometimes in construction streamed from him, sometimes they contained rather exotic words like "cocksuredom" and no-one as yet knew with any
precision what he was talking about. The atmosphere grew
a little tense, and the members of the Chitchat, sitting very
demure and attentive, felt that it was not wise to catch each
other's eyes. There came a pause: the lecturer slapped his
forehead and confessed that he had forgotten exactly what
he meant to say on that topic. So he launched out on something cognate, and then remembered what he had forgotten
and went back to it. The exquisite grace of Greek sculpture
— that was it: it reflected the charm and the urbanity and the
breeding of that superlative race. Gentlemanly-ishness no
less than genius was characteristic of sculptor and model
alike. There was that statue of the Discobolus which illustrated what he meant as well as anything, and he threw
himself into a semblance of the famous pose, and his mortar-
board cap dropped off. He picked it up. "It's no use."
he said, "you should see me naked." At that intense moment
when everybody might have been statues too, so still they sat,

Dr Cunningham of Trinity happened to be drinking claret
cup, and he burst.   The liquid squirted from his mouth,
and nose, he hooted with laughter, and seizing his cap and
gown he hurried from the room.   Through the open window
he could be heard roaring and slapping his leg in the court
below.

Like O. B., Waldstein was addicted to eminent persons
and the two competed in a sort of Royal Hunt Cup, or we
might call it a boxing match. Royal visitors constituted the
points scored by the antagonists.   A prince of the House of
Greece came to lunch with Waldstein, and afterwards his
host took him to see the museum of classical casts, which
would remind him of Athens.   O. B. countered this by
brandishing an English Royal Highness in Waldstein's face,
and taking him to the Union, which would remind him of the
Houses of Parliament.   That required some beating, but
Waldstein's blood was up, and one day there was a red carpet
on the steps leading to his rooms, and the Crown Princess of
Germany walked along it: this was the third round.   It was
very chic of O. B. to have no red carpet at all, when, in the
fourth round, he landed a stunning blow on Waldstein with
H.R.H. the Duchess of York, for her visit was thus quite
private and informal.   Upon this two or three undergraduates laid plans for having a fifth round, and knocking out
both O. B. and Waldstein, the puny creatures !   They arranged that one of them who was short and stout should dress
up in a black bonnet and a black silk gown and be seen to arrive at the porter's lodge at King's in a carriage and pair;
another of them who was slim and slight in build, would be
sitting on the front seat, fashionably dressed as a young
woman.   There would be a bath-chair waiting at the porter's
lodge.   A hint as to the identity of the little old lady in black
would already have been given to O. B. and Waldstein, so
that it would be certain that they would be looking out of
their windows, when the bath-chair propelled by one of the
conspirators, with the lady-in-waiting walking behind it, was

wheeled round the court, to the entrance of a certain set of rooms in Fellows' Buildings, where another of the conspirators lived. But the courage of these ingenious young gentlemen failed them, and, as a matter of fact, this fifth and final round in the boxing match never took place. They feared they might be clapped into the Tower of London and shot for high treason.

To DESCEND from thrones, there was a visit of Robert Browning to Cambridge, to which a memorable incident is attached. His admirers there had started a Browning Society ("There's a Me Society down at Cambridge," to quote from one of the most brilliant parodies in the language, written by Jim Stephen), which met to discuss and elucidate the poet's more difficult moods, and he attended one of these meetings, but was said to be unable to throw any light on certain of the conundrums of his own making which were referred to him. There was present at it a young lady of Newnham College, who was a most enthusiastic member of the Society, and, greatly daring, she asked Mr Browning if he would come to tea with her and a few friends at Newnham, and afterwards read some little piece of his own to them. He loved appreciation, and liked young ladies, so he said he would be delighted. There were waiting for him some dozen of eager adorers, and he was given his cup of tea (or it might have been cocoa) and a piece of muffin. Then his hostess, in a frenzy of diffidence and devotion, told him that she had woven a crown of roses for him, from which all thorns and unpleasant moistnesses had been banished, and might she have the extreme honour of placing it on his head. The poet most good-naturedly consented, and with trembling hands she deposited the decoration on that august brow. So there he sat, bland and ruddy, and slightly buttery from the muffins, with the crown of pink roses laid upon his white locks, and looking like a lamb decked for sacrifice. By his side was an occasional table on which were placed the volumes of

his complete works, and opposite him on the wall there happened to hang a mirror.   When tea was done he was asked
to fulfil his gracious promise and read.   None knew what
he would choose : some hoped for a book or two of "The Ring
and the Book," the more advanced for "Sordello," and some
for "Saul."   What he chose was the "Serenade at the Villa,"
and the young ladies (since there were not enough chairs)
grouped themselves gracefully on the floor round those revered feet.   He began reading from the book, but he found
he knew the poem by heart and closed it.

> *When the firefly hides its spot* [said Mr Browning]
> *And the garden voices fail,*
> *In the darkness thick and hot —*

And just then he raised his eyes and saw in the mirror the
image of himself crowned with pink roses.   He broke into
a peal of the most jovial laughter.   "My dear young ladies,"
he said, "shall I not read the "Patriot" instead ?   'It was
roses, roses all the way.' "

He came to dine one night with my parents in London :
if the family had been allowed to commandeer the presence
of whom they would, as guest, the vote would probably have
been cast for him, for not only was my mother an ardent
Browningite, but one of her daughters knew really prodigious
quantities of his work by heart, and was willing if anyone
doubted it, to go on repeating his poems till there could be no
question about her claim : while one of the boys, a year or two
before, had devoted the money for a prize he won in some
athletic competition at school to the purchase of the six-
volumed edition of his works, instead of buying a silver cup
with his own name enwreathed in *repoussé* ferns.   The guest
was immensely genial, he ate and drank and talked with a
juvenile pleasure, as if the world held many joyful surprises
for him still.   Then one of these pert creatures asked him
what he thought of Austin Dobson as a poet, for there were

strong differences of opinion in the family about him. He
laughed, he sipped his port, and then he said, "Well, some people do like carved cherrystones." His audience approved of
that, for they found it characteristic of one who in his entrancing "Men and Women" told you with huge gusto not what he
thought, but what fifty other people thought, and did not
say a word on his own account till the last poem of all. Just
such a word he said on his own account that evening quite
at the end of dinner, and it is for that reason I am telling
the story, since to this day it stands in greater need of inter-
pretation than anything he ever wrote. He guessed, I imagine, that everybody wanted him to talk about himself (so
plain had the hints been) and now he asked my father which
class of his poems (as he had been so kind) most appealed
to him. My father without hesitation said "Your lyrics."
Browning bounded in his chair, "Lyrics ?" he said. "I've
got deskfuls of them."

Here then we are confronted by the puzzle: what has happened to those lyrics ? After that evening, when he said
he had "deskfuls" of them, no further volume was published
during his lifetime except the one slim book "Asolando"
which came out actually on the day of his death, and since
then there has been no posthumous publication of lyrics.
Are they in existence still, slumbering in some forgotten cup-
board of his beloved Palazzo Rezzonico ? In this sad autumn of English poesy when the melody of its nightingales
is mute, what would we not give for some staves of that lyrical song of the springtime ? It is surely possible that
even now they may be found to make new magic for a new
generation. Or (I have sometimes thought) did Browning
only mean that in his brain there was still the bird of "lyric
love" ready to break into song ? But if that was all, why
did he say "deskfuls ?" That is surely too concrete a word
to use for songs yet unwritten. Certainly that volcanic
spirit which "loved well because it hated," was a-fire still beneath the surface-cooled age, and once again, at the very

end of his life, it broke out again spouting lava and withering flame. For there had been published a volume of letters by the translator of "Omar Khayyam," Edward Fitzgerald; in it was one in which he wrote, "Thank God Mrs Browning is dead; we shall have no more 'Aurora Leighs.'" It was a bitter cross-grained way to put it, but all Fitzgerald really meant was that he did not like Mrs Browning's poetry. He knew nothing of her, for they had never met, and there was no personal attack on her. But it was a crime to publish it during Browning's lifetime, for though the chance of his seeing it was small, the chance existed. He did see it, and instantly the old fire flared up. "I felt as if she had died yesterday," he said to a friend, and he published in the *Athenæum* the following lines:

To Edward Fitzgerald

I chanced upon a new book yesterday;
I opened it, and where my fingers lay
'Twixt page and uncut page these words I read,
Some six or seven at most, and learnt thereby
That you, Fitzgerald, whom by ear and eye
She never knew, thanked God my wife was dead.

Aye, dead! and were yourself alive, good Fitz,
How to return you thanks would pass my wits.
Kicking you seems the common lot of curs,
While more appropriate greeting lends you grace.
Surely to spit there glorifies your face,
Spitting with lips once sanctified by hers.

It is impossible not to feel a certain savage satisfaction. There was the old man nearer eighty than seventy, close on thirty years had passed since the death of his wife but to him it was as if they had been but a watch in the night. Except possibly for the dedication of "Asolando," this was the last poem he ever wrote.

WHILE O. B. in the later years of the eighties and still in the very zenith of his vivaciousness, was becoming a legend at Cambridge, another very notable figure at Oxford, Dr Benjamin Jowett, Master of Balliol, had already become a legend, though one of an exceedingly different sort. About him there was no kind of fatuousness (fatuousness withered in his presence) which made it easy to invent stories about him which would help the legend to crystallize, though Mr W. H. Mallock, in that early and amazingly brilliant book of his "The New Republic," presented under the name of Dr Jenkinson, a portrait of him which was wicked just because it was so appallingly truthful in essentials. But the ordinary observer would never have ventured to concoct a story about Jowett, for it would have rung false: the expert would have detected it in a moment. For this reason the Jowett-saga of the day could be relied on. It was certainly true, for instance, that the orthodoxy of his Christian faith was suspect (owing to his contribution to *Essays and Reviews*) when he was appointed to the Regius Professorship of Greek, though he was a clergyman of the Church of England. He was therefore asked whether he would sign the thirty-nine Articles as set forth in the Prayer-book, and he expressed his perfect willingness to sign forty if they wished. Nobody could produce a fortieth on the spur of the moment and so Jowett asked for a pen. "Give me a pen," he said, and signed all the Articles that there were. His style, in his official dealings with dons and undergraduates alike, was marked by this rather arid incisiveness; when he delivered his terse ultimatums there was no more to be said. He dealt in this way with my friend Dr David Hogarth, who as a junior don at Magdalen, was in charge of the production of one of Aristophanes's comedies, which was to be performed by the undergraduates. Dr Hogarth had cut out of the play certain witty lines which bore on the Athenian code of ethics with regard to boys; he just struck them out. The Master heard that this had been done, and requested Hogarth

to call on him. "I hear you have been making cuts in the
Greek play," he said. "Aristophanes wrote it. Who are
you?" Again there had come to Oxford under the leadership of Professor Blackie a deputation from Edinburgh
University, and the Master had mentioned to him a certain
want of urbanity and polish that he found about the visitors.
Professor Blackie genially replied: "Oh, you mustn't think
too hardly of us, Master." A still small voice answered him,
"We don't think about you at all." This withering de-
meanour, not really representing the greatness of the man.
was rather childish; intercourse with him was like being invited to taste a bottle of wine of noble vintage and finding it
slightly corked. He liked snubbing harmless and well-
meaning folk, and, had he ever known it, he would have found
it very disconcerting to realize that these raps on the knuckles
so far from rendering him formidable, afforded the ingenious
youth of Oxford a fearful joy. Like Whistler, they used
"carefully to exasperate him" in order to add to the collection
of those brilliant little gems. He often asked undergraduates of the College to breakfast with him alone, and sometimes he would not speak. In order to break the portentous
silence, one of these young gentlemen, as he nervously chipped
his bacon high into the air, threw a fly and remarked that it
was a fine day. Jowett said nothing whatever till his guest
rose to go. Then he said, "That was a very foolish observation of yours." But he had contributed a treasure towards
the legend.

Dr Jowett liked promising young men (except Mallock),
he liked lively visitors from outside, and he used constantly
to entertain rather distinguished parties for the week-end at
Balliol. It would do his friends good to see the Oxford mode,
and it would do Oxford good to see poets and Prime Ministers. At these parties he had a very good idea of the duties
of a bachelor host, and though he seldom or never laughed,
he became companionable. One day he told a small intimate
circle that there were three men to whom he owed a great

deal, men who had moulded and formed his mind, and made him what he was. The first of these was Gladstone; Gladstone's views on the Church were illuminating. It ought to be disestablished, and then sedulously cherished: also Gladstone's reverence towards the classics, especially Homer, had led the Master to a worthier appreciation of them. The second of these prodigious minds to which he owed so much was that of Darwin. Darwin's "Origin of Species" had opened to him a new conception of ethics, it had revealed to him that the progress of mankind lay in complete resignation to the Divine Will, and in obedience to the laws of nature in conjunction with it. This was all terribly interesting, and no-one wished to break the pause that followed, for it was supposed that some rare and deep upwelling of emotion had caused the Master's silence. Eventually one of the circle broke the silence (for he like everyone else was eager to hear more) and most sympathetically asked who was the third of those who had so powerfully influenced him. "I've forgotten the third," said the Master.

But he who had so often silenced others once made a man in difficulties speak. This occasion was in Balliol Chapel one Good Friday, for which day special psalms are appointed. There was no music and the officiating chaplain repeated one verse and the congregation the next. The first psalm had been finished: the Chaplain gave out the second, but he could not find it in his prayer-book. A sort of nervous myopia seized him, he turned his leaves backwards and forwards but still the fortieth psalm eluded him. Then came a penetrating little weary voice from the Master's stall. "I waited patiently," it said, and instantly the Chaplain found his place. "I waited patiently for the Lord," he recited, "and he inclined unto me and heard my calling."

Jowett had no pretensions whatever to be a great scholar: he would have thought it imbecile to spend his time like Walter Headlam, who, like the "Grammarian" whose funeral oration Robert Browning so nobly pronounced, would count

any day well spent that had enabled him properly "to base
οὖν." Jowett knew that οὖν meant, more or less, "therefore," and that was sufficient for him. Why bother any
more about a Greek particle ? But he spent years of useful
labour in his translation of the history of Thucydides, and
of the dialogues of Plato, and produced exactly what he
meant to produce, namely readable English versions of exceedingly interesting books, which gave very fairly the sense
of the original. He did not set himself to solve the more
human problems that arise out of Thucydides's narrative, nor
did he attempt to reconcile, for instance, that historian's
view of Alcibiades, with Plato's or Plutarch's: his business was
to provide intelligent English readers (not scholars nor
specialists) with an admirable version in English of what
Thucydides wrote. He took the utmost pains to find out
which was the most reliable text, and having done that proceeded to translate it, freely but faithfully, into dry and
weighty English, recognizing, as he says in his introduction
to the dialogues of Plato, that literal translation does not
always give the English equivalent, and that the particles
with which Plato betrews his sentences are often not trans-
latable at all. Strangely enough, in a man who had spent
so many years in studying Greek, he was by no means accurate, and knowing his frailty in this regard, he had his
translation carefully revised by other scholars. Among these
(though I think the Master does not mention him by name)
was the poet Swinburne: probably Swinburne was only an occasional reader of his proofs, when he was staying with the
Master at Balliol. But there was a certain humour about
the situation, for Swinburne had left Oxford without taking
a degree, and there he was again looking over the Master's
classical work for him. And the humour became even more
manifest when he was engaged at his task. One morning
the Master was in his study going through with their authors
the English essays which the undergraduates had sent in for
his perusal and criticism: Swinburne was sitting, with proofs

of a Platonic dialogue, in a small adjoining room, the door between the two being open. It was the Master's habit sometimes to make rather withering remarks to these young essayists, and today one of his most biting observations was interrupted by a joyful crow of laughter from the next room and Swinburne's exultant voice exclaiming, "Another howler, Master !" "Thank you, Algernon," said the Master meekly, and gently closed the door.

Of the kindness of his heart there could be no question, his loyalty and his generosity to his friends was invariable, but always masking that to the world was that metallic tang of his tongue which liked scoring cheap successes. Was it perhaps an attitude of defence on the part of one who shunned intimate contact, and who wore his heart not on his sleeve, but in his innermost pocket ? It had been hurt once; the object of its adoration had been Florence Nightingale. Such a conjunction seems more like the fantastic situations in the pleasant game called "Consequences," than a romance of real life, for the imagination boggles at the picture of Miss Nightingale as the wife of an Oxford don, and, not less, at that of Jowett seeing that the lamp was trimmed.

CHAPTER VIII

ATHENS

THE FOCUSSED point of life for me had shifted from Cambridge to London and other places far more remote before my Cambridge days were over. The stream of those impressions which for three years had carried me along really heedless of what happened outside that adorable flood of friendships and games and rapt observations of Nixon and O. B., joined that of the world outside, and the Cambridge current seemed to edge away into a very pleasant backwater. It was still delightful to leave the main stream and float quietly there under the bank, but all that had appeared so swift and strenuous now seemed leisurely, quietly eddying. I had won decent distinction in the Classical and Archæological Triposes, and already there was a novel which I regarded as finished, written on loose sheets of foolscap, reposing somewhere in a drawer, which a year or two later I picked out again, and wrote the second half of it. But for the present archæology was the passion and for three years in succession Cambridge most amiably gave me grants and travelling studentships for the pursuit of antiquity. Chester and its walls, in which were embedded the tombstones of the Roman legions which had interested Mr Gladstone, was the first field for research, and I spent three winters as a student in the English school at Athens.

What an enlightenment was there ! Those dreary hours devoted at Marlborough and at Cambridge to learning irregular Greek verbs, to racking the brain for crabbed scraps of phrases from Thucydides and Plato for the decoration of Baboo versions of Greek prose (thus earning occasional approving smiles from tutors), were suddenly seen to be exer-

cises, however mis-begotten, to acquire the tongue not of a
dead folk long perished, but of the wondrous people who had
built the Parthenon, and whose spirits, still intensely alive,
wandered in its ruinous colonnade, sat on the mellowed marble
seats in the theatre, and rode in peerless squadrons up the
sacred hill of the Acropolis, to do honour to Athene on her
birthday. The plane-trees and the *agnus castus* had perished from the bank of the Ilyssus and its stream was dwindled, and the washerwomen scolded and rinsed their linen by
its shrunken pools, but it was here in very truth that Socrates had sat and told young Phædrus of the chariots of the
soul, and when his tale was done had prayed "Beloved Pan,
and all ye deities that haunt this place, give me inward beauty
of soul, and may the outward and the inward man be at one."
My year of studying archæology at Cambridge, and above all
intercourse with Walter Headlam and Professor Middleton,
who instead of lecturing gave me Greek gems and fragments
of red-figured vases to examine, had begun the vivifying work,
and now the dry bones of that arid valley of education were
all a-stir, and they came together, bone to his bone, and were
transformed into a host of swift and comely presences. I
do not mean to suggest that every boy who is about to be
taught Greek should be taken out to Athens, before he learns
his first declensions, but merely to remark how dismal was
the system, which, expunging all human interest and beauty
from a subject that is instinct with humanity and loveliness,
taught a language, and that the most flexible of all human
tongues, as if it had been a series of algebraical formulæ.
How willingly would those dry irregularities have been
learned if the imagination had first been kindled by photographs of the temples of the beautiful people and by repro-
ductions of their statues: there would then have been an in-
citement to know how the poets and historians of the folk who
made those things, talked and wrote. But at the time when
I was learning Greek, the methods of tutors resembled that
of those who by making their pupils chop up dry faggots of

wood, hoped to teach them what was the nature of the trees that once the wind made murmurous on the hillsides of Attica.

Apart from its ancient inheritance Greece in these years just before the war with Turkey which broke out in 1896, was an astonishing little kingdom, the like of which, outside pure fiction, will never again exist in Europe, for fresh forms of democracy, constructive and destructive alike, have rendered it obsolete. It was not rich, but it had great undeveloped resources, and financially it had a far better credit than most of the great European States of today, for the value of its drachma (nominally equivalent to the franc) stood at about thirty to the pound sterling.   Gladstone, the lover of Homer, had on the accession of King George of Greece, given back to it the lovely Ionian islands, and its independent status as well as its exchequer, was guaranteed by the great Powers. There was scarcely a trace of the old Hellenic blood on the mainland, so ruthlessly had it been overrun by Romans, Venetians, and Turks, and the population of Athens and the towns of the Peloponnese were largely of that mixed blood which by way of a formula we call Levantine.   Their merchants were very acute business men, a good match for the Jews and even the Armenians of the Eastern markets, and many had made large fortunes in Cairo and Smyrna and Alexandria.   There was also in the northern half of Greece, especially in the country districts, much of the robust Albanian blood, and all over Greece a strong national spirit justly proud of those stubborn ancestors who, seventy years before, had risen, under the leadership of Petrobey and the Mainats, and thrown off the damnable yoke of the Turks, kindling by that most heroic insurrection European sympathy with Hellenism, of which the immortal mouthpiece was Byron.   He was regarded as a national hero, and his name was still known and honoured in the remotest parts of Greece.   Once, travelling in the Peloponnese, when I came into sight of the Gulf of Corinth, my young mule-driver from Sparta doffed his cap, and pointed to

the hills of Missolonghi, where "our Byron" died, and where
his heart was buried. He was very keen also to know about
Queen Victoria, the report of whose amazing wealth had
reached him. I told him that she was remarkably well off,
and attempted to express the Civil List in terms of drachmas.
He listened almost incredulous and said "I suppose she can
have tinned meat every day !" His imagination could not
picture a more sumptuous extravagance.

But the national spirit in Athens was prouder yet of its
earlier ancestry: the people considered themselves to be the
modern representatives of the race that had conquered the
Persians and built the Parthenon, and all the little Levantine
boys were christened Agamemnon and Theseus and Epaminondas. They were quite convinced that the whole world
was in their debt as being the lineal heirs of the ancient Hellenes, and they permitted Germany and France and America
and England to excavate the classical sites, and restore to the
rightful heirs the treasures they unearthed. Schliemann had
dug up Mycenæ and the Central Museum at Athens gleamed
with the gold-studded swords and decorations of their ancestor the conqueror of Troy. Germany, too, had recovered
the riches of Olympia for their rightful owner, and the Her-
mes of Praxiteles stood radiant on his pedestal: the French
were permitted to dig up Delphi and recover the bronze
charioteer. America under Dr Charles Waldstein was doing
its duty at Argos, and England at Megalopolis. All these efforts on the part of artistic Europe fostered the national
pride: by the favour of modern Greece the nations were permitted to render their homage to it, by giving back to it its
ancient glories. But Germany and England were rather
shabby folk, for the one had rescued the marbles of Ægina
from destruction, and taken them off to Munich, and England had filched the greater splendour of the Parthenon, at
which, when *in situ*, Turkish soldiers took pot-shots to see if
they could hit the nose of Zeus or the breasts of Athene.
That the frieze and pediments would probably have perished

had Lord Elgin left them there was not relevant; he had had
the inestimable privilege of saving them, and now England
ought to send them back.

Further, it was the privilege of the Powers to establish
the heirs of Agamemnon and Pericles in an inviolable land
and to give them a reigning house of royal blood to hold rule
over Greece and the isles of the Ægean.   Otho of Bavaria
had been the first king, but his despotic methods were intolerable, and in 1862 a fresh king was given them, George I,
then seventeen years of age, who was still on the throne in
these years of the nineties.   Greece, indeed, was furnished
with a very well-connected royal family : their king was the son
of the King of Denmark, and brother of the future Queen of
England and of the Empress of Russia, his wife Queen Olga
was the daughter of the Imperial Grand Duke Constantine,
and their eldest son Constantine was married to Sophia,
sister of the German Emperor.   Europe had really done its
best to give them a reigning family, not unworthy of their
ancient glories, and all these eminent personages with the best
will in the world set themselves to be truly royal and thoroughly democratic.

The effect was inimitable.   Athens, with its high-born
princes, and its national pride, and its army dressed in Albanian costume (embroidered jacket, fustinella, like a ballet
skirt, fez, white gaiters, red shoes with tassels on the toes
like the seed of dandelions), its fleet of three small cruisers,
its national assembly of bawling Levantines, and its boot-
blacks called Agamemnon and Thucydides, was precisely like
the fabulous kingdom of Paflagonia in the "Rose and the
Ring," or some Gilbertian realm of light opera.   King
George lived in a monstrous white palace overlooking the
square; a bugler was stationed by the front door in the long
portico of Doric columns who blew soul-stirring blasts in a
great hurry whenever a royal personage emerged from
within.   Sometimes the royal personage was only a royal
baby in its perambulator, and the slightly self-conscious nurs-

ery-maid hastened to convey her charge into the garden
away from these trumpetings of advertisement. The affable
King gave audience to any foreigner, who, through his legation, asked to have a quarter of an hour's conversation with
him, the Queen was equally willing to talk to those of her
sex, and aspiring American ladies flocked to Athens because
(as one of them stated to me with the most engaging frankness) "The royal family of Greece is the easiest royal family
to become acquainted with."

Here was the democratic side: this open access was useful
to Greece, for it brought visitors, but Royalty also asserted
itself. These fortunate foreigners must be suitably clad
for their interviews: ladies who visited Queen Olga must wear
high evening-dress with a lace mantilla, or something of the
sort on their heads; gentlemen who visited King George must
be decked in top-hats and frock-coats, but since few travellers
carried such articles in their luggage, they were permitted
to wear dress-clothes and white ties. Hence about eleven
o'clock on a broiling morning one might observe the pleasant
spectacle of an obese pilgrim emerging from the Grand
Hotel in a dress-suit (slightly green in the strong sunlight),
pumps, and a straw hat, and making his way across the small
stony desert in front of the palace for his chat. The King
received him in a room with a purple Victorian wall-paper
sprinkled with gilt stars, and he stood during the whole interview see-sawing backwards and forwards from toe to
heel. That movement was as infectious as yawning, and it
was only by a strong effort of self-control that the pilgrim
prevented himself from following the royal example. When
a long catalogue of simple questions and answers had been
correctly repeated, the King gave a little bow and the cate-
chumen a low one, and he then left the palace. If the bugler
on duty was an ardent fellow, he probably started tootling
without waiting to make sure who came out, and all the way-
farers and loungers observed with well-merited sneers this
attempt of a man in dress-clothes and a straw hat to imper-

sonate royalty. He slunk back to the Grand Hotel past
the garlic-savouring congratulations of the porter, and, having changed his clothes, sat down to his lunch with its strange
native menu of fried baby-cuttle-fish, and stew of nameless
meat and a bowl of curdled sheep's milk. Stranger yet was
the native beverage, a white wine in which the flavour of the
grape was imperceptible below that of the resin which was
lavishly mingled with it. National tradition proudly accounted for this monstrous concoction by affirming that in
the days of Pericles and Aspasia wine was stored in sheep
skins caulked with resin, and hence was derived the liking for
the taste of turpentine which their descendants inherited.
They liked what Pericles liked. King George, however, was
not sufficiently Hellenic to like what Pericles liked, and had
vineyards of his own up at his country seat at Tatoi, where
he made a very decent wine called Deceleia, which was innocent of the traditional ingredient, and he sold it at considerable profit to the restaurants and hotels of Athens in bottles
bearing a label with the royal crown. Just so might the
King of England start a brewery at Windsor with the lion
and the unicorn on its label to distinguish it from other
brands.

Often on a Sunday afternoon, there would be a small
compartment reserved on the steam train that ran between
Athens and the shore of Phalerum; it stopped opposite the
palace. Then came a prodigious tootling from the bugler,
and King George and several of his family came out and
walked briskly across towards it. If they did not come at
once, or if they loitered, the driver touched the whistle, and
they made better speed and climbed quickly into their compartment so as not to keep the lieges waiting. Had they not
done so, the driver, after this warning, would undoubtedly
have moved off without them, leaving them to wait for the
next tram or take a cab, and so they hurried. This royal
simplicity pleased the Greeks: that was what a king should
be. The Dowager Empress Frederick of Germany who was

spending a long time in Athens, waiting for the birth of the
baby which her daughter the Crown Princess was expecting,
was very simple too.   There would be a quiet, comely woman
plainly dressed in black, sitting all the morning on a fallen
block of column on the Acropolis, busy with her sketching.
A semi-circle of tourists and idlers stood round her, but she
did not mind that, and if they knew anything about painting
they would easily see that this lady was no ordinary amateur,
but an artist, as Lord Leighton once told me, to be judged
by professional standards.   She had little imagination, he
said, she was a second-rate artist, but, so admirable was her
technical skill she could not be considered an amateur at
all.   So there she sat very busy, and they all stood round
her spitting and smoking, till her gentleman, Count Secken-
dorff, who had also been sketching, came and told Her Majesty that the fiacre was waiting.   He stood bareheaded as
he spoke to her, until she told him to be covered, and so the
crowd recognized who she was, and off they drove in a little
jingling one-horsed victoria.

One morning, casually, she sent round word to the English
legation, where I was staying, that she would like to lunch
there, and though the occasion was quite informal, diplomatic
etiquette seemed to demand that I should wear a frock-coat
of which I had no specimen.   The butler therefore, kindly
lent me his, and as we went down to lunch, I suspected from
the whispers and giggles that went on between the Minister
and the Empress, that this sartorial secret was being divulged.   And so it was, for as we sat at lunch she began to
admire my frock-coat; she had never seen such a beautiful
frock-coat and how well it fitted. . . Directly afterwards Sir
Edwin Egerton had to go to see the King, and I was left
alone with her, and had a glimpse, tragic and sudden and
disconcerting, of the tumult that raged underneath that
tranquil manner.   She talked for a little about an uncle
of mine, who had lived for many years in Germany, and of
whom she was very fond.   Then she was silent a moment,

and suddenly broke out, "But Willie is mad !" Again she paused, then pointed an emphasizing finger at me "I mean just what I say," she cried, "It is literal: Willie is mad."

To all of them Athens was a sort of holiday home; the Empress Frederick came to be with her daughter, the Czarina came to see her brother, the Princess of Wales to see her sister, the Czarevitch to see his uncle and his cousins, and all the Greeks thought they had come to render homage to the land of Hellenic culture. They could relax at Athens, and forget about their crowns, just as they relaxed at Copenhagen, and though, when a family gathering was going on, the bugler outside the palace was sadly overworked, for they all kept popping in and out unattended to do their shopping, and the demand for his music was incessant, they much enjoyed these hours of ease. They romped and unbent; one day a young Englishman who had the privilege to sit and laze in the royal garden heard the sound of tripping feet and male laughter and female cries of dismay, and round the corner of the rose-pergola where he sat came King George, kicking in front of him what had once been a hat. Behind him tripped the Princess of Wales, shrilly protesting. "I beg you not to, George," she cried, "It is my hat: so rude of you !" The young Englishman was in a *cul de sac,* he could not flee, and presently he was apotheosized into an umpire. "But she had an ugly hat," pleaded the King, "and I did not like it. So I took it off and I kicked it." Then the plaintiff stated her case. "It was my hat, and it was so rude of him, and now I can never wear it any more. . ."

This astonished umpire had lately been at Corfu and now they asked him about his experiences there. They had been rather remarkable, for he had been bidden to call on the Empress of Austria who at that time had a big house on the island called the Achilleion. He presented himself there, and was told that Her Majesty was in the garden, and thither he went, conducted by a great golden major-domo. Presently he heard the boom of an intoning voice, and as it came nearer, he perceived that it was reciting the majestic hexameters of Homer. Then round a clump of oleanders came the Empress dressed in Albanian costume, and behind her walked her Greek secretary reading aloud to his mistress, while she took the air, this masterpiece of Greek literature. After a word of greeting, the visitor fell in beside his hostess, the major-domo behind the reader, and to the sonorous music of the Odyssey, this remarkable phil-Hellene procession marched back to the Achilleion.

Then perhaps there was a State ball, but still the suspicion of *opera bouffe* was there, for it seemed almost incredible that the man who had been kicking his sister's hat down the garden path was a real king, or that the woman I had seen coming out of the dentist's yesterday with a rueful face, and who now appeared resplendent wearing a girdle of emeralds so large that they seemed highly improbable, was a real queen: they were playing at being kings and queens and the emeralds were a stage property. The same sense that it was a toy kingdom over which they ruled was present everywhere. For this ball was in honour of the King's name day, and that morning there had been a review of troops in front of the palace: lusty and well-favoured men they were in their ballet skirts and tasselled shoes, but obviously supers. An incident had occurred which, though almost too extravagant even for comic opera, must have required a great deal of rehearsing, for a perfectly trained horse standing in a cab rank near by suddenly bolted, and charged straight through the flower of the Greek army which scampered nimbly away behind orange trees and places of convenience. Right across the square it galloped amid the shrieks of the populace, and was stopped by a courageous boot-black who slung his blacking-box in its face: the army then re-formed for the march past. The incident was recorded in the evening papers with much florid detail, in columns of Thucydidean prose, under the heading "Zeto Epaminondas" ("Here's

to the health of Epaminondas") that being the name of
the boot-black.

Was it not also pure operetta that, when the Greek fleet
of three cruisers was ordered to sail to the Peiræus from
Nauplia where it was stationed, to salute the Russian squad-
ron accompanying the Czarevitch Nicholas who was arriving on a visit to his uncle, it was found, on the eve of this
naval display, that there were not sufficient stokers to enable
the entire fleet to move together ?   Two ships therefore were
brought into the Peiræus, and as soon as they had anchored
there, a contingent of stokers was bundled back to Nauplia,
over-land, in order to bring the third cruiser.   So when the
Russian fleet arrived, there was the Greek navy ready for it.

Patriotic pride and national sentiment are most admirable
qualities; no country can get far without them.   But it is
possible to have too much of them, as of other good things,
and they must be balanced by some sobering weight of sense,
which in these early years of the nineties was sadly wanting
in Greece.   It was not altogether her fault, for the Powers
had done their best to spoil her, and they had, unhappily,
succeeded only too well.   They had given her back the Ionian
Isles, they had guaranteed her loans, they had provided her
with a royal family which, in those days when Kings really
counted, was closely allied with the ruling families of England, Germany, and Russia, and the national pride of Greece,
as embodied in the man in the street never suspected (or at
least instantly put such an absurdity out of his mind) that
all these benefits had anything to do with the balance of
power in Europe or with a check on Turkey, that "sick
man" who, an English premier had once rather rashly stated,
should be put out of his misery.   The Powers (such undoubtedly was the opinion of the Greek cafés) were very
properly paying by instalments the infinite debt which civilization and culture owed to the Hellenes.   In reality the
Powers had stabilized the kingdom of Greece with much the
same object as they might have set up a clock-work mechan-

ism to control the flow of water through the sluices of some reservoir.

Greece, not quite realizing this, felt she must make some gracious gesture of acknowledgment to the tributes paid her, and the suggestion was made that the Olympic games should be revived, and be celebrated at Athens. Athens took the notion up very warmly, for athletes of all nations would certainly flock there, in order to have the honour of competing with the Hellenes, whose forefathers had been the originators of contests in bodily prowess. Originally the Olympic games had been open only to those of true Hellenic blood, but Romans had been permitted afterwards to compete in them, and now they were to be thrown open to the entire world, after being in abeyance for fifteen hundred years. It was decided to include in the events not only such ancient feats as the throwing of the discus but newer athletic acts of physical valour like bicycling. The youth of Athens, not hitherto remarkable for bodily activities, instantly went crazy over athleticism, for Greece was challenging the whole world. Strings of young men in shorts trotted about the streets of Athens all day, occasionally bursting into sprints: they practised long jump and high jump: they put weights, using large stones if they could not procure the standard instruments; the extremely bumpy roads to Phalerum and Kephissia were thick with flashing bicycles, and one day I saw two stout and elderly gentlemen solemnly wrestling together by the columns of Zeus Olympios. But the blue riband of the games would be the race from Marathon to Athens, in commemoration of the day when Athens had hurled back the might of Persia, and Pheidippides had run from Marathon to the city with news of the victory, expiring as he panted out his message. The race would be run over the sacred soil (more or less) which Pheidippides had actually traversed. A patriotic millionaire renovated the ancient stadium, there was a running track round it, a space within the track for such events as jumping and discus throwing, and tiers of seats,

hewn of the marble from the bowels of Hymettus, were provided for spectators, and all was ready by the spring of
1896. The King performed the opening ceremony, the
hymn to Apollo recently dug up at Delphi by French excava-
tors was chanted in the Dorian mode, and the games began.
There was a fair sprinkling of athletes from foreign countries, though there were few, if any, of the first class, but all
these, in the popular view, contended with the Hellenes: it was
Hellas contra mundum. There was a good deal of friction
of one sort and another; defeated Hellenes argued passionately with the judges, disputing their decisions and threaten-
ing them with corporal violence, but the national pride which
was rather humbled by the result of most of the events was
amply restored by the Marathon race. It was easily won by
a young Greek called Loues, who happily did not expire like
Pheidippides, but reached the Stadium in wonderfully good
condition. So far ahead was he of all other competitors, and
so phenomenal was the time in which he had covered the
twenty-five miles from Marathon, that there were some ugly
conjectures whispered about that he had possibly been assisted by occasionally putting his hand on the stirrup of the
Greek cavalry officer who rode beside him with words of encouragement. Without doubt the suggestion was false; indeed it was refuted next year when the victor once more
proved very definitely (as we shall see) his unrivalled power
of speed and staying. He was hailed as a national hero,
he was crowned with a wreath of wild olive by the King.
Pindaric odes were written in his honour, the municipality
voted him a free dinner every day till the end of his life, and
the Athens-Corinth railway a free pass, for he had re-estab-
lished for Greece the athletic supremacy which had been her's
two thousand years ago.

Late that year, arising out of Turkish barbarities in Crete,
there broke out the Greco-Turkish war. In 1897 the Turks
invaded Thessaly from the north, and high flamed the fiery
spirit of Hellas. The Crown Prince Constantine was ap-

pointed Commander-in-Chief of the Greek armies, and went to the front. All over Greece there raged a delirium of war-fever, the most gratifying news was issued hot and hot from the press, and though as yet there was no Turk within fifty miles of Volo, the sea-port in the south of Thessaly, excited youths rushed into the cafés there carrying fezzes impaled on knives. They cried out that they had taken from the heads of the Turks they had slain, and though everybody knew that this was rubbish, they were much applauded. But at the front things were not going so well: the Greeks were in-capable of making any sort of stand against the enemy, the Crown Prince retreated from his headquarters at Larissa, and the Turkish armies marched quietly on till at the end of a few weeks the whole of Thessaly was in their hands. Refu-gees from the Greek army — they could hardly be called de-serters for the army no longer existed at all — poured into Athens, and the first to arrive, easily distancing all competi-tors, was Loues, the winner of the Marathon race the year before. He had silenced for ever all doubts about his run-ning.

The collapse was complete. Streams of homeless, penni-less families poured into Athens on the heels of the army, though the majority of the Thessalian peasants, lacking means of transport, remained in their villages. The troops of the occupying Turks behaved to them with exemplary kindness and consideration and their worst enemies were brigands of their own race, who overran the country. I had been commissioned to distribute the alms of an English fund for the relief of the Greeks in Thessaly, and, as it was quite impossible to move about the country without some small armed guard, I applied to the Greek government to furnish me with one.

Endless difficulties and delays ensued; I was passed from one department to another, and despairing of getting any-thing done in Athens, I went up to Volo, where Edhem Pasha, the Commander-in-Chief of the Turkish forces, had his headquarters, and told him what the object of my mission was. There stood out the high-breeding of the Turk; he was delighted that any help should be brought to these poor Greek villagers, whose soldiers had given him so little trouble, and he instantly provided me with the escort the Greeks would not give me for the relief of their own countrymen.

Then once more the Powers stepped in, and ordered Turkey to evacuate this province of Thessaly which she now occupied, for she could not be allowed to increase her holding of European soil. In fact, the only result of this war, if it could be called a war, was that Crete was put under the protectorate of Greece. The great Powers wound up the works of the toy-kingdom again, and it was soon ticking away as merrily as before.

THOUGH a very decisive thaw had melted the more ludi-crous of the early and mid-Victorian frigidities years before the last and liveliest decade of the reign, there still remained the tradition of a certain splendour and dignity, which ex-pressed itself in the particular type of woman known as "a great lady." She is scarcely definable, though she was very easily recognizable — in fact she could not be mistaken for anything else — and she is now as extinct as the Great Copper butterfly. It is not that the intrinsic qualities which com-posed her have failed, for there are probably just as many women in London now who have them all, but it is rather that, just as the draining of the fens in Cambridgeshire deprived that noble butterfly of the environment and grazing ground in which its caterpillar thrived, so the breaking down of the whole Victorian setting of dignity and fine manners deprived these great ladies of the stage on which they so magnificently functioned. There were also material props and scaffoldings to that stage: great houses in London where they entertained were part of it, so too was the willingness of their guests to set themselves to the stately key. That is not the mode now: the thirst for immediate and lively amusement is more in-sistent, and publicity (to be heard and seen of men, and to resound at restaurants) is a larger ingredient in entertain-ment than it used to be. To give a dinner at a hotel and take her party to a dance-club afterwards would have seemed to the great lady a most extraordinary proceeding: she could never have been a figure at such functions, though they were far less trouble and expense than a dinner and a dance in her own house. Then when a season of three months in

London was over she settled down fairly solidly till after Christmas in her house in the country, and gave parties for her friends at which the men went out shooting and the women drove in landaus to points of interest in the neighbourhood. Autumns in London, lip-sticking in public, winters on the Riviera, the kippering of her arms and legs, bosom, and back on the sands of the Lido, and inability to remain in one place for more than a week, were not habits of the great lady. Above all, she was possessed of that queer old quality called dignity.

Indeed it is far easier to get near the definition of her by excluding what she was not, than by the inclusion of what she was. She was not in a blazing hurry all the time, she did not run a hat-shop or sit in the House of Commons, she had no push, because there was nowhere to push to, for as regards position she was there already by birth or marriage or both, and the craving that everyone should know how much she was there, could not exist in her, for nobody could doubt it. Therefore she did not permit, still less encourage, the public press to regale its readers with chatty paragraphs about the decoration of her "boudoir," the tiles in her bathroom, and the diet of her dogs, nor did she order her dressmaker to show the author of the column signed "Jezebel" or "Hermione," the dresses she intended to wear at Ascot. She did not want to be advertised or her doings daily to be mirrored, and she had no ambition (the odd, old-fashioned creature) that next morning everyone whom she did not know by sight should be told how she had entertained a distinguished company to dinner, or that her guests sat at two round tables decorated with sprays of "Aurora Borealis" and "Delirium Tremens," from her greenhouses at Widdicombe Royal. There were others, effulgent and beautiful and fashionable creatures who liked that: their photographs appeared in all shop windows and they were called "Professional Beauties," and as they walked in the Park, people stood on the chairs to see them. But no "great lady" ever desired that sort of publicity, and Jezebel and Hermione might have died of starvation on the doorstep before they were resuscitated with such succulent domestic morsels as are now pressed on their jaded and fastidious appetites, for her private life did not concern the public.   Unlike the hostesses of a later day (and, for that matter, many hostesses in her own day) to whose bountiful hospitalities London owes so much, she did not cadge and scheme to collect her glittering assemblies.   It was enough that she gave a party, and instead of exerting feverish efforts to secure a galaxy, she had only to decide whom she was obliged to leave out owing to lack of room.   She was not concerned with making a position for herself by enticing notable folk to her house, for the position was hers already, and she did her social duty by it.   Sometimes it rather bored her, but she must play the part for which she was cast in the pageant.   She had power, she mattered, and that was her unsought reward in the performance of her duties. With the disappearance of such women, there vanished every nucleus of social power, the very idea of which today is an antediluvian notion.   "Society" (in the sense of inverted commas) has so broadened out that, becoming quite flat in the process, there is not the semblance of a peak left.   To suggest that anybody matters now, or wields any social power, would imply as complete a misunderstanding of modern conditions as would the failure to grasp the fact that in the eighties and the nineties there were in existence these great ladies who mattered very much indeed.

Three women out of many may be taken as instances of the vanished type which was possessed of an extreme distinction and wielded this effortless though obsolete power.   In many respects they were exceedingly unlike each other, but essentially they had this classical but indefinable quality in common.   The Duchess of Manchester who became Duchess of Devonshire was one, the late Lady Londonderry was another, the third was Lady Ripon, at that time Lady de

Grey.   All of them had to a very high degree a sort of regal
personality, which could manifest itself in graciousness or
imperiousness, but was always dominating, and all of them
(though that had very little, if anything, to do with their
greatness) had been at one time strikingly beautiful women.
Lady Ripon retained that personal splendour to the end of
her life.   But beauty was only a casual, outward expression
of that quality, undefinable as is a colour, which all can
recognize but none explain, except by saying that it is itself.
Certainly they were all extremely capable women, and we may
take it that their high intelligence was a tool with which this
quality worked.   But it was not the same as the quality.

The Duchess of Devonshire was German by birth, Countess
Louise von Alten.   Those who knew her when she was young,
said that no-one who had not seen her then could possibly tell
how beautiful a woman could be.   It is the irritating habit
of old people to say that sort of thing, but early portraits of
her seem to give support to it.   As a young woman when she
first came to England, she used to take delight in walking
alone about the streets of London, a thing which was not done
then, especially by duchesses, but it amused and interested
her, and a story of a little adventure that once happened to
her on one of these excursions, which she told of herself, was
evidently characteristic.   Naturally there would often be a
man, hopefully following this radiant and unaccompanied
vision, and she gave one of these a salutary lesson to leave
her alone.   She had stopped to look in at the window of some
smart bonnet-shop, and the hopeful follower asked her if she
would not like to have one of those nice bonnets.   She said
she would like one very much, and they went in together and
she chose one, for which the follower paid.   So, of course,
he said he would carry it home for her, but she said he must
not trouble himself to do that, for they would send it to her,
and she gave her name, the Duchess of Manchester, and her
address.   He would thus learn not to pester respectable young
ladies who were taking the air: it would do him good. . .

There was something (as may thus be conjectured) of the unswerving relentlessness of a steam-roller about her, neither kindly nor unkindly, but crushing its way on, and flattening out the unevennesses of the road it intended to traverse. With the same quiet fixity of purpose, she intended, should the day arrive when she was free to do so, to marry her second husband, who was her devoted admirer. But long before that day came, while he was still in the House of Commons as Lord Hartington, she made him pull his weight in the political world, and she appreciated very correctly what his weight could be. Under the spur of her ambition for him, he became one of the most powerful units of influence there, not because he was possessed of any very exceptional genius or had great political dexterity or because he was personally ambitious. Indeed it was exactly because he was indifferent to personal motives, because he had no enthusiasms (the happiest moment of his life, he was reported to have said, was when his pig took a first prize at some agricultural show) that she saw what a tremendous force he could become. He had no axe to grind, and that was why he could deliver such stunning blows with it. His bitterest opponents could not accuse him of self-seeking because it was obvious that he wanted nothing for himself, for the man who, in the course of nature will become Duke of Devonshire, and inherit colossal wealth and a quantity of noble possessions has not very much that he can covet for himself among the vain trappings of the material world. So, when, with his great position and very sound judgment, he made up his mind (which took time) on any political question, it was because he thought that such a course was right, and probity, when all is said and done, remains the most valuable equipment in any career. It was largely she who made him use this weight: he could use it equally well sitting down. Sometimes, of course, when he was in office he had to stand up and make a statement of policy, uninspired always, but full of plain common sense, and always to be listened to as the con-

viction of a perfectly honest man with regard to the welfare
of his country. No wizardry of speech, no sophistically
attractive argument liable to be torn to shreds, no ridicule
of his opponents, in the modern mode, gave spice to these
laborious pronouncements; once he yawned heavily in the
middle of a statement, and accounted for this lapse by explaining that what he was saying "was so damned dull." He
found it so himself, and that was partly why it was impressive. Later, when as Duke he came into his enormous prop-
erties, he preserved an engaging ignorance born of complete
indifference, as to what was his. A friend of mine one day
going down to stay with him for a week-end at Compton
Place near Eastbourne, left London in the morning in order
to ramble in the country and in especial to visit the noble
ruin of Pevensey Castle, which belonged to the Duke. He
told his host that evening what he had been doing, and how
deeply impressed he was by Pevensey. The Duke was
vaguely interested but he had heard the name before.
"Pevensey ?" he said. "Whose is Pevensey ?" But the
Duchess knew.

Most people found her rather formidable, for she could
be unexpectedly ruthless in her ways. They never quite
knew, and so they were careful. One day a couple of young
men drove over from Gisburne to lunch with her at Bolton
Abbey. Afterwards she drove them out in a waggonette with
a pair of horses to see the Strid, where the river Wharfe
bustles down, swift and deep, between narrow rocks. It was
raining, a cheerless day, but she would like a breath of air,
and she carried no umbrella, only a stick. As she was getting back again into the waggonette, after having majestically observed the Strid, one of the horses moved on a step,
then was checked again, and she was thrown forward on to
her knees in the carriage. Without a word she hit her coachman smartly over the back with her stick, and then seating
herself said to her companions, "As I was just saying — "
On another occasion, when there was some rumour about that

Devonshire House was to be sold, a friend, rather imprudently, asked her if it was true. She said very drily: "Yes, perfectly true. We are proposing to live at Clapham Junction instead. So convenient a train service." This was the steam roller at work, neither kind nor unkind, but just crushing this slightly impertinent obstacle. Later (for she lived to be an old woman) she became the wraith of what she had been, and still be-wigged and be-diamonded and be-rouged, she was rather like the half ruinous shell of some castellated keep, with flower-boxes in full bloom on the crumbling sills. She had had enough of it all (and indeed she had had a good deal), enough of power, which she had loved most of all, and of wealth and of position: playing-cards and race-cards were the toys to beguile the last lap of her superb course. She did not care any more, and in the absence of any external stimulus, she became almost a piece of still life, expressionless, speechless and motionless. Up till the end that luck which had always attended her, still held, for she knew nothing of death when it came. She had a stroke while at a race-meeting at Sandown, and never recovered consciousness.

Lady Londonderry was equally enamoured of power, and had a far keener appreciation of its insignia. She revelled in personal splendour, she frankly and unmitigatedly enjoyed standing at the head of her stairs when some big party was in progress, with the "family fender," as she called that nice diamond crown, gleaming on her most comely head, and hugging the fact that this was her house, and that she was a marchioness from top to toe and was playing the part to perfection. She was of course far younger than the Duchess and quite lacked the subtlety of the other. She liked violence and strong colour, and sweeping along with her head in the air, vibrant with vitality. She did not plot or plan or devise, she "went for" life, hammer and tongs; she collared it, and scragged it and rooked it like a highwoman in a tiara, trampling on her enemies, as if they had been a bed of nettles —

and occasionally getting stung about the ankles in the process
— incapable of leniency towards them, or of disloyalty to her
friends.   She did not want to forgive her enemies, nor did
she want any peace-conferences with them: she hated them
with a genial sincerity, and loved her friends without reserve.   She was in the great style and liked to know that the
Talbot blood which was hers, was described by some mediæval Latin chronicler as the most unbridled strain.   She had
the stuff in her of autocratic empresses, the kindliest heart
towards those to whom she was well disposed, and a vitality
which, like a bracing wind to those who can stand it, raised
the vitality of any who were exposed to it.   But if they
couldn't stand it, it merely flattened them out.   She lived on
a plane of high-pitched sensation of the most catholic kind:
sailing a small boat in a gale of wind, the twelve o'clock Communion at St Paul's Cathedral, the state coach in which she
attended the opening of Parliament, a loud noise on the
organ, all these were of the quality which gave her sustenance.

Naturally (being what she was) she wanted to manage
everything for everybody, and though she would always do
her best that her friends should get their hearts' desire, she
distinctly preferred that she should compass this for them in
her own way.   She was always very conscious of herself (a
very different thing from being self-conscious in the usual
sense of the word) and she continually remembered who she
was: you might almost say that she impersonated herself (she
was an inimitable mimic) with realism and gusto.   Then in
the middle of this exposition of her imperious will and her
ebullient blood and her arrogant certainty, she would suddenly turn over a new leaf in this illuminated manuscript
of herself, and you saw written there (in the margin and
minutely) little tender things.   A tiny instance must suf-
fice though perhaps it may not seem so significant to others
as to one who knew her well.   The King had come to tea with
her one afternoon and that evening she happened to be
dressed rather early for dinner, and came into her drawing-

room before her time, and saw that her housemaid was still
tidying it up. The girl had not heard her enter, and she
was employing herself, duster in hand, in sitting down on
all the chairs, one after the other. Lady Londonderry instantly guessed what was the purpose of these odd sessions,
and pointed to one of the chairs. "That was the chair the
King sat on," she said. "Sit down on it."

The third of these great ladies, Lady Ripon, had little
in common with the two others, except that she was also of
the grand style, superb in dignity and manner. Unlike the
Duchess of Devonshire she regarded everything connected
with politics with a sort of weary repulsion; unlike Lady
Londonderry she neither had nor wished to have a great London house for stately and magnificent entertaining. During
the years of the nineties, she was still in the zenith of her
youthful splendour. She was very tall, a full six feet, but of
so matchless a grace that the effect was not that she looked
tall, but that most other women looked squat. Her beauty
was of the quality that can only be described as dazzling;
when she was there the rest appeared a shade shabby. They
wanted a touch of the sponge or duster. She had a series of
beautiful names: first she had been Lady Gladys Herbert,
then she was Countess of Lonsdale, now in the nineties she
was Countess de Grey, and presently became Marchioness of
Ripon — who ever had such lovely names or so well became
them ? Henry James who had a passion for nomenclature
appropriate to the style of his heroines, could not have named
her more aptly. At this time she had a small house in Bru-
ton Street where she entertained with a touch of that apotheosized Bohemianism of which nobody else ever quite had the
secret.

One such evening, though it must be nearer forty than
thirty years ago, has its lights still brightly burning for me.
It was the last night of the opera season, and Edouard and
Jean de Reszke came on to a little party there. There were
not more than fifty guests all told, the Duke of Cambridge

was among them, and he, sitting on a very low chair, was sunk in the condition which hypnotists call "light trance"; not asleep, at least not at all sound asleep, but slightly oblivious to external impressions.   Then Alick Yorke came tripping in, with a little rouge and an eyebrow and a stupendous carnation in his buttonhole, not much more than five feet tall.   He looked up at his hostess who had done her hair in some amazing manner, piling it on the top of her head while somewhere near the summit was a diamond crescent; indeed for once she looked almost too tall.   Alick Yorke surveyed her critically, blinked up at the crescent, and with a little lisp he said, "Dear Gladys, I like the way you've done your hair tonight.   It gives you what you've always wanted.   Height."   Oscar Wilde came drifting largely along, and caught sight of some new arrival.   "Oh, I'm so glad you've come," he said. "There are a hundred things I want not to say to you."   Then Réjane recited "La Poupée," and after a few trifles of that kind, all rather informally bestowed, Lady de Grey, purely for a joke, said to Edouard de Reszke; "Won't you sing something?"   He, instead of answering her according to her folly and saying he hadn't brought his music, said "But certainly I will, though I have never sung in so small a room. I will sing you 'Le Veau d'Or' from Faust."   He had a prodigious volume of voice when he chose to open it out, and now he sang "Le Veau d'Or" as loud as he possibly could, and the windows rattled, and the crystal festoons of the chandelier quivered.   He sang it with extravagant operatic gestures, parodying himself, with an eye all the time on the Duke of Cambridge, but he never disturbed the light trance.   And then Jean de Reszke fired by this noble exhibition, and slightly jealous said, "But I want to sing too.   I will show you how I sing the 'Preis-lied.'"   So he found two footstools and placed them in the middle of the room, and insecurely perched on them proceeded also to parody himself.   He sang it as he always sang it, but with some absurd exaggeration of gesture and caricature of the way he took his high notes.

Never was anything quite so ludicrous, and before he had finished his singing there was not, quite in the Victorian manner, a dry eye in the room except those of the Duke of Cambridge. . . Bohemia in excelsis: Bohemia in tiaras.

Now possibly Réjane might have recited at a party of the Duchess of Devonshire's or of Lady Londonderry's for some colossal fee and, just possibly, the De Reszkes might have consented to sing there, but there was no-one but Lady de Grey for whom they would have rollicked like this, just for the fun of it. They were not stars at this remarkable party, they were merely her guests in the *milieu* which they all loved. At heart she was Bohemian, while socially a great lady on a pinnacle which, in the eyes of the world, was higher than any other. But the pageant of her existence was to her merely a painted background. It was pleasant to have it there, and probably she could not have done without it, but it was only her setting and did not make her life, for she had far too much ability and brains to be content with it. She hated politics, she did not care for such pastimes as cards, and her mind, though exceedingly subtle and perceptive was not of the blue-stocking order that can immerse itself in literary or artistic study, and she abhorred the high-brow. Her husband was one of the best shots in the world, possibly quite the best, but to entertain shooting-parties all the autumn at her father-in-law's house at Studley Royal was wearisomeness, for she had not the smallest interest in sport. She was essentially urban, she yawned in the country, and the "vernal wood" provided her with no impulses or ecstasies. She disliked any form of physical exercise, though when bicycling became for a brief space one of the fashionable crazes of the nineties, she took it up for a while. But she did not want to trundle through rough country lanes and listen to the cuckoo. It was fun sometimes in the evening, when there was no traffic in the city to skim over the asphalted ways with a few friends and return to a supper party, but she soon had enough of that. All such things, with which many women fill their lives, her own distinction, her own pinnacle in the world, the never-ending round of social engagements, were all trivial to the eagerness of an unsatisfied though not dissatisfied mind.   She wanted a definite "stunt" to occupy her, and a year or so before that party of her's about which I have spoken, she took up the Opera.   Opera was urban, there was the touch of Bohemianism about it, and in itself its pageantry and artifice suited her sophistication.

At this time in London it was languishing in an incredible tawdriness.   Rossini and Donizetti and Gounod were the chief masters in the repertoire of Covent Garden and the performances were ill rehearsed, ill staged, and interpreted by a wretched orchestra and squawling singers to shabby and sparse houses.   Once it had been a great institution in the days when Queen Victoria and the Prince Consort came to the Haymarket to hear Mario and Grisi, or Jenny Lind, and since then there had been great singers such as Adelina Patti, but it had fallen from its high estate and the whole affair, both in front of the footlights and behind them, must be revitalized.   Opera must be made the fashion: boxes must gleam with the jewels of beautiful women, and the stage must resound with glorious voices singing noble music.   About music technically Lady de Grey knew nothing, nor was she musical in the sense that it was a need of her nature.   She could not, without aching weariness, have sat out a symphony of Beethoven unless she had been a personal friend of the composer or the conductor.   But now when in this regeneration of the opera, which was mainly due to her, great artists flocked to London, Edouard and Jean de Reszke and Ternina and Melba, her friendship with them gave her stunt a living interest which mere music did not possess for her.   It was her beloved Melba who was enchanting all the gleaming boxes with her flawless singing as Mimi, and it was Jean de Reszke who, "ritterlich" as no other Lohengrin had ever been, came down the Scheldt and bade farewell to his swan.   And when he called for his swan again to ferry him away, there was

no longer any such catastrophe to be feared as had once
been presented in the shabbier days to the astonished stalls,
when, after the Knight had taken his stand again between
its wings, the swan did not glide away on its motif as Wagner
had directed that it should, but remained planted very firmly
in the centre of the stage.   The orchestra held on as long
as it could to the final chord, by which time the swan should
have made its exit, and various tuggings and wheezings of
ropes behind the stage were heard, but the bird heeded them
not.   Then, with a smart explosion, the head and neck of
the swan broke off, and flew into the wings, as if discharged
from a catapult, leaving a decapitated bird and an agi-
tated knight to be tugged away by a workman in shirt-
sleeves.

Nor were surprising musical accidents to be expected any
more from the orchestra.   Richter conducted the Wagner
performances; he had worked at Baireuth under the Master's
tuition, and the orchestra swayed by the spell of his magic
wand, became the voice of one melodious presence.   The
quality of the singers also who equally responded to his inspiration was, irrespective of the great primos and primas,
far finer than that at Baireuth, and Richter frankly said that
it had always been his belief that Wagner's music would one
day return to Germany, sung and not barked and yelled, and
now he knew that it would be England who set the example.
The "Ring," "Tristan," "Meistersinger," and the rest (not of
course "Parsifal") were nobly given, and it was here at Covent
Garden that Ternina, the most peerless artist of them all,
sang her swan-song as Isolde and thereafter was mute.
That night I was with Lady de Grey in her box, and for the
first time, perhaps, opera profoundly moved her, for she
knew that her friend Ternina would never sing again.   And
never was the Liebestod sung as she sang it then: she sang it
quite privately, bending over Tristan's dead body, and at
the end she died herself to all that had been life to her.

It was not that Lady de Grey made sure for herself that

the swan's neck in "Lohengrin" was robustly joined to its body
or that she swung in the Rhine maidens' trapezes, or tried
Jean de Reszke's voice, or criticized the wood-wind in the
orchestra, or told Hans Richter that he must go to bed if he
was to be fresh for "Siegfried" next day, or even insisted that
her friends should take boxes at the opera and wear their
tiaras, but it was directly due to her that this regeneration of
the opera took place. She wanted it, she intended to have
it, and hers was a personality that usually got what it wanted.
Somewhat similarly, as one of his staff told me, Lord Kitchener sat at the War Office in the early days of August
1914, and rapped with his knuckles on the table and said
"I want a million men," until he got them. That was the
effect of his personality: and it was thus that Lady de Grey
sat in the centre of the web in touch with it all. Seemingly
rather effortless but appreciative, she was the initial and
effective force. An apparent casualness was her chief
weapon; she would do no more than mention how magnificently Melba had sung last night, and how pleasant it was to
see so many friends in the full tiers. In reality she was taking endless trouble, though it looked (she did it so easily)
as if she was merely leading the life of pageantry that was
natural to her. She had a house now down at Coombe, easy
of access from London, people came down there to have tea
and stroll about and dine, and it seemed almost accidental that
on the evening when the Princess of Wales came down to
dine with her, it happened to be an off-night at the opera, and
in consequence Melba and Jean de Reszke were there too, and
so, after dinner there was a little singing. It was not so easy
to hear either of them except at the opera, for Melba only
took one private engagement a year when she sang at the
house of Mr Alfred de Rothschild for a suitable sum, and
Jean's appearance at a private concert was just as rare.
Those folk therefore who were privileged to hear them like
this in mufti were very apt (and with good reason) to tell

everyone how marvellously they had sung, and that was very good for the opera, while the divine choristers had been delighted to sing for the Princess of Wales. Such an entertainment seemed quite social and fortuitous, though as a matter of fact, these parties gave Lady de Grey torture-hours of anxiety, so desperately keen was she that everything should go swimmingly, and all her guests enjoy themselves. Above all it was done privately ; the searchlights of the Press never succeeded in getting Coombe on to the illuminated area, nor did "Hermione" and "Jezebel" ever recount how they had chatted with friends on Lady de Grey's lawn, and saw her smoking a cigarette out of an amber holder. She completely evaded the limelight, and though she immensely enjoyed entertaining her royal guests, and having the evening stars to sing to them, she had not the faintest desire to let the public know all about it. In this respect she differed from Lady Londonberry who loved driving in the family coach through crowded streets to the opening of Parliament. If Lady de Grey had ever dreamt of attending such a function, she would certainly have gone there in a four-wheeler with the blinds down. Nothing was more alien to her than the desire to astound the citizens by her splendour or regale them with news of her parties: she would as soon have done conjuring tricks with a rabbit and a pack of cards in Piccadilly Circus. She did not think of them as "canaille" or anything of the sort, but like Dr Jowett she did not think of them at all.

It was inevitable that since she was not musical she should have tired of her creation when it was finished. She had done what she set out to do, but that was not primarily to enjoy a first-rate operatic performance any night during the season, but to clean and wind up this shabby old clock and set it going and striking the hours. The greatest singers of the time appeared here now, Wagner was sung here as nowhere else in the world, and, perhaps hardly less of an achievement,

the house now on a gala night or on a Melba night was a
scene of almost barbaric splendour, and that too was part of
her creation.   She had no sort of sympathy with the indi-
gent music lover (not being a music lover herself) who
wanted his opera cheap, for if he wanted that he could go to
Germany, and she would have sickened at the thought of the
stalls being invaded by men in Norfolk jackets, or of the
foyer being peopled by short-skirted women smoking cigarettes: her opera at Covent Garden was not for such, it was
an expensive piece of luxury for the wealthy.   For English
composers and English singers, similarly, she had no sympathy at all: she thought of them vaguely as people who
wrote and performed oratorios in Cathedral towns.   By
nature and taste she was very cosmopolitan, and, like most
cosmopolitans, she preferred foreign products to native;
opera to her connoted something coming from abroad.   But
the relentless years ticked on, the velvet of the voices of the
two de Reszkes began to show signs of wear, and like wise men
they did not outstay their warning.   She took less trouble
now over what she had inaugurated, the business part of it
was in excellent hands, and she did not care to take up new
singers and play the gorgeous Bohemian godmother over
again.   But when the Russian ballet appeared in England
her interest in the affairs of Covent Garden swiftly revived.
This form of art was new to her, it was violent, it was intensely artificial, it was exotic and Bohemian, vivid as a
gorgeous butterfly, and it excited her in itself in a way that
music had never done.   But there was no proselytizing to be
undertaken here, for it took London by storm.   Then came
the war, and she discarded ballet and opera and the whole of
her past modes of life like worn-out toys.   She showed what
noble stuff, what humble zeal for service lay below her
pageantries, and up till the time when a disease, cruel and
hideous, wholly incapacitated her she spent every day and
all day in the management of the military hospital in Water-
loo Road, capable and tender and beloved.

TIME, the mere lapse of it, performs the function of a telescope; through its extended tube one perceives things at a distance in very clear shape and outline, whereas more recent happenings for the scrutiny of which no such telescope can be used, are often far more fluid and undetermined. They have not yet "set," they shift and slide under the eye, various lights, which confuse as well as illuminate, play upon them, and they have not yet undergone that quasi-crystallization which more remote, more documented objects have acquired. The latter have somehow shed the topical trappings which dangle before us irrelevant issues, they appear in a drier and more distinct light, and their main outlines, focussed through the telescope of time are firmly fixed. Unfortunately the telescope has two ends, and the observer may be applying one or the other one to his eye (he never knows which for certain) and the objects he brings into its focussed field may now appear to be bigger than they really were, or very much smaller. The clumsy fellow in fact never can be quite sure whether he is exaggerating or whether he is missing a larger significance than the objects appear to him to possess. He can only give an account of them based on what he believes himself to see, and perhaps these figures of great ladies here presented, were not so remarkable as through his telescope he fancies them to have been, nor perhaps was Mr Gladstone so cosmic and overwhelming a personage. But they and others like them persist in appearing larger than those contemporary figures which now occupy their position and offices, and he insists that the late Lord Salisbury also belonged to the larger breed. Other Prime Ministers have steered the country through far more perilous waters, and far vaster responsibilities have lain on their shoulders than ever burdened the statesmen of the nineties, but the sight of Mr Asquith going down to the House of Commons in the early days of the war or of Mr Baldwin knocking out the ashes of his pipe seemed less an embodiment of the majesty of imperial affairs than Mr Gladstone waving his umbrella to arrest a cab, or Lord Salisbury labouring on his tricycle through St James's Park in the early hours of the day. His was the grand style, something Elizabethan, and he wore his office with the same indifference as his Garter robes, and that very indifference, the naturalness of it, were impressive. One admirable instance of it was when he consulted my father about some appointment. There were two candidates discussed, whom we will call Mr Smithson and Mr Jameson, and my father recommended Mr Jameson. Lord Salisbury acquiesced and said he would make the appointment. A day or two later my father had occasion to write to the Prime Minister again on the matter, referring in his letter to the newly appointed Mr Jameson and received the following reply:

"I do not know which of our memories was wrong, but I thought it was Smithson not Jameson we had agreed upon. Both are Liberal M. P.s. Unfortunately before I received Your Grace's letter, I had sent in Mr S.'s name to the Queen. But I daresay it will do as well."

That surely was in the grand style: all Liberal M. P.s were clearly much the same sort of person, and if, in addition, their names were so very similar, who could be expected to distinguish between these dim specimens? And, in any case, whoever was responsible for the confusion, it could not much matter which of them was appointed. But behind this superb indifference to such minor accidents in patronage, there was a very stubborn obstinacy from which it was very difficult to move him if he thought the question was really important. The Queen also could be equally immovable if she too had made up her mind, and on one occasion certainly she was too much for him. For the Bishopric of Durham, one of the very greatest positions in the Church, had fallen vacant, owing to the death of Bishop Lightfoot in 1890, and the Queen, after consultation with my father, had felt sure that the right man for the post was Bishop Westcott. But Lord Salisbury, who, as Prime Minister, had to make his recommendation to her, refused to put forward his name and told her so. He added that "he had been looking into some of Westcott's works, and thought he would be unsuited to Durham." Though there was a humorous side to the picture of Lord Salisbury adopting the rôle of the conscientious theological student and, after purchasing and perusing Westcott's "Gospel According to St John," deciding that the author was not fitted to occupy an important See, there was a deadlock of an embarrassing kind. He was determined "not to be pushed," the Queen was equally averse from being pulled, and she therefore prepared to remind him, quite in the style of Queen Elizabeth, that "when all was said and done she was Queen of England." She told Sir Henry Ponsonby that "she intended to prevail," and asked Lord Salisbury to come down and see her at Windsor. The interview took place (Queen Bess and Burleigh over again), and though we can only guess what she said, the effect was that the Bishopric of Durham was at once offered to Westcott.

On the other hand, in a year's time another bishopric fell vacant, that of Winchester, and once more the Queen and her Prime Minister could not agree as to the appointment. She wanted Dean Davidson of Windsor to be appointed to Winchester, for she had an immense opinion of his wisdom, and he would thus take his seat at once in the House of Lords; also Windsor and Osborne were both in that diocese. She wrote two strong letters to Lord Salisbury on the subject, but he would not hear of it, though he was willing to offer Rochester to Dean Davidson: he assigned reasons which the Queen thought "most extraordinary." So she wrote to my father asking him to back her up, and without allusion to her wishes in any way, to express a hope that Lord Salisbury would appoint Dean Davidson to Winchester. She thought this independent recommendation would have great weight. But it proved to have none whatever, and Lord Salisbury had his way. . . He was a master of ironic humour: one of his notable phrases, very thoughtfully delivered was "the Draconic character which usually marks philanthropic legislation."

Again when he was asked for what sort of reason he had appointed Mr Alfred Austin to be Poet Laureate in the place of Lord Tennyson, he is reported to have said (again with thoughtful candour) "I don't think anybody else applied for the post." His opinion both of the candidate and of the office to which he had presented him, could thereby be accurately gauged.

MY FAMILY were deeply interested in this appointment, for a short time before it was announced the Poet had stayed with us at Addington. In anticipation of his visit we had acquainted ourselves with some of his pieces, and these had filled us with a horrid joy. We soon saw that he as well as his work was worth study, for at dinner he told us (as already recounted) about his talks with Tennyson, and how he had found fault with certain of his lines, and how Immortal Bard had confessed that these criticisms were just. That was promising, it boded well, and I am afraid we formed the design of drawing out Mr Austin when he came to the smoking-room that night and getting all we could out of him. But there was no need to put this treacherous scheme into practice, for Mr Austin poured himself out, of his own spontaneous uncorking, with a fullness and a foam that our clumsy handling could never have accomplished. He laid himself down, all five feet of him on the sofa and as feast-master directed a wondrous symposium entirely about himself; *ipse fecit*. He told us how he had once been an occasional leader-writer to the *Standard*: forty-five minutes was the time it took him to write one of these leaders on whatever subject was required. Mr Bryce was once staying with him, and Mr Bryce very rashly expressed his firm conviction that nobody could write a leading article in forty-five minutes. Oddly enough there arrived at this precise moment a telegram for Mr Austin in which the Editor of the *Standard* requested him to supply them with a leader on some particular subject without delay. He went at once into his study, and Mr Bryce, having noted the time, sat in the garden to wait for him. As soon as he had finished his article, he went out to show it to Mr Bryce. There it was complete, and Mr Bryce looked at his watch. "To be quite exact, forty-three minutes," he said. "I could not have believed it."

But leader-writing was a mere toy (continued Mr Austin), a piece of child's play, and when the *Standard* offered him £3000 a year to become a regular writer for them, he could not entertain the idea. Then he wrote two novels: "they were dreadful rubbish" he said, and at that our faces fell for this was not the Ercles-vein we wanted. But presently we were comforted, for Mr Austin began to tell us of "It." "It" was the poetic inspiration. Sometimes It left him altogether, and when that first happened he was terribly upset, for he feared that he would be able to write no more poetry, since he never wrote a line except when It directed him. But he had learned since then that, though It might leave him for awhile, It always returned, and so he waited without fretting or attempting to produce uninspired stuff, until It came back. "It left me once," said Mr Austin, "after the second Act of "The Human Tragedy." I had just written the lines:

As for the twain they vanished in the rattle
Of jolting tumbrils and the joy of battle

when It went. I could write no more and so I put my pen away and waited. Then It came back and I went straight on. Let me see: how does the third Act begin ? Can any of you remember it ?" Of course it was on the tips of all our tongues, and we snapped our fingers and said, "Tut ! how stupid !" But then Mr Austin luckily remembered it himself.

Now this noble evening took place after Lord Tennyson's death, and I have a suspicion that Mr Austin had already

sent in his application to Lord Salisbury, for when, in a
rather thoughtless manner, we hazarded guesses as to the successor of Immortal Bard, he preserved a very tactful silence.
Great was our joy when the appointment was gazetted, for
now we all felt sure that It would be with him when some imperial occasion demanded that the heart of England should
make itself articulate. These bright hopes were splendidly
fulfilled for in 1897 Mr Austin published that remarkable
poem "Who would not die for England ?" (Sub-title
Whippingham-Sandringham February 1896.) It brought
up to date, the duties of the national bard to the Royal
House which Mr Austin thought had fallen into arrears,
for in its comprehensive stanzas it deplored the recent death
of a member of the Family, it recorded the poetic vision of
"veiled Fate like muse inspired" addressing the cradle in
which lay the infant Prince of Wales, in those lines beginning "Another Albert shalt thou be," and it paid the following tribute to the memory of the Prince Consort who had died
thirty-five years before —

> *Sweetest Consort, sagest Prince*
> *Snows on snow have melted since*
> *England lost you: — late to learn*
> *Worth that never can return:*
> *Learned to know you as you were,*
> *Known till then alone to Her !*
> *Luminous as sun at noon,*
> *Tender as the midnight moon:*
> *Steadfast as the steered-by Star*
> *Wise as Time and Silence are.*

We felt that It had been strongly functioning when such
lines as these were born, and waited eagerly for more. The
Jameson Raid inspired a fugitive composition and It was
surely there when Mr Austin wrote:

> *They went across the veldt,*
> *As hard as they could pelt,*

To him, too, is ascribed, though with what certainty I know not, a wonderful couplet concerning the national suspense during the illness of the Prince of Wales in 1870: the internal evidence strongly supports the theory:

> *Across the wires the electric message came,*
> *He is no better, he is much the same.*

That sounds very like It: that sounds like Mr Austin at his very best. He never wrote a line except when It was directing him, and never fell below the standard of what he considered his greatest work, "The Human Tragedy," from which (as it has been suffered to fall into an ill-merited oblivion) I must allow myself one more quotation. The Poet is describing (under It) how the rejected Godfrid receives a letter from the mistress of his heart:

> *He tore it open with a trembling hand,*
> *And with a greedy eye its message read,*
> *Written, it seemed, in haste and quickly scanned:*
> *"I write to tell you my last news, instead*
> *Of leaving it to gossip's busy hand.*
> *I am engaged and shortly shall be wed.*
> *Congratulate me, won't you ? All here send*
> *Their best regards. I fear that I must end."*

All these gems, incredible but authentic, gave fresh impetus to our scheme of bringing out a slender volume (suitable for a Christmas present) called "Leaves from the Laurels of the Poets Laureate" which should entirely consist of precious fragments from the official bards of England. Laureate the

Reverend Laurence Eusden would lend us those striking lines in which he addressed George II on his coronation:

> *Hail mighty Monarch, whom desert alone*
> *Would without birthright, raise e'en to the Throne,*
> *Thy merits shine conspicuously nice,*
> *Ungloomed by contiguity to vice.*

and Tennyson should contribute:

> *O darling room, my heart's delight,*
> *Dear room, the apple of my sight,*
> *With thy two couches soft and white,*
> *There is no room so exquisite,*
> *No little room so warm and bright*
> *Wherein to read, wherein to write.*

and Wordsworth should tell us how

> *And five times to the Child I said*
> *"Why, Edward, tell me why!"*

With these promising samples to show I once submitted the scheme to our beloved Edmund Gosse, who gave it his high approval and promised an enthusiastic review. But he begged me to include among these gems a poem written by a housemaid of his wife's, which, he maintained, in the matter of triumphant bathos was quite up to the mark of our Laureates. No doubt she would have been laureated had it not been her misfortune as regards sex: "Besides," said he, "think of Sappho: you would not leave Sappho out of a Greek anthology: so do not be so narrow. . ." This young lady had no time to do her menial jobs among slops and soap-dishes for she was busy writing poetry, and Gosse pleaded with his wife not to dismiss her, for poetesses (see Sappho) stood outside the laws that applied to the common rabble. But she continued to write so much poetry and to empty so few slops that at length Mrs Gosse would stand it no more, and gave her notice. She took her manuscripts with her, but when her room was being made ready for her meaner successor, it was found that she had overlooked one precious leaf on which was written the quatrain which Gosse implored me to include among the jewels of the Laureates. It was an "Address to the Moon," and ran as follows:

> *O Moon, lovely Moon, with thy beautiful face,*
> *Careering throughout the boundáries of space,*
> *Whenever I see thee, I think in my mind,*
> *Shall I ever, oh ever, behold thy behind.*

"It is bathos," said Gosse, "of the purest ray serene, and incidentally it contains the statement of a profound astronomical problem."

But our volume was of Laureates only, and though recognizing the quality of these lines, I could not include them any more than I can include in it certain gems that Mr Gerald Gould, poet and critic, has lately given us. On him the mantle of Elijah has fallen, and though I know Mr Austin's style very well, I should certainly have attributed to Elijah such lines as:

> *And now we have a boy — like me, they say;*
> *Also I think a little bit like you.*

or the even finer conclusion to a poem about Lancelot and Guinevere:

> *The eyes and cheeks of her grew hot,*
> *The hands and mouth of her grew dry:*
> *Her heart was clamorous for reply,*
> *But asked not, and was answered not;*
> *Till in a sudden dreadful shout*

His passionate "Guinevere" rang out
To meet her pitiful "Lancelot."

That's the true stuff, and I would that it was eligible for my
book.   Perhaps an appendix. . .

Edmund Gosse was of that rare breed, a natural and instinctive man of letters, and English literature will always
be in his debt for the acuteness and sanity of his critical
faculty.   The particular quality of it is rather hard to describe: I may perhaps get nearest it by saying that he was
not appreciated in America.   He wrote one book, rather
a cruel one, of first-rate merit, "Father and Son," and one
poem called "Tusitala" addressed to R. L. Stevenson, which
will live long in English anthologies, but he had neither that
tragic grip on life nor that deadly seriousness of aim out of
which alone arise masterpieces.   As he himself said in one
of his graceful poems, "I hold it best in living to take all
things very lightly," and he had no taste for "the singeing
and the smoke," the struggle and the suffocation of soul in
which great original writers constantly labour.   Nor did he
really care for the fruits of such portentous travail, nor for
what we may call the blasting masterpieces of literature,
works like the "Divine Comedy" or "Wuthering Heights," or
"The Brothers Karamosov."   Though he had a sincere reverence for such and for the genius of the huge brooding
minds which made them, he did not devote himself to the
study of such large movements.   In many ways he was more
like a tremendously intelligent child who, playing on the
seashore, did not concern himself with the sweep of the great
tides, but splashed ecstatically in the less menacing ripples
with the keenest of eyes for the adorable jetsam they flung
up.   He was not at ease nor at his best in the presence of high
tensions, they made him feel uncomfortable, as if a thunder-
storm was brewing.   So, skipping lightly from their neighbourhood, he devoted his taste, his knowledge, his acumen to

less cosmic phenomena. It was not that he liked the second-rate in literature, for no-one disliked it more, but he liked the first-rate in its less violent manifestations. Though it took a Pheidias to conceive and execute the great presence of the Parthenon, it also took a very great artist to paint an Attic vase or carve a fine intaglio, and the vase and the intaglio were more to his taste, first-rate work on a small scale. He would never have dreamed of writing a commentary on Isaiah, but he could bring to light all sorts of hidden charms in the work of excellent though minor prophets.

There were the roaring masterpieces: anyone who had a taste for being roasted alive, might go and impale himself on a spit in front of these sombre furnaces, but for himself he preferred the cool and pleasant glades and gardens of literature, its smoking-rooms, its libraries, its fire-sides and arm-chairs. But he did not pass mere hours of dozings and relaxations among these, he was extremely active and wide-awake in such surroundings, exercising to the full his powers of penetrating observation. But there was nothing to be said about the more torrid masterpieces; he was not equipped for them, but for conveying in a light and urbane style the most entertaining suggestions and speculations about less perilous stuff and in this field he was quite unrivalled. Should you happen to be in need of very accurate information based on dry scholarly research, there were no doubt many safer guides than he, but if you wanted the brilliant gossip of an amateur on a subject, there was no-one so stimulating. Thus, though as a critical historian he made no important contribution (except perhaps in his life of Donne) to literary knowledge, he gave you by means of that dancing will-o-the-wisp light of his, both in speech and written word, a constant galaxy of enchanting glimpses. For some years before his death he wrote a weekly review in the Sunday *Times*, which exhibited his method and style of criticism at its very best, urbane and cultivated. His first object, always apparent, was to put himself in sympathy with his author, and then, turning himself into a delightful Master of the Ceremonies, to introduce his reader to him as a charming fellow. Like all good critics he was always advocate rather than judge, and never found it worth his while to assume the black cap or thunder from the critical Olympus. His object as a critic was to point out what was to be praised; there were plenty of myopic reviewers who could see nothing beyond motes in their author's eye by reason of the beam in their own and triumphantly detected small misprints or lapses of grammar. Most of all he detested an attitude of pompous self-assertiveness in a critic, that pontification with tiara and *sedia gestatoria* and its flatulent pronouncements. Gosse never called attention to himself when he spoke of other people's books. He chatted in his arm-chair, but anyone could see how sound his critical faculty was.

His companionship had all the charm and the stimulus of his writing, wit and humour and a most delicate and airy perception of the ludicrous. Occasionally, a little wariness was needed with him, for something went awry, some sensitiveness of his was stung, something offended him, and he would suddenly dry up, and sit glaring glassily through his spectacles and bow silently with a slightly acid smile, if a remark was addressed to him. Mrs Gosse knew perfectly how to deal with such a mood, for the symptoms were clear to her, and if he was really vexed she would let him be and divert attention from him; if she saw that his disturbance was superficial she would say in a comfortable voice, "Edmund is being tiresome, just poke him," and the glassy aspect melted, and at once he was the joyous talker again. He had known with a revelling Boswellian intimacy most of the great literary figures of his day and would tell you how Swinburne came to him one morning chuckling and twitching and snapping his fingers. "Emerson will be surprised," he said, "to receive the letter I wrote him last night, for I reminded him that he was a debilitated and now toothless ape, who, once hoisted into prominence on the shoulders of Carlyle, now spits and gibbers from a platform of his own finding and fouling." * He had been intimate with R. L. Stevenson from the time of the gallant invalid days of his youth, and to the end of his life had a boy's hero-worship for him, not only and perhaps not chiefly as an author (for I think that some faint doubts, instantly suppressed, occasionally assailed him as to whether R. L. S. was quite so supreme a master as he always maintained) but as the most entrancing personality he had ever come across. "The gods had come down in the likeness of men," and he was to Gosse the most radiant of all his memories.

Or he would tell you how the late Lord Houghton had been present at a dinner given to George Curzon by his friends, to congratulate him on his appointment to one of his earlier political posts. Lord Houghton had got very drowsy as sometimes happened, during the speeches that followed, and woke up just as the hero of the evening, now in the middle of a suave and polished oration, was assuring his admirers that any success that had come to him was entirely due to his having made it a rule of his life only to associate with his intellectual superiors. This was a very apt and pretty compliment to everybody present, and they gently preened themselves on being his associates. But Lord Houghton saw it in another light. "By God!" he exclaimed, "That wouldn't be difficult," and the unerring tact of the future Viceroy of India prompted him to pursue that line of thought no further.

Unlike most people who talk exceedingly well and many who talk exceedingly badly, Gosse had never the slightest desire or tendency to monopolize. He much preferred that the ball of conversation should be thrown backwards and forwards, and when it came to him he made his brilliant catch, and instead of retaining it, threw it lightly away to some other player. Of the three wittiest talkers I have ever

---

* This was Swinburne's account of his own letter to Edmund Gosse. The actual wording of it, I believe differs slightly.

known he stood midway in habit between the two others, namely Harry Higgins, who in later years, owing to an operation on his throat, spoke only in a whisper and did not join in general conversation, and Oscar Wilde who also seldom joined in general conversation because he conducted the most of it himself. Of the three for sheer wit in making *mots*, and in comments, *obiter dicta*, always sharp as a needle and possibly Rabelaisian, Harry Higgins was without rival. He did not like Gosse keep the ball of conversation in the air, he did not like Oscar Wilde hold the table entertained with spoutings and eloquence and amazing fireworks, but in that confidential whisper there came from his lips, as from the mouth of the good little child in the fairy tale, a pearl or a gem each time he opened them. It was quite inimitable: nobody else had the secret of those ludicrous and humorous thrusts. There was once, for instance, in connection with the opera syndicate of Covent Garden of which he was the business manager, a question as to the engagement of a very notable lady to sing there, and to him fell the task of discussing with her the terms for her appearance. Notable as she was as a singer, with a fine though not a superb voice, she was perhaps even more notable (in fact she had a European reputation) for her beauty, her temperamental nature, her charm, and her broad-minded views. When the question arose as to the terms of her appearance, she asked a really prodigious sum, a sum, so it seemed to him, out of all proportion to her quality as a singer. So with infinite tact and politeness, he whispered to her, "But we only want you to sing. . ." One night I met him on the steps of the Garrick Club, and he suggested we should dine together. A particularly odious book of reminiscences had just come out in which the author had published the current private affairs of his friends with a good deal of malice and mischief, and the victims were justly furious, but rather vociferously so: everybody had anathema to hurl at him, even if he had said nothing particularly objectionable about them. As we sat down at our table Harry Higgins said to me, "Have you read that brute's book ? I've looked at the index, which is the same thing, and found I was mentioned seventeen times. So I turned them all up and saw that on each of these occasions he had been to dine with me. Now what right has the man to tell the world that ? It's monstrous: I've been trying to conceal it all my life. . ."

Lady Randolph Churchill, whose friendship will always remain so dear and vivid a memory to me that sometimes still I find myself thinking that I must remember to tell her some witty trifle I have heard, had something of the same swift aptness. She once asked our most pungent critic and dramatist to spend a week-end at her house. He had lately been lifting up his voice against the practice of week-end parties, and, scenting advertisement, he scribbled a refusal on a postcard with the query, "Why this assault on my well-known principles about week-ends ?" Instantly she seized a telegram form and wrote on it, "I know nothing about your principles, but hope they are better than your manners." One night she was playing bridge with me, and after hectic hours of hard work she won exactly a shilling. She greedily seized it. "Is all that mine ?" she said. "Someone will want to marry me for my money."

Of the third of these witty men I will tell presently.

CHAPTER X

TWO SCANDALS

THERE were during the period of the nineties, two scandals accompanied by trials in the law courts, both of which produced an immense sensation and a din of public hooting. The first of these which was the more openly and vehemently discussed was the Tranby Croft affair in 1891. The second, to the sequel of which is attached a remarkable literary interest was the trial of Oscar Wilde four years later. To both of them I have a little material not generally known to contribute.

I

WITH regard to the first, the main facts, briefly stated, were as follows. The Prince of Wales (subsequently King Edward VII) went to stay at Mr Arthur Wilson's house, Tranby Croft, near Doncaster, for the St Leger meeting in September 1890. There was a large party in the house, most of whom, after dinner on the first evening of his visit, amused themselves with a game of baccarat. There were counters denoting various sums of money up to ten pounds, which, as usual, players purchased at the beginning of the game, and accounts were settled at the end of it. The counters used were the property of the Prince of Wales, and the game was conducted in the ordinary manner. It was entirely the concern of the people who played it, but owing to an unfortunate incident that occurred on this and the next evening, there developed out of it a most prodigious scandal.

On the first night they played at a make-shift table, and during the progress of the game Mr A. S. Wilson, a son of

the house, observed, so he thought, that his neighbour, Sir
William Gordon-Cumming, Lieutenant Colonel in the Scots
Guards, was cheating. He whispered what he had seen to
Mr Berkeley Levett, who was sitting on his other side, and
who was a subaltern in the same regiment. They then both
watched him, and again saw him cheating, withdrawing or
augmenting his stake, under cover of his hand, according
to the value of the cards he received. When the game was
over, Mr Wilson told his mother the same night what had
occurred, and next morning also told his brother-in-law,
Mr Lycett-Green, who told his wife. There were thus five
persons already who knew about it. As there would probably be a game of baccarat again on the second night, Mr
A. S. Wilson procured a table of more convenient shape, on
which it was hoped that cheating would be impossible.
Though at the subsequent trial all these five persons denied
that there had been any agreement between them to watch
Sir William, in order to see if he would cheat again, they all
did watch him, and though there may have been no agreement
to do so, such was their intention.

Now that was not a very pleasant thing to do, and assuredly none of them could have liked doing it. A party of
friends and of guests in the same house was to sit down to
a cheery little game of cards, and all the time, *au dessous les
cartes*, there would be going on this grim piece of criminal
investigation. Some men, no doubt, would have felt that
whatever course was taken, it must not be that, for detective
work among friends would have appeared to them a pro-
hibitively ugly business. Moreover, in making this plan,
they omitted to consider that supposing on this second occasion they saw nothing to confirm their suspicions, there
would always have been left in their minds the belief that
this man had cheated the night before. They could not possibly have rid themselves of that notion, and while additional
evidence would convict him, the absence of it would not (in
their minds) have really cleared him, for two of them were

perfectly certain that they had seen what the five now, though without a formal agreement to watch, were on the lookout for. On the other hand it was very difficult to know what else they could do. It would have been useless to have taxed Sir William with having cheated the night before, for he would have denied it, even as he subsequently did when they had obtained a far higher degree of certainty than they at present possessed. It would have been equally useless, as regards the object they had in view if their suspicions were confirmed, to arrange that there should be no more baccarat that night, for the suspect would then have been free to continue his practices, and that they were determined, if his guilt was established, to stop.

So on this second night they sat down again to this damnable friendly game of baccarat: the Prince of Wales, as on the night before, took the bank. All five of the observers saw that on more than one occasion Sir William put his stake close to the line which is drawn round the table and separates the counters that are staked from those the player has in hand. If he got a good card, he supplemented his stake, if a bad one, he withdrew it or a portion of it. Their suspicions ceased to be suspicions at all, for they were convinced of the truth of them.

Next day, after further confabulation, those who had watched told Lord Coventry and General Owen Williams, who was a close friend of Sir William Gordon-Cumming's, what they had seen, and it was decided first to tell Sir William and then the Prince of Wales, who up to this point knew nothing whatever about what was going on. This was done. The Prince then interviewed Sir William in the presence of Lord Coventry and General Owen Williams, and afterwards those who had seen the unfair play. They all regarded a man who cheated at cards as a pest and an intolerable danger to his friends, and they determined to stop his card-playing. With the Prince's concurrence he was sent for and given a choice of two alternatives, and a declaration was written out in

which he promised on his word of honour not to play cards
for money again. If he would sign that, the committee
promised him on their part that the matter would go no further, and that no one outside themselves should ever know
about what had occurred. If he refused to sign, no such
secrecy would be binding on them. Thereupon, though protesting his innocence, he signed the declaration, and it was
witnessed by ten persons, of whom the Prince was the first
signatory. The declaration was then put in the hands of
the Prince, who sent it up to his private secretary in London,
by whom it was placed, unopened, among his personal papers.

Some member or possibly members of this committee, who
had obtained Sir William's signature on the definite promise
that the matter would never be heard of again, must then
have given this pact away, for before the end of the year,
he received an anonymous communication from Paris, which
showed him that the secrecy had been violated. A more
odious treachery can hardly be conceived, and the victim of
it brought an action for defamatory scandal against Mrs
Arthur Wilson, Mr A. S. Wilson, Mr and Mrs Lycett-Green
and Mr Berkeley Levett, who were, it will be remembered, the
five persons who on the second night had observed his play,
and, in consequence of what they saw, had told Lord Coventry and General Owen Williams, who in turn told the Prince.
Sir William cited the Prince to appear as witness, and when
the trial took place in the following June 1891, he took his
place in the witness-box, and was examined by Sir Edward
Clarke, counsel for the prosecution. It was not a pretty
company to appear in: one of his friends had cheated at
cards (so ran the defence), several had partaken in a friendly
game to make sure that he was a swindler, and of the ten
signatories, one certainly had broken his word of honour
that he would never divulge what had passed. Human nature being what it is, a secret shared by ten persons is pre-
cariously placed, and in this case it did not preserve its balance for long, but the individual traitor is none the less

ugly for that reason. According to an ingenious theory, lately advanced by an eminent solicitor, there was no such traitor, but it was observed next day at the Doncaster races, that Sir William was looking anxious and depressed, and that the rest of the party, notably the Prince, had no converse with him. From this (it is argued) suspicion was aroused that something very unpleasant had taken place, and the true story gradually took shape. A fatal objection to this theory, apart from the remarkable clairvoyance required, is that the entire Tranby Croft party dispersed next day, in consequence of a death in the family, and that not a single one of them went to the races at all.

At the trial the evidence which most told against the plaintiff was the fact that he had signed this paper promising never to play cards again and that was certainly most awkward, for this did not look like the conduct of an innocent man. His explanation was, that though innocent, he wished at any personal sacrifice, to keep the Prince's name out of the affair. This view his counsel Sir Edward Clarke believed to be true. Sir Edward Clarke also argued that if the Prince of Wales and General Owen Williams had believed that Sir William had cheated, they were bound to have reported it to the military authorities, and this they had not done. He inferred therefore that the Prince had not believed him guilty. A juryman, however, asked the Prince whether he believed him guilty or not, and the Prince said he had no option, in the face of such support, to do otherwise. For the defence there was the impregnable argument that five persons, and those his friends, were sure they had seen him cheat on more than one occasion, and unless there was some monstrous and incredible conspiracy on their part, or unless they were all the victims of a collective hallucination, there was no explaining it away. The verdict was exactly that which might have been expected, and the case was given for the defence.

The scandal that followed was colossal. Not only in Eng-

land but abroad the Press teemed with it. A German comic
paper produced a cartoon showing the great door into Windsor Castle, surmounted by the Prince of Wales's feathers, and
the motto "Ich Deal." French papers had columns of far
more acid matter, and the Prince's private game of baccarat
became the business of the whole world: you would have
thought that baccarat was the sin that could never find remission. It was all very unpleasant but what really mattered was the universal disgust of the English Press. The
incident was made the occasion of the most virulent attacks on
the Prince: Stead, in his *Review of Reviews*, applied the test
of the "Prayer Gauge." He calculated with ruthless arithmetic how many times in the various churches of the United
Kingdom prayer had been offered during the last fifty years
on behalf of the Prince of Wales since the day of his birth,
and how many people had sincerely said "Amen," and drew
the conclusion that the baccarat scandal had been the only
answer vouchsafed from on high to these millions of petitions.
If the Prince himself had been detected cheating, he could not
have been more savagely sentenced. In particular all papers
of a serious or religious turn, especially Church papers and
Nonconformist papers, trumpeted their horror, like great
moral elephants piously running a-mok. They told their
readers that the Prince carried gambling counters with his
Royal device wherever he went, that he insisted that the party
should join him in high play: that his host at Tranby Croft
would never allow gambling in his house, but had been obliged
to yield to the Prince's wishes: in a word he was made scapegoat for all that had happened and all that was invented, and
was denounced as the ringleader in that odious vice of gambling which was undermining the morals of the country. He
was exposed to an unparalleled tempest of abuse, and, owing
to his position, he could not say a single word on his own behalf, though, as it turned out, he had plenty of very just observations to make. Doubtless in these attacks there was
much genuine indignation that the heir to the throne should

have been mixed up in so unsavoury an affair, but it was obvious that in these attacks there was a great deal of insincere gusto. It was not every day that a leader-writer in the *Camborne Chronicle* could lecture so exalted a personage, and he felt a smug Pharisaical satisfaction in joining loudly in the booing and thanking God that he had never played baccarat himself, nor even whist for money. But other more responsible journals felt the same, and *The Times* published a leader at the end of the trial, which, in conclusion, expressed regret that the Prince, as well as Sir William Gordon-Cumming, had not signed a declaration that he, too, would never play cards again. *The Times* in those days wielded an influence which no group of papers can rival today, and this expression of its opinion might be taken as the voice of all serious and respectable people who had read the account of the trial. Though the Prince had known nothing about the cheating and the watching, it was he who drew the barrage fire of all these moralists, and publicly, owing to his position he must be dumb. And then, privately, he spoke.

One morning when the hooting was at its shrillest, my father received a message from him that he would like to see him at Marlborough House. My father already knew that there was something brewing, for the day before he had received a telegram from the Prince's private secretary, when he was in the country, asking him to make an appointment, but this had been followed by a cancelling telegram. Now, on this second invitation he went straight off to Marlborough House, and the Prince, without any ado, stated his business. He had seen that the whole of the religious and Church Press was condemning him "as a gambler and worse," and he believed that my father had been instigating this campaign. He therefore wished to discuss the whole matter with him in person, and give my father an opportunity of affording him an explanation.

At that moment two highly exasperated people faced each other. How the Prince had got hold of the notion that my

father had been doing anything of the sort is quite unex-
plained, and he had no curiosity to inquire into that, but con-
tented himself with telling the Prince that there was no truth
of any sort or kind in the accusation.   He had on the contrary
been particularly careful neither to say nor write a single
word of comment on the whole business, and had forbidden
any discussion of the case in his own house.   What he
thought about it was a very different matter, and that was
his own concern, but he would be delighted to tell the Prince,
if he wished, what he did think, or if His Royal Highness
preferred, he would write him a letter about it.   He had
considered before now whether he had not better do so, but
decided that while there was so much virulent and unwarrantable language flying about, he had better wait.   But there
was not the faintest justification for what the Prince had
supposed.

They then discussed the whole affair.   The Prince was
eager to state to an old friend of his, who was also head of
the Church, what he had to say in answer to the fierce attacks made on him in the Church papers.   He strongly affirmed that he was no gambler, that gambling, as he understood the word, was hateful to him, but that playing cards
for small sums was no such thing.   But he would never try
to put down betting, there was a national instinct for betting, and every small boy in a grocer's shop put his sixpence
on the Derby.   "Very bad developments that leads to," said
my father.   "Certainly it does," said the Prince, "but there's
no harm in playing cards for money in itself.   And one of
the first men I ever played cards with was Bishop Wilber-
force."   At which, I imagine they both smiled.

The Prince then spoke of certain points in these attacks
which had been made on him, which he particularly resented.
The Press howled with horror at the idea of counters belonging to him being used at this game of baccarat.   "They
say that I carry about counters, as a Turk carries his prayer-
carpet," he said.   "But the reason why I carry counters is

to check high play. High sums are easily named, but these counters range from five shillings to five pounds,* and that can hurt nobody." Probably that did not much appeal to my father as an argument, for he hated all betting on principle. But admitting, as most would do, that there is no harm in people playing cards for such small sums which are well within their means, the contention is a very sensible one. Counters, if you play baccarat, are as necessary to the game as a pencil and a scoring-sheet at bridge.

The second point of which the Prince justly complained was the statement, freely made in the Press, that his host disapproved of cards and forbade them in his house, but that in spite of that the Prince had insisted on playing. He now affirmed that he had been absolutely unaware at the time that Mr Wilson had any objection to games of cards being played in his house, and that when in consequence of these statements, he had inquired into it, he had found it was not true. Mr Wilson had never forbidden cards in his house, and the only foundation for his supposed prohibition was that when his sons were quite young, just growing up, if he found them playing recklessly he said to them, "You don't understand the game, you don't play it properly, and I won't have you play it." On that alone was founded the accusation that he himself had insisted on playing baccarat against his host's wishes.

It was quite evident then that in these points, of which the papers had made much, the Prince had been the victim of malicious and repeated slanders in the Press, and he said that if such things were believed of him, the whole country would be against him. They then settled that my father should write him a letter, putting before him, better than could be done in a conversation, the views of sensible and serious men who were not disposed to join in shrieks, for the whole scandal had deeply shocked many whose opinions must

* My father evidently made a mistake here in his account of this interview, for, as it came out at the trial, the counters ranged up to ten pounds.

A Quiet Round Game

Key to the portraits as far as they can be ascertained: Mr. Arthur Wilson (looking through the curtains); at the left end of the table, Mr. Lycett Green (with the eyeglass); Mr. Jack Wilson. From left to right on this side of the table: Mrs. Lycett Green (or Miss Wilson); Sir William Gordon-Cumming, Lady Coventry. Gen. Owen Williams, Lord A. (?) Somerset (it is possible that these last two names should be reversed). At the farther side of the table, from left to right: Mr. Berkeley Levett, Lord Coventry, The Prince of Wales, Mrs. Arthur Wilson. At the right end of the table: Mr. Reuben Sassoon.

Reproduced by permission from the 1891 Christmas number of *Truth*, the London weekly newspaper.

be treated with respect. "Very well," said the Prince, "we will consider that settled. And we're old friends." And as such they parted.

My father therefore wrote the following letter:

Sir,

The utterances of various religious bodies have been so painful and ill judged that I am anxious to assure Your Royal Highness more explicitly than seemed possible in our conversation, how entirely erroneous are any assertions that I had in any way countenanced or encouraged such tone of criticism.

These utterances were well calculated to advertise the various speakers and their "connexion," but equally well calculated to defeat any serious object beyond low political aims. And my attachment to the person and honour of Your Royal Highness is so heartfelt and of such long standing that it would give me the acutest pain to think that you supposed I sympathized with their proceedings. The Church has, I am sure, felt throughout that if there were a word to be said about the Tranby Croft affair it must be said in a perfectly different spirit and manner.

I cannot say how grateful I was for the two points which Your Royal Highness impressed on me as the facts. They have been useful to me. But I should ill repay Your Royal Highness's kindness as regards my own loyalty, if I did not in a few words assure you how keen and anxious has been the feeling in the Church roused by the controversy, and how many and keen have been the representations made to the Bishops and leading men of every order. It is not the way of the Church to be vociferous, but whatever touches the throne and those near it, touches the Church and affects the peace of its best members.

Some twenty years ago it was made evident by discussions in Parliament and outside, that the evil of intemperance among working classes and women was growing intolerable.

*It is not too much to say that what intemperance was then,
gambling is now, and I was not surprised to hear Your Royal
Highness express yourself as abhorring the spirit of it.   It
is proving itself the hopeless ruin of young and old among
the poorer classes.   All alike who, without holding any absurd views as to minute acts, are in earnest on the subject
would be encouraged and their hands strengthened if you
would take any natural opportunity which might present
itself of saying what you said to me, while fully distinguish-
ing what is innocent from what is bad.   Your Royal Highness is foremost in all movements for the good of the working
classes and the poor, and never more so, I am sure, than in
the present year.   I do earnestly venture to say that the
least thing said or done (without forcing the occasion but
taking it as it came) which would show the people what your
real mind is in respect of these thoughtless but most dangerous habits would do a world of good and evoke a world of
good feeling.*

The Prince answered this with great friendliness, formally
stating the views he had expressed at the interview, but declining, perhaps wisely, to make any further utterance on
the subject of gambling.   His letter is given in full by gracious permission of H. M. King George V.

R. Yacht Osborne
Cowes, August 13, 1891

My dear Archbishop,
    *Your kind letter of the 10th has touched me very much as
I know the kind feelings which prompted you to write to me
on a subject which we have discussed together and which you
are aware has caused me deep pain and annoyance.*
    *A recent trial which no-one deplores more than I do and
which I was powerless to prevent, gave occasion for the Press
to make most bitter and unjust attacks upon me, knowing
that I was defenceless, and I am not sure that politics were*

*not mixed up in it. The whole matter has now died down,
and I think therefore it would be inopportune for me in any
public manner to allude again to the painful subject which
brought such a torrent of abuse upon me not only by the
Press, but by the Low Church and especially the Noncon-
formists.*

*They have a perfect right, as I am well aware, in a free
country like our own to express their opinions, but I do not
consider they have a just right to jump at conclusions regarding myself without knowing the facts.*

*I have a horror of gambling and should always do my ut-
most to discourage others who have an inclination for it, as
I consider that gambling, like intemperance, is one of the
greatest curses which a country can be inflicted with.*

*Horse racing may produce gambling or it may not, but
I have always looked upon it as a manly sport which is
popular with Englishmen of all classes, and there is no reason
why it should be looked upon as a gambling transaction.
Alas! Those who gamble will gamble at anything. I have
written quite openly to you, my dear Archbishop whom I
have had the advantage of knowing for so many years.*

*Again thanking you for your letter and hoping you will
enjoy your holiday,*

Yours sincerely,
ALBERT EDWARD

It is impossible in the light of the above interview and exchange of letters not to feel the utmost sympathy with the
Prince of Wales. Not only had the Press made savage
capital out of this incident, but it had libelled him, making
public statements about him which were definitely untrue, but
to which he could not reply. He had been execrated as a
gambler, who was determined to have his baccarat whatever
his host's feelings were, and whose luggage, according to
comic prints, chiefly consisted of boxes of gaming counters,
but his reiterated statement that he was not a gambler and

that he abhorred gambling carries complete conviction for its sense and sincerity. A game of cards for such stakes as he and his party had been playing, was not, according to his view, gambling at all. Gambling was playing for stakes which a man could not afford and had no business to risk, and this view must surely commend itself as sound to anyone who has played domestic bridge for a shilling a hundred. Gambling is not an absolute term, nor is it to be defined by one fixed set of figures. It is a question of proportion, and while a bet of a sovereign on the Derby is culpable gambling on the part of a man whose wages are thirty shillings a week, it would be a ludicrous misuse of language to call the same bet gambling if made by a man who had ten thousand a year. The use of alcohol furnishes an excellent parallel, for drinking only becomes a vice when it is indulged in to excess, and the question of excess is part of a personal equation, similar to that concerning stakes at cards and the income of the player, and no one but a faddist could object on principle to a man taking a glass of wine with his dinner. The rigid moralists of the Nonconformist Press had failed to appreciate this, and their homilies based on a misconception of the case, and decorated with ripe juicy falsehoods must have been intolerable to the Prince. He had been put in pillory for the whole of the ugly story, the cheating and the watching, which took place before he came into the affair at all, and a private game of baccarat in which he was perfectly at liberty to indulge in a friend's house resulted in these attacks from which he was powerless to defend himself. And all the time his views about gambling and about horse-racing would have commended themselves to at least ninety per cent of reasonable folk. But reasonable folk had no opportunity to hear what he had to say, and until the supply of gossipy inventions ran low, the Press continued to regale the public with these morsels. They felt that they had been given a real glimpse, more lurid than the most sumptuous imaginings of Ouida, into the private life of exalted personages, and the shock they professed to have experienced was certainly spiced by a high degree of enjoyment. It was not so pleasant for those more immediately concerned, and a letter which Queen Victoria wrote to my father, later in the same year, in reply to his felicitations on the engagement of Prince Albert Victor of Wales to Princess Victoria Mary of Teck, our present Queen, perhaps faintly reflects what she thought about it all.

Osborne
Dec. 21, 1891

My dear Archbishop,

I must thank you very much for your kind letter, and congratulations on the engagement of my dear grandson Albert Victor to Princess Victoria Mary of Teck, which promises to be a happy union. 'May' is a charming girl, with much sense and amiability and very unfrivolous, so that I have every hope the young people will set an example of a steady, quiet life, which, alas, is not the fashion in these days. The wedding is to be at St George's Chapel, on the 27th of February. I hope you will perform the ceremony.

In conclusion, let me ask you to accept the accompanying card and with best wishes for Christmas and New Year for yourself and family,

I am,

Ever yours affly,
*VICTORIA R & I.**

II

THE second of these two scandals which caused such a commotion in the nineties was the trial of Oscar Wilde on a criminal indictment. A very remarkable literary interest both directly and indirectly, attaches to it and to the savage punishment to which he was sentenced, for they were among

* By gracious permission of H. M. King George V.

the causes which combined to establish his reputation as a writer and a dramatist, and caused it to soar, especially in Germany and Italy, to a height which it is most improbable that it would ever have reached otherwise.

Up till that year, 1895, he had written (apart from the plays of which I shall speak presently) little that had attracted serious attention. His poems had enjoyed a great success when they were published, but they had long been forgotten, and of the rest "Dorian Gray" and the "Happy Prince" had been his only books, at the time of his tragic debacle, to pass into a second edition. He used to say, with a charming gaiety, that while the first editions of most classical authors were those most coveted by bibliophiles, it was the second edition of his books that were the true rarities, and even the British Museum had seldom been able to secure copies of most of them. In England there was a small but most enthusiastic band of artistic and literary folk, who saw in him the greatest genius of the age, but outside England he was absolutely unknown as a writer, whether in prose or poetry, while the English critics treated his publications with the scantiest contempt. "Dorian Gray" had been fiercely attacked, but otherwise they scarcely troubled to point out to an indifferent public the feeble and ineffective plagiarizations in his poems, and the tawdry glitter of his prose.

This was not very discerning of them, for there were far more noticeable qualities in his work than plagiarization and glitter: these were its defects and not its merits, for in spite of the glitter there was brilliance, and in spite of the plagiarizations a truly original note. Nobody else could possibly have written his "Decay of Lying" or his "Critic as Artist" which were the gems in "Intentions," but neither the taste of the literary public nor that of its directors perceived that these two dialogues, though possibly only trifles, were little masterpieces of airy wit and mockery, and had a very individual quality of their own. A live voice spoke in them. Then, about 1890, when Wilde was getting on for forty years old, he turned his hand to comedy for the stage and not for the study, and in the next four years wrote "Lady Windermere's Fan," "The Ideal Husband," "A Woman of no Importance," "Salomé," and "The Importance of Being Earnest." "Salomé" was written in French; Sarah Bernhardt had undertaken to produce it in London and it was actually in rehearsal when the censor of plays for the Lord Chamberlain's office, in a spasm of feverish conscientiousness, refused to license it. The reason for the refusal of the licence was that it presented on the stage Biblical characters, and that was sufficient. The four other plays were brought out in London. George Alexander had a notable success with "Lady Windermere's Fan"; the two following it, "The Ideal Husband" and "A Woman of no Importance" had a moderate success, but none of them were considered more remarkable than the majority of theatrical pieces which had a fair run. They were neatly constructed, they were light and witty, but they contributed nothing new to the history of dramatic art. Then in February 1895, a few months before his trial, "The Importance of Being Earnest" was produced, again by George Alexander, and that was far more notable than anything that had preceded it. The critics, for the most part, still thought scorn of his work (indeed their sneers had become fixed like Kundry's laugh) for they had made up their minds about him, and nothing that he wrote could alter their verdict, but the public signified its high approval, and stalls and gallery alike revelled in this very amusing piece. It scintillated with witty fireworks and characteristic fantasy, it was constructed with brilliant and farcical ingenuity, it was admirably played, and though the critics called it rubbish, the playgoers whispered "Sheridan!" Mr Bernard Shaw, it must be remembered, had not then come to the rescue of the English stage, and audiences had not yet been taught to think, but were satisfied with being amused. Then suddenly the scandal flared up, the author's libel action against Lord Queensberry melted into the criminal prosecution of himself, and what was to be done with the play ?

Mr George Alexander was in a difficult position, and very gallantly he attempted a solution which was in the true spirit of Victorian reticence and unconsciousness of anything disagreeable. Both for his own sake and that of the author he did not want to withdraw a popular play that was running strong, but it was unwise to flaunt outside his theatre the play-bills which advertised "The Importance of Being Earnest by Oscar Wilde," for people might not like to come to see the work of that wretch. So with a high ingenuity he caused the offensive name of the author to be pasted over with opaque strips of fair white paper, and so his patrons could come to see "The Importance of Being Earnest," without unpleasant associations being aroused; they could enjoy this amusing, anonymous piece, and refrain from wondering who the author was. This was truly Victorian, and quite after the pattern of the Duchess of Beaufort admiring the picture of her husband's mistress, and calling it a fancy portrait. But already such lofty reticence was a little out of date; besides, the public had learned from the baccarat scandal what entertainment can be derived from scapegoats and moral indignation. Or Mr Alexander had not hit upon the precise brand of Victorianism that was required to meet the situation, and his sense of the importance of being tactful did not meet with the success it deserved. The play could not be saved, and he had to take it off.

The crash then with regard to Oscar Wilde as author, dramatist, and citizen was complete. It was years before any play of his was staged again; his books were withdrawn from library lists; the sale of them, such as it was, ceased altogether or was confined to those who collect gruesome relics, and critics and public alike thought that they had heard the last of the ways and works of a man whose name must not even be mentioned in polite circles. Yet had not this landslide of ruin buried him, it is more than possible that by now

he would have been forgotten.   For his plays, which were
the most successful of his productions, had never been produced abroad up till then, and they have since proved very
disappointing in English revivals.   They have aged rapidly
and become out of date, their wit to us seems tight-roped and
acrobatic, and now no-one in England will listen to them.
His ruin, however, which everyone thought had consigned
him to an execrated oblivion, was one of the chief factors out
of which should develop a fame which he had never previously
known.

THE whole tragic business sprang from that act of inconceivable folly, when (his life having been what it was) he
brought a libel action against Lord Queensberry for leaving
at his club a calling-card on which he had written the words
which constituted the libel.   Then in the witness-box, when
being cross-examined by Sir Edward Carson, he made the
further deplorable error of being flippant, and though he was
both dexterous and witty, this was a ghastly mistake.   He
said that he put the society of charming young men as even
more pleasurable than the privilege of being cross-examined
by an elderly Queen's Counsel: when asked whether iced
champagne was a favourite drink of his he acknowledged
that it was, though strictly against the doctor's orders, and
when Carson rapped out, "Never mind the doctor, Mr
Wilde," he said, "I don't mind the doctor."   It was all very
amusing and there were roars of laughter, but the entertainment was madly out of place and most prejudicial to him,
for these answers were given to questions which clearly had
a very ugly significance, and a more unsuitable occasion for
jests could not be imagined.   But he was still intoxicated,
even in that sobering experience, by his megalomania: he saw
himself as a man of fashion and of genius strolling amateur-
ishly into the witness-box, and in this brilliant extempore
manner making the ministers of the law the disconcerted butts
of his wit.   It was a bore to have to come here at all, but it

would soon be over, and though he might miss an amusing
luncheon party or two, how he would keep the dinner table in
convulsions of laughter at the expense of Mr Edward
Carson !

For three days the trial lasted, and then the prosecution
was withdrawn and the jury gave the verdict in favour of
Lord Queensberry as having proved justification for the
libel.   Other trials followed, for such was the nature of the
evidence of which he had made a jest that the Home Office
ordered a prosecution against him for indecent offences.   At
this second trial the jury disagreed, and the Home Office
under the direction of Mr H. H. Asquith instituted a third.
He had already lost friends, position, and reputation, his
career, as far as could be foreseen, both as author and play-
wright was finished, but the law had to take its course.   At
that third trial he was convicted, and the judge passed on him
the most severe sentence that the law permitted.   That
probably reflected the bulk of public opinion in England, and
a plebiscite would have approved any amount of trials in
order to obtain a conviction and the severest sentence possible.   The wave of retribution towered and curled over and
smashed him; he had been made a scapegoat, and now the
wretched animal was dragged ceremoniously off into the salt
desert of tribulation.   He was ruined, disgraced and bank-
rupt, and the moral sense of the hooting public sang Ho-
sanna.   But the actual offence for which he was condemned
was not in most European countries a crime at all, since
public indecency was not alleged, and in consequence of the repeated trials followed by this relentless treatment, there
began to awake instantly in Germany and Italy an interest
in him and his work.   Most of this work had been accessible
to the world for several years, and some of it for twenty, and
hitherto it had not aroused abroad the slightest sympathy
or even curiosity.

The second factor which contributed to his fame was the
publication, during Oscar Wilde's lifetime but after his

release, of the "Ballad of Reading Gaol," which he had written when in prison. It sprang directly from his catastrophe, for if we may judge from his previous poems, it seems unlikely that he had got it in him to write it before. No-one could fail to be impressed with that wailing from the wilderness, for technically it is a masterpiece, ranking high among the finest ballads in the English language, and through it runs the venerable inspiration of bitter suffering.

The third factor, arising from the newly awakened interest in him abroad, was the performance in Germany in the year 1901, of his one-act play "Salomé." It had been banned by the Censor in England on the eve of its appearance on the stage, its publication in book form had been hailed by the critics with a more than usual measure of abusive contempt, and though his French (in which language it was composed) had satisfied Sarah Bernhardt, it was far from pleasing to those who knew so much more about the language than she. One critic translated some of the lines for the benefit of English readers, so that they might judge for themselves, but his rendering of Salomé's cry, "C'est de la bouche que je suis amoureuse, Iokanann," by "It's your mouth I like, John," was really not quite fair to the French. But now "Salomé" was selling largely in Germany, and its production on the stage was received with the greatest enthusiasm. Richard Strauss set a German translation of the libretto as an opera, and we must suppose that the blood-lust and savagery of the music was held to hallow it, for the Censor subsequently relented, and allowed it to be seen at Covent Garden. Following its production in Germany, it was translated into and acted in most European languages, its bibliography is almost as long as the text, and today it and Oscar Wilde's other plays are given in Germany more frequently than the works of any other foreign dramatist.

The fourth and the most potent factor of all in establishing the fame of a modern author who was rapidly becoming classical, first abroad, and now also in England was the publi-

cation in 1904 after the author's death, of the book to which
the editor gave the title of "De Profundis." It is part of a
far more substantial manuscript which Oscar Wilde had
written while he was still in prison, and which was as direct a
result of his tribulation as was the "Ballad of Reading
Gaol." It records in admirable and at times masterly prose,
rather intentionally purple in places but always of great
dignity, the effect that his bitter punishment had had on him;
how he accepted it without complaint, fear or reluctance;
how he realized that he must grow to be worthy of his suffering instead of considering it an indignity; how he must, at
the sacrifice of all else, keep love alive in his heart; how, owing
to this spiritual awakening, a new hope had been born out of
his anguish; how Christ is to be found in all art and in all
romance. Though some readers were astonished that this
enlightenment had brought him no sense of regret for the
misery he had brought on others as well as himself, and that
he regarded his past life merely as the due development of
his own nature, the book made an enormous sensation, passing through edition after edition, for the scapegoat, by the
miracle of love and the study of the Gospels, had transmuted
the salt of the desert into an exceeding sweetness, and rested
content beside the waters of comfort. It had an immense
sale in England, and the translations of it in Europe, and,
while arousing the most poignant sympathy with the author,
established him as a classic.

It was Mr Robert Ross, Oscar Wilde's executor, who
brought out this book, and before proceeding to the real
history of it, it must at once be stated that there was never a
stricken and disgraced man more lovingly and unselfishly
ministered to than was Wilde by this devoted friend. But
the book itself, "De Profundis" in the form in which it was
given to the world by Mr Ross, is the most gigantic literary
fraud. In his preface, he refers to "instructions" he had received about the publication of it from Oscar Wilde (though
he does not give the smallest hint as to what those instructions

were) in which, addressing Mr Ross, Wilde alludes to "De Profundis" as "my letter," and goes on to say how grateful he is to the governor of the prison "for his permission to write fully to you, and at as great length as I desire." The plain inferences from this are that this letter was addressed to Mr Ross, and that it was published (more or less) in its entirety. But both these inferences are incorrect. "De Profundis" was indeed a letter in the sense that it began in the ordinary form of a letter, "My dear — ": but it was not addressed to Mr Ross at all, but, by name, to Lord Alfred Douglas, and little more than half of it (if as much) was published at all. But to publish the whole of it was obviously impossible, for the omitted pages contained tirades of the bitterest vindictiveness against Lord Alfred, bringing against him a farrago of preposterous accusations. Not only would a libel action against the publisher and the editor have been the well-deserved and immediate result, but the text, if complete, would have entirely defaced the sublime impression produced by the rest, and, instead, have presented one far less edifying though of a unique and tragic interest. Since such publication was impossible, Mr Ross made these elegant extracts (for they are indeed no more than that) though he knew that they must convey an absolutely different picture from that which the author actually painted. Oscar Wilde, in these extracts, revealed himself to Mr Ross as humbled and softened and sweetened by suffering, as having love in his heart and love only, whereas the whole letter would have shown him as still harbouring resentments the most petty and the most unjust against the man to whom it was really addressed. I do not say that those published sentiments (some of them of an almost infantile simplicity) were not sincere, but the bitter and vindictive moods with which the entire letter abounded were certainly just as genuine.

Finally, after making his extracts, Mr Ross, in order to render himself secure against any immediate disclosure of the whole, presented the complete manuscript to the British

Museum, with the proviso that it should be sealed and sequestered there until the year (I think) 1960, by which time,
presumably, both he and Lord Alfred Douglas, against whom
it brought accusations which no doubt could have been proved
libellous, or at any rate mistaken, were dead.   Possibly he
received instructions in this sense from Oscar Wilde, but in
that case it is impossible to understand why he did not say
so in his preface, and thus justify his action.

Again if Oscar Wilde had intended that this bitter and
vindictive letter of his should be presented to the world as
this patchwork of sweetness and spiritual illumination, there
cannot possibly have been any reason why he should not
(with Mr Ross's help) have brought it out himself, when he
published the "Ballad of Reading Gaol," unless he desired a
posthumous sanctification of himself.   But this is frankly
impossible: *poseur* in many ways he was, but that sort of
pose was not one that could have appealed to him in any
mood.   He could feel the attraction of many attitudes, but
that of a saint in a stained-glass window which he would never
see, would always have seemed grotesque to him.   Indeed, on
Mr Ross's lines an editor would be almost justified in omitting the negatives in certain sentences of his text, and thus
reversing their meaning, if he thought that the moral tone of
the whole would be thereby improved.   No doubt he
thought it his duty as literary executor to secure the best
possible sale for a most remarkable manuscript which, without substantial omissions, could not be published at all; he
may also have said to himself, that these fulminations of
abuse did not represent Wilde in his true light and were only
moods of passing passion.   But there comes a point when
"*de mortuis nil nisi bonum*" merges into "*de mortuis nil nisi
bunkum*," and the version of "De Profundis" as given to the
world does not represent what Wilde entrusted to him.
Though he wrote every word of what Mr Ross published, he
wrote in that same document so much besides and in so different a spirit, that the omissions cannot but be held to falsify

the whole of it. In the absence of further evidence, it is, in fact, scarcely credible that the "instructions" to which Mr Ross vaguely alludes in this misleading preface to the book, enjoined on him to do what he did.

It is difficult also to understand the mental processes of the authorities of the British Museum, who accepted this bequest under the condition of sealing it up for more than fifty years. Presumably they were acquainted with its contents, for we cannot suppose that they accepted a sealed gift without acquainting themselves with it, and they therefore knew that it abounded in violent and bitter accusations against a man who, when the period of its privacy was over, would be dead and therefore unable to reply to them. Doubtless they saw that the manuscript was a masterpiece of writing and both was then, and would be in the future of great literary interest, but would they, on the same principle, accept a manuscript, let us say, of Mr Bernard Shaw's which contained a brilliantly written account of the terrible wrongs he had suffered at the hands of Mr Rudyard Kipling, with the stipulation that it should remain in sanctuary there until some future date when Mr Kipling would no longer be able to defend himself ? Whatever Oscar Wilde's unknown instructions to Mr Ross were, even if he told him to deal with this manuscript exactly as he did, it is hard to comprehend how it was given harbourage on such terms. By law, of course, it is impossible to libel the dead, but it may by such measures be easy to give unwarrantable pain to descendants of the dead who are living.

It may be asked how I can vouch for the vindictiveness of the complete manuscript and for its incongruity as a whole with the extracts which have been given to the world. The answer is very simple, for there are in existence, as is now known, copies of the holograph which reposes in the British Museum, and I have studied one of these with the greatest care. It is a marvellous and a terrible piece of writing; stony-hearted would he be who could read unmoved the ac-

count of that dolorous way, but it is not the work of one who
has been made regenerate by suffering, nor can anybody who
has read the whole of it think that the published portion is a
legitimate abbreviation of it.   It is the exceeding bitter cry,
de profundis indeed, of a very gifted, a very sensitive and a
very self-conscious man, who has bartered his birthright and
who, tortured by loneliness and privation, *imagines* love and
beauty (as set forth in Mr Ross's extracts) springing from
such fiery experience as had been his.   He could see himself
in imagination wandering on the hills of .Galilee, beholding
the lilies how they grow, and learning humility and charity
from the words of Christ, and recognizing in Him the type
of the supreme artist.   No doubt those aspirations were quite
sincere, but then, with pen not yet dry, he indited blistering
reproaches against the friend he had loved, taxing him with
perfidy and ingratitude, and denouncing him as the cause
of his own ruin.   Then the venomous stuff (omitted by Mr
Ross) was spent, but it had been as sincere as the other, and
now he took up his pen again, and forecasted how, on his release, he would be a very lonely man and friendless, and how
he would hide himself from the eyes of the scornful in secret
valleys where he would weep undisturbed.   Nature would
hang the night with stars for him and cleanse him in great
waters, he would sleep in the cool grass in summer and in
winter under the lee of a haystack.   But even as he wrote
that he must have known that he had no intention of sleeping
under haystacks and that he was indulging in forecasts which
he was quite incapable of fulfilling, for tribulation had not
changed his tastes.   He was drawing an imaginary portrait
of himself and though, soothed and self-intoxicated by the
beauty of the phrases and paragraphs that flowed from his
pen, barred till now when the privilege of writing was restored to him, he only pictured such impulses.   It was the
passion for writing a fairy tale and not for living it which
possessed him.

His manuscript was finished before he left prison, but he

never sent it to the friend to whom it was addressed, and who still remained ignorant of its existence: eventually it passed into Mr Ross's possession. Phantasmal became to him at once, now that he was free, the self-induced dream which had peopled his cell with bright presences, and touched their drab walls with the colours of an opal, and he knew that he was unchanged. No miracle of grace had been wrought in him, skilley and solitude had not cured him of a psychological abnormality for the indulgence of which he had suffered as a criminal, but which, owing to that same abnormality he could not himself think of as morally wrong; nor had he in "De Profundis" even hinted that his nature had undergone any sort of conversion to the ordinary tastes and passions of mankind. Prison life and all he had suffered there had been a punishment, savage in the extreme, for offences against the law, and neither those who framed that law, nor those who inflicted that punishment can possibly have supposed that it would do anything more for him than torture him. Once free, he sought the arc lights of Paris cafés in preference to the shimmer of stars, and cleansed himself not in Nature's great waters, but in innumerable tumblers of absinthe. For a while his brain and his perceptions were clear enough to record in the immortal verses of the "Ballad of Reading Gaol," the eating of the iron into his poor tortured soul, and we owe to his anguish a wonderful poem. Prison and its forced abstinences had renewed him physically for the time, but morally he was not changed, and soon, with the removal of discipline, the slime of intemperance and perverted passions gathered upon him again, till the wheels of his soul were choked with it. No decent man can feel anything but sheer pity and sympathy for one so gifted and so brittle and withal so lovable.

From his youth it had been a passion with him to be conspicuous and stand in the limelight, and for the sake of that he had always laughed at ridicule and held contempt in scorn. He had passed through his undergraduate years at Oxford with credit and distinction, taking a first in his schools and winning the Newdigate prize poem, and he had there come under the influence of Ruskin. The Slade professor had told some of the young men that they wasted their time and energies in playing games: let them exercise the vigour of their bodies to better purpose, and make a road instead of making runs, and he would talk to them as they cut sods and plied pickaxe and wheel-barrow. A well-made road, so ran his message, was a thing absolutely and divinely beautiful; it was a highway in the wilderness and a path in the desert. Though Oscar Wilde had never wasted a moment playing games, he went out with the road-makers, and listened to Ruskin. But the road did not get very far, for the flanelled fools went back to wickets and the muddied oafs to their goals, and it came to an end in the middle of a field.

Then, coming up to London, Oscar Wilde worked at his poems and at journalism, and presently espied in the æsthetic movement which had grown out of the pre-Raphaelite school, with Ruskin as its prophet, a far more promising chance of limelight than road-making. He consecrated himself high priest of the cult, and anointed himself its king, and dressing himself, in the service of beauty, in a velvet coat with cut-steel buttons, knee breeches and white stockings, and brandishing a sunflower in his hand, he speedily attained notoriety. These antics drew on him the favours of the comic press, but to make any mark, however ludicrous, was infinitely better than making none. He extended his operations by a lecture tour in America, and spoke to amazed but limited audiences about the beauty of life and of William Morris's furniture. But even outside his own country this prophet was not received with honour, while in it the opera "Patience" from which so much might have been expected, as an advertisement, called attention to the wit of Mr W. S. Gilbert rather than to the object of his satire. Similarly his journalistic duels with Whistler only made the public perceive what a droll person Mr Whistler was. Wilde went on writing, though making, as we have seen no great mark for himself, until the success of his plays brought the limelight full on him.

He was widely known already as a very brilliant talker, but this was something more substantial, for there was fame, and there was money, and it was as the man of genius and fashion, careless and gay, witty and elaborate, that he loved to appear in those halcyon days of the early nineties. He envied that particular *insouciance* which he thought to be the habit of those who have been brought up in certain traditions, and he aped the manner of it, without having the instincts that render it natural. There was no more of the flamboyant charlatanism of sunflower and velveteen breeches, a garb of ultra-conventional propriety best fitted the man of the world who happened also to be a consummate artist. He played his part without the slightest touch of pomposity (for the *clou* to it was this care-free gaiety) but with a childlike zest and gusto. Every morning his hansom was waiting for him to be at his disposal all day, and in he stepped with his shining hat and his cane and his great tie-pin and his frock-coat, and his earliest errand was to a fashionable florist's, where there was ready an immense buttonhole for himself, and another, slightly smaller, as was meet, for the decoration of his driver. He often stayed at the Savoy Hotel, for Tite Street where his wife and children lived was a long way off and he gaily explained that he could not go home that night because he had forgotten the number of his own house, though he knew which Whistler's was. Besides, to stay at the Savoy was part of the make-up of the character which he played with such huge enjoyment: it gave him a naïve and costly delight to write to a friend and tell him that he had got a new sitting-room and that his bill for the week was prodigious. It was part of the fun to throw money about, and to point out how beautifully, as if to the heedless manner born, he was doing so. He lunched at some suitably distinguished table, entrancing his hostess's guests by his wit, or perhaps he lunched at the Café Royal, and sent for the *chef* afterwards to compliment him on his curry. The festival would be prolonged with liqueurs and innumerable cigarettes and marvellous talk, till the winter's day was on the wane. Then he would dine at Kettner's, drinking oceans of the most admired brand of champagne that could be procured, looked in perhaps for an act of one of his own plays, prominent in a box to be seen by all men, and then it was time for supper. He took his own Dorian Gray as his model, and saw in himself the exemplar of the truly delectable life, denying himself no pleasure, full of wit and laughter, rejoicing in heedless extravagance, even adopting the ancient kings of Ireland as his ancestors to give birthright to this regal sumptuousness, and by some strange lack in just perception believing that he was realizing for a drab world the ancient Greek ideal of the joy and beauty of life. Nothing could have been less like what he was doing, for the Greek genius for exquisite living was founded on physical fitness and moderation in all things, while he based it on the unbridled gratification of animal appetites. He took Plato's "Symposium" as the text for his life, but expurgated it by omitting all that Socrates stood for, which was continence and the sense of the sacredness of beauty. Effortlessly, cursorily (such was his pose at the time) and with the ease of casual conversation he scribbled the plays that filled his pockets with gold. A few weeks of airy work saw each complete, and he shook them from him like the drops of water the wild duck shakes from his feathers as he rises for his flight.

These triumphant and ludicrous progresses in a hansom with buttonholes, this life with its gorgings and drinkings, its very various companionships, its luncheon parties and its laughter, its largesses of jewelled sleeve links and gold cigarette cases, its Dorian-Gray pageantry in which he was the principal figure, sound in the telling of them more like the antics of one dressed up for some preposterous charade than the normal behaviour of a man of fashion leading the delectable life, and they were conducted, it must be remembered, on the smoking sides of a volcano which might burst into eruption at any moment. He was doubtless the victim of a monstrous megalomania; he thought himself a man apart, exempt from the laws that govern others, and set above the thunder. He says as much, indeed, in "De Profundis," speaking of himself as one, "who stood in symbolic relation to the arts and culture of his day, and acknowledged and felt so to be": he compares himself to Byron, though Byron, he notes, was symbolic of things less vital and permanent. He tells us, for his own greater splendour, that his father and mother "had bequeathed me a name they had made noble and honoured not merely in literature, art, archæology and science, but in the public history of my own country, in its evolution as a nation." But in truth these are all figments of his egotism, for Sir William Wilde was a surgeon of possibly doubtful reputation and his wife a highly theatrical and second-rate poetess, and they neither of them had anything more to do with the national evolution of Ireland than Oscar Wilde himself. He believed himself to be the Lord of Life and the Lord of Language, and as such he might order his goings as he pleased, and the world would only gape at and applaud his radiant hedonism. Mayfair was his washpot and Piccadilly was glad of him. The desire to appear magnificent is no doubt a quality common to both sexes, but these gewgaws, these glittering trappings and millineries of which he, like Dorian Gray, was so much enamoured, point perhaps to a feminine trait in him, which is not without significance.

Yet it seemed almost right that any vain excess or extravagance should be condoned in so lavish a maker of mirth, who talked as he could talk. It was no wonder that his brilliance should dazzle and intoxicate himself as well as his listeners. It soared and sparkled, it was ἀνήριθμον γέλασμα, it passed into shadow and grew serious, and then its gravity cleared again as some bomb of absurdity exploded in the middle of it; and so ingenious was he that he could, when challenged, defend

the most outrageous of his paradoxes. Like Vivian in his
"Decay of Lying" he was prepared to prove anything.
He loved a string of jewelled phrases in his spoken word as
well as in his writing, and if possibly they sometimes sounded
like a recollection of Walter Pater, as perhaps they were,
who cared so long as the Pied Piper continued to flute ?
How like was his talk to the play of a sunlit fountain ! It
rose in the air constantly changing its shape, but always
with the hues of the rainbow on it, and almost before you
could realize the outline of this jet or of that, it had vanished
and another sparkled where it had been, so that you could
hardly remember even the moment afterwards, what exactly
it was that had enchanted you. Like all talk, it is completely
unreproducible, for gesture and voice had no small part in it,
and, essentially so, his own glee in what he said. Mr Laurence
Housman, in his admirable dramatic sketch, called "Echo
de Paris," may perhaps recall to those who heard Oscar Wilde
talk, something of the manner of it, but even then it lacks the
colour and the personal element which gave it individuality.

Or he told stories, but of these again the narrator was a
part. The first time I ever saw him he recounted to me some
miracle play which he had lately seen in the south of France
acted by peasants and if, as I feel sure was the case, he im-
provised the whole, what did that signify ? The charm of
it lay not in what he might or might not have seen in a booth
near Napoule but in the peerless narration of what he had
probably invented. Talk in his mouth was not as with
Whistler, a rapier making shrewd and telling thrusts and
always gleaming with menace: for the heedless butterfly had
as sharp a sting as any wasp, and indeed he was less like a
butterfly than an aeroplane dropping bombs, little bright
delicate bombs, full of mustard gas. Oscar Wilde, on the
other hand, was always genial, he was lambent but not burning, he neither barked nor bit, his gaiety was not barbed for
wounding, and his laughter (except when he spoke of
America) was always kindly. Behind the brilliance of his

talk, behind and infinitely more charming than his poses, in
those days before his bitter ruin came on him, was an ex-
traordinarily amiable and sunny spirit which wished well to
everyone, and the sense of that gave him a charm that many
of those who distrusted him and found him sinister were unable long to resist.   Months before the crash came, there had
been unpleasant mutterings and whispers about him; he was
bloated and flabby in person, his dandifications were rather
terrible, but then the charm of his talk began to work, and in
how short a time even those on whom these other things made
a disagreeable impression were disarmed by the wit of it, and
the geniality from which it flowed.

That same gaiety of good humour marks his critical work,
especially when, as in "The Decay of Lying" it is cast in a
conversational form.   He pokes fun at the most admired
literary reputations of the day, but with so light and laughing a touch that none could be hurt, and his ridicule had no
sting in it, like that of Whistler or of George Moore, who in
his "Confessions of a Young Man" goes round his book-
shelves with a little bottle of corrosive acid, which he drops
first on this volume, then on that, and sets them all smoking.
. . . Oddly enough, though he had so keen and just a sense
of the music in spoken or written words, he had absolutely
no sense of music itself, being practically unable to distinguish one tune from another.   But, as the apostle of beauty
in all its forms, he was bound to profess an appreciation of
music, and his total ignorance of it did not prevent him from
speaking of the "passionate, curiously-coloured fantasies of
Dvořák": the phrase pleased him, for Dvořák seemed a likely
person to write curiously-coloured music and he embodied it
in one of his dialogues.   Again he wrote of those to whom life
wears a changed aspect because they have listened to one of
Chopin's nocturnes, or, having heard someone speak of the
deferred resolutions of Chopin, he would refer, not very
felicitously to the "deferred resolutions of Beethoven," which
does not make very good sense.   But music always presents

the most insidious traps for those who regard the appreciation of it as a social equipment. Once at a concert I sat next to a woman who had a tremendous reputation as a music-lover: it was meat and drink to her. An item on the programme was Beethoven's "Appassionata" to which she listened with clasped hands and steeped far-away eyes. She had heard no doubt that a sonata consists of not less than three movements, but no one had told her that in the "Appassionata" the second and the third movements are played without pause between them. So when the third movement had been finished, and all was over, she thought (so naturally) that there had been only two movements and recalling herself from her rapt intensity she whispered to me, "And now for that heavenly third movement."

But indeed I am not sure whether Oscar Wilde's most individual conversational gift was not that well-spring of nonsense, pure and undefiled, which perennially flowed from him. He announced with great gravity that he was very busy just now on a small volume of ethical essays, moral tracts they might be called, which was designed to fulfil the needs of thoughtful people of small means, who wished to give their friends little tokens of good-will at Christmas time. The Bishop of London had kindly consented to write a preface in which he expressed the hope that these little trifles would carry their message of sadness into many otherwise hilarious homes. The book would be published at the price of one guinea, and would be No. 1 of the "People's cheap guinea series of Great Thoughts." The first of these ethical essays (just completed: that was why he was late for lunch) had for its subject "The Value of Presence of Mind," and it took the form of a parable. . . There was a play being performed at a West London theatre which was proving exceedingly popular: boxes, stalls, dress circle, gallery and pit were always crammed, and the queues for the cheaper places extended to Hammersmith. In fact, he added, the play was at Hammersmith. One night during that tremendous scene in

OSCAR WILDE AT WORK

Caricature by Aubrey Beardsley, reproduced from Stuart Mason's
"Bibliography of Oscar Wilde"

which the flower girl of Piccadilly Circus rejected with scorn
the odious proposals of a debauched Marquis, a huge volume
of smoke, intermixed with flames, poured out of the wings.
The fire-curtain was instantly let down, and the audience rose
in panic, and rushed to the exits of the theatre. They
shoved and pushed, skirts were trodden on, and dress-shirts
irretrievably injured: they were all mad to get out, and there
was serious danger that in this wild stampede some of the
weaker might be trampled on. Then in front of the fire-
curtain there appeared the noble figure of the young man
who was the true lover of the flower girl. His voice rang
out (as they had heard it before that night) and commanded
the attention of these panic-stricken folk. He assured them
that the fire had already been got under, and there was no
danger any more from that. The only danger now to them
was that with which their own unfounded panic was threaten-
ing them. Let them all go back to their seats, and recover
their calm. So ringing was his voice, and so commanding his
gestures that they ceased to crush round the doors, and returned to their places, leaving the exits free. The brilliant
young actor then leapt lightly down over the footlights and
ran out of the theatre. Not a single other person left the place
alive, for the flames poured in from every side, and they were
all burned to death.

Such nonsense was rich in decoration of phrase: sometimes,
as above, it was highly dramatic, for who could guess the
dénouement of this moral tale till it was divulged, or fail to
be entranced with it when it came? Sometimes it was sheer
nonsense, unharnessable to any idea. He was arranging a
symposium and hoped I would come to it. "Everything nowadays is settled by symposiums," he said, "and this one is to
deal finally with the subject of bi-metallism: of bi-metallism
between men and women. . ." Again, he had just been introduced to the lady he was to take down to dinner and his
hostess had impressed on him the solemnity of the occasion,
and had told him that flippancy of any sort would be sadly

out of place. For his partner was a serious woman and expected everybody else to be serious too. She was also highly
intellectual, and had lately published a long novel, which at
that time was supposed to have delivered a staggering blow
to Christianity. As they descended the stairs to dinner arm
in arm on this wintry night, she said to him:

"What terrible weather we are having," which was surely
a very judicious opening for serious talk. To this he replied
with great earnestness,

"Yes, but if it wasn't for the snow, how could we believe in
the immortality of the soul ?"

This sounded most promising, at the same time she was a
little puzzled.

"What an interesting question, Mr. Wilde," she said.
"But tell me exactly what you mean."

"I haven't the slightest idea," said he. . .

Or he would find himself at some week-end house party
of athletic tendencies, and agreeable occupations for Sunday
afternoon were being discussed at lunch. Everybody
wanted to be out of doors, and to play some game. There
was golf, there was tennis, there were boats on the river for
those who could row, and water in the river for those who
could swim. When asked to say what he would like to do,
he sighed:

"I am afraid I play no outdoor game at all, except
dominoes," he said. "I have sometimes played dominoes
outside French cafés."

Once at the end of one of his admirable stories, which he
said he had made up that morning, some well-informed
creature asked him if it was really his own: had it not appeared a year or two ago in the *Mercure de France ?*

"Very likely indeed," he said, "but I believe it came
originally from the Dutch. I made another, too. Once
upon a time . . ."

One did not know whether to revel most in the apt absurdity of the reply, or the scholastic mentality of the

questioner. The latter resembled that of the seriously
minded small boy who after earnestly watching Mr George
Robey preparing to play golf on the stage, and getting held
up by a piece of adhesive paper which stuck to the face of
his driver and his ball and the back of his hand, turned to his
mother and said, "Mummie, is Mr Robey a *good* man ?"
That had precisely as much to do with the entertainment as
had the question whether one of Oscar Wilde's stories came
out of the *Mercure de France.*

His witty gaiety never left him even in the darkest days,
for when the late Lord Haldane, who held very strong views
about the brutality of his punishment, went to see him in
prison and recommended him, now that he had so much
leisure, to embark on some considerable work, he plucked up
at once, and said he was preparing a small volume of table-
epigrams.

Such, apart from that side of his life for which he so bitterly paid, was the manner of his days in the early nineties.
Later, after the crash, he asserted that nothing of these
pomps and social successes had been of any worth to him
compared with his art, but then he also said that he had only
given his talents to his art, and had devoted his genius to life
and to talk. The two statements are irreconcilable, and it
is probable that the latter was nearer the truth. He did not
live the life of one to whom the call of art is supreme, for he
must have known that such a manner of existence as his was
suicidal to an artist. He made phrases to justify it: he said
that the artist should realize every mood, and gratify himself
in every desire in order to render himself complete, but he
knew that he was only making the shallowest excuses for his
own uncontrollable appetites. Then straight from his tread-
ing of "the primrose path to the sound of flutes" he passed
into the grim isolation of his cell. That phrase which is his
own, and is applied by him to the years we have been speaking
of, conveys the image which he formed of himself as the
central figure or at least the hierophant of the god in some

Bacchic pageant.　But unless ruin had thus come upon him, it may justly be doubted whether the artistic and literary world, especially of Germany and Italy, would ever have begun to take that interest in his work which has led to his now being considered a classic.　It was that which woke their interest in him, and it was that which made out of an exceedingly witty trifler the poet who wrote the "Ballad of Reading Gaol."　Perhaps it was the harrowing of his soul which created the power, or perhaps it only turned it up, as the plough of woe cut its way through the grosser soil of his nature.　It may have been merely dormant hitherto, while he devoted his wits and delightful gifts to the service of self-indulgence and trivial success, but in these years of anguish and solitude he found himself, only, alas, to lose himself again when he was free.　When the crash came, there was never a man so bitterly mocked and execrated as he, but out of the number of his real friends, who knew what lay below his follies and his vices, there was none who failed to stand by him.　There is much to be said for judging a man by his friends.

CHAPTER XI

ORTHODOX English artists who had won for themselves a recognized position as Associates of the Royal Academy or as Academicians enjoyed during the sixties and seventies and eighties a period of unique commercial prosperity : never before or since have they found it so easy to sell at high prices, the works which were hung "on the line" at the annual exhibition at Burlington House. The lean years were over in which Constable could not find a purchaser for his landscapes, and Victorian art, as we know it, was at the zenith of its popularity. It seems impossible to us now, so complete has been the slump in the work of most of the artists then so much admired and eagerly purchased, that the tide will ever again return to float off the hulks of those stranded masterpieces, and yet who would venture to make any pronouncement concerning the artistic tastes and fashions of the future ? Who, twenty years ago, would have been so rash as to prophesy that Mr Epstein's statue of night would be erected outside the underground railway instead of inside it ? Even Presidents of the Royal Academy itself may have their most solemn dictums disproved, for when Lord Elgin brought home from Athens the marbles from the Parthenon frieze and pediments, Benjamin West, P.R.A., made an official examination of them and pronounced that these statues and reliefs were not Greek work at all but late Roman.

But no doubts ever troubled those eager purchasers and admirers when year by year they saw the "line" at the Royal Academy filled with masterpieces. How glorious were those walls, the whole wide acreage of which up to the very ceiling, was inlaid, as neatly and completely as a finished jig-saw

215

puzzle, with the pictures that had been judged worthy to hang there ! Even a place at the very top where distance and foreshortening made one of moderate size appear like a glazed postage stamp, conferred a cachet on its exhibitor, for it had been hung at the Royal Academy and the artist's friends turned their telescopes on it, and congratulated him on the honour. But the line was the Holy of Holies; there (at one time or another in those halcyon days) were exhibited stags in the mist by Sir Edwin Landseer, R.A., or some dogs, or some ptarmigan under a rock. There were Highland cattle standing knee-deep in the heather by Mr Davis, R.A., and quantities of sheep by Mr Breton Riviere, R.A., portraits by Herkomer, battle pieces by Ernest Crofts, Greek youths and maidens reclining on marble benches, and reading to each other from rolls of manuscript, with glimpses of a blue, blue sea through pink flowering almond trees, by Mr Alma Tadema, family parties having tea in the garden beneath an ivied wall or young ladies suitably unclad for medical examination visiting a shrine of healing, by Mr Poynter, interminable surfaces of the English Channel by Mr Moore, and of Bible history by Mr Herbert. All these pictures were painted by artists who knew their business and had got a sense of line and colour, and they had given them appropriate titles ; the "English Channel" by Mr Moore was "Britannia's Realm," and Mr Alma Tadema's picture was "A Reading from Homer" and Mr Croft's "The Retreat from Moscow." Nothing could be more like the sea than "Britannia's Realm," nothing more like marble than the translucent benches on which Greek youth and maidens sat and read Homer to each other, or more like ivy than the tidy creeper that covered the wall where the family party had tea.

Of course, there were among them pictures which we still believe, and which we think that future generations will believe to be of the first rank. Millais, for instance, was exhibiting then, but no-one would class Millais among those whom we call Victorian artists any more than they would class Whistler among them. But it was of these true Victorians that the line was as full as is a railway line of wreckage and corpses after some terrible accident. Perhaps some may be resuscitated, but for the present most of those admired works will seem to us as dead as anything can possibly be.

Then somewhere on the line there was the greatest annual masterpiece of all, which was known as "the picture of the year." I vividly remember the "Slave Market" by Mr Long, R.A., which attained this distinction, and he sold it for £6000, which was precisely the sum for which, not many years earlier, Ruskin could have bought for the nation Tintoret's picture of the Crucifixion in St Cassian's in Venice. It was too much for the nation to pay for one of the world's masterpieces, but Mr Long's "Slave Market" found a ready purchaser. The blue riband of the Academy was probably awarded on the day of the Private View, when the smart and privileged crowd in frock-coats and bustles and waists were really more intent on pictorial art than on each other. They clustered, they broke up, they formed again, and soon they arrived at the verdict which the popular taste generally endorsed, when next day the gallery was open to the public. It was always an exceedingly well-painted picture, but it was always by one of those artists whom we now consider typically Victorian. The most famous of all the series was undoubtedly "The Derby Day" which was exhibited in 1858 by Mr Frith. It was not only the most popular picture of the year, but for many years the most widely known picture in England: there was not a coffee-room in any inn that had not a print of it. The coaches, the gipsies, the fortune teller, the sky, the book-makers, the horses were all rendered with the most minute finish, every quarter-inch of the picture was in focus: you might say it was an infinite number of little pictures put together with extreme skill. It was bought by the nation, and Oscar Wilde, in a voice full of reverence, asked if it was really all done by hand. Mr

Frith followed it up by the hardly less famous "Railway Station."

Victorian art reached the zenith of its popularity in the eighties, during which decade Sir Frederick Leighton was President of the Royal Academy. He was himself a most accomplished artist of that school, and in person an incarnation of it, picturesque and urbane, and highly finished. Even if he had been no artist, there could not have been found an apter figurehead, but as it was, his pictures were among the most admired of all. "Wedded," "Psyche," and "Hit" were undoubtedly pictures of the year. Modern art became so popular, that perhaps what Edmund Gosse (speaking of the work of Miss Marie Corelli) once called "the taint of popularity" was partly responsible for its decay. Yet the fact that an artist is popular need not necessarily imply that he is worthless, any more than the fact that an artist is not thus tainted is a proof that he has distinction, and Miss Corelli possibly had this in her mind when she replied to Mr Gosse's criticism by pointing out that though her works might be tainted with popularity, no-one could offer such an unfavourable comment on his.

But if these Victorian masters were thus tainted with popularity, M Gustave Doré was positively crawling with it. He made a larger fortune with his paintings than any artist in the whole of the history of the world, and, incredible as it may seem now (and doubly incredible if his pictures were exhibited here again), he had a permanent gallery of his works in Bond Street called the Doré Gallery, where for many years winter and summer alike, his prodigious canvases were on view. In his unregenerate days he had made illustrations for Balzac's "*Contes Drolatiques*" the sight of which, so dreadful was their drollery, had made Ruskin physically sick. But the Doré Gallery was not of such, there were sacred subjects on an enormous scale, there was one of Christ leaving the Prætorium, another of the entry into Jerusalem, another of angels hovering above the arena of the Colosseum, where in the dusk lay the bodies of Christian martyrs lately killed by lions. The lions had been interrupted at their meal by this disconcerting vision, and prowled uneasily about. . . It was not for a few brief weeks in the summer, as at the Academy, that this gallery was open, but all the year round the turnstile clicked to the shillings of the serious. Before the most important works there was a row of chairs and, if you were lucky, you could step into a vacant seat and reposefully drink in the solemn thoughts produced by these masterpieces. They had all the technical merits which were characteristic of the period; even the pre-Raphaelites admitted the carefulness of their execution and the sublimity of their subjects, and in terms of paint, they were exactly on the level, in terms of ink, of the novels of Miss Marie Corelli, in terms of the stage, of the dramatic art of Mr Wilson Barrett, and in terms of the pulpit, of the sermons of Dr Farrar, then Archdeacon of Westminster. All these in their various lines were admirable technicians, since technique means the ability to render precisely the effect that the artist wishes to produce, and the source of their inspiration as of that of Victorian art generally, was that species of sentiment and feeling which we now call sentimentality. We detect below the prismatic brilliance of the surface a certain oiliness, as when a motor, which has been gently leaking, covers the asphalt of the street with the hues of a rainbow. But no such oiliness was perceived then: the colours seemed to be laid on the hard black asphalt, which stood for power. "Very par'ful" was a common term of praise for Victorian masterpieces and the rest were "Perfectly sweet."

But from far back in the Victorian Epoch there had been a fellowship of artists in revolt against the smug conventions which in their opinion rendered all modern art quite futile and meaningless. This was the school of the pre-Raphaelites which was founded in the forties by Holman Hunt and John Everett Millais. Dante Gabriel Rossetti joined them so soon afterwards that he may be counted also as a founder. The whole history of the progress of Art is, necessarily, a history of revolts against conventions, but the rebels, we may remark, are of two classes. One of these consists of hooligans whose delight is merely in smashing, but who have nothing else to offer in place of what they consider worthless. The other class is of those whose iconoclasm makes room for something worthier, which they profess themselves ready to supply, and of such were the pre-Raphaelites. They held that up till the year 1848, Raphael had been the last of the inspired painters, and their aim was to bring Art back out of the wilderness where commerciality and charlatanism had driven it. They formed a Brotherhood with this end in view, and every Brother on admission had to subscribe his name to their creed. This creed consisted of a list of thirteen names, some of which were distinguished by various numbers of stars or asterisks, in the manner in which Baedeker's guide-books point out the degrees of excellence in the notable objects which they recommend the tourist to visit. Jesus Christ (in this creed) received four stars: the author of "Job" three: Raphael, Coventry Patmore, Elizabeth Browning, the author of "Stories after Nature" and Longfellow one each, while the remaining names, undistinguished by stars, were those of Newton, Bacon, Michaelangelo, Joan of Arc, Pheidias, and Tintoret. Then followed the declaration to be signed by all members of the Brotherhood: "There exists no other immortality than what is centred in these names."

The ground thus then was very conveniently cleared for future operations. Shakespeare, Dante, Leonardo da Vinci, Holbein, Titian, Velasquez were not of the stuff which merits immortality, though Longfellow and Mrs Browning were held worthy, and the Brotherhood set to work to produce pictures of the starred class and to ally to itself other artists who had within them the seed of immortality. Their aims were of the loftiest, their pictures were to be inspired by moral as well as artistic beauty, the utmost finish and accuracy in detail must be bestowed upon them, and the subjects must in themselves be of an elevating character. Keat's "Eve of St Agnes," for instance, was pronounced by Holman Hunt to be a fit subject for a picture, "because it illustrates the sacredness of honest, responsible love, and the weakness of proud intemperance," and the same process of moral selection inspired his "Converted English Family Sheltering a Christian Missionary from the Druids," his "Triumph of the Innocents" and his "Light of the World." He also regretted that Millais had not chosen a better subject than "Two Lovers Whispering by a Garden Wall." Their creed and their practice in fact were the precise opposite of the artistic principles of today, for today an elevating subject is enough by itself to damn a picture, while if it has not got that fatal defect, the fact that it is painted with care and finish, is sufficient.

Other Brothers joined them (indeed Rossetti discovered immortals with an almost embarrassing frequency) Woolner, the sculptor, Ford Madox Brown and, most notable of them all, Edward Burne-Jones. To these must be added William Morris, whose aim it was, in an annexe of this great hall of regenerated art, to produce beautiful books, and to restore beauty to modern domestic life. Chairs, tables, tapestries, carpets, glass and wall-papers were to shed their Victorian ugliness, and be replaced by work of exquisite design and honest manufacture, made of vegetable dyes and seasoned wood, that should be a durable joy in daily life. William Morris was also their poet, and for prophet they had Ruskin, who with the full force of his authoritative eloquence proclaimed the splendour of the new dawn now beginning to light the face of the Artless earth. Like them he held that, with the exception of Turner's landscapes, no divinely-inspired works of art had been produced since the fifteenth century. Rembrandt he regarded with unfeigned horror, Claude with contemptuous ridicule, the great English portrait-painters,

Reynolds, Romney and the rest were mere nonentities, but he saluted Burne-Jones as the direct and immediate artistic heir of Giorgione and found the true Hellenic spirit incarnate again in him.

Now the Royal Academy had always been the throne-room, so to speak, of English art, and to appear on its walls was a kind of presentation at Court, conferring on the aspirant a definite certificate of artistic soundness and respectability. But in the late seventies the pre-Raphaelite school made the Bolshevist move of setting up a Court of their own, and of pledging themselves not to submit their applications to the Lord Chamberlain of Burlington House at all. Sir Coutts Lindsay, a wealthy banker, and himself an artist of moderate merit, opened for them a rival Court at the new Grosvenor Gallery in Bond Street, where their work would be the principal feature, and here year by year were mustered the forces of the rebels and their defiance of the obsolete Victorian traditions. This first exhibition also contained Whistler's "Nocturne in Black and Gold," about which, before long, much more was to be heard. In spite of the defection of Millais from their ranks, and the death of Rossetti in 1882, their cult, this new religion of Art, spread rapidly, and when in 1888, the Grosvenor Gallery was closed, another centre was found at the New Gallery so that there was no break in the public exhibition of the pre-Raphaelite ideal. To believe in it and to profess it became a stamp of artistic sensibility, and a season ticket to the New Gallery was a sort of documentary certificate to that effect. There the elect would feed their souls on Rossetti's collected canvases, full-blown matrons with their sumptuous shawls, their downcast eyes, their great red lips, their full white throats, and the finished furnishings of their surroundings: there, too, were companies of Burne-Jones's wan and willowy maidens, exquisitely painted, who faltered up and down the Golden Stairs, or sadly observed their perfect features in the Mirror of Venus. Certainly all trace of Victorian convention was banished, not a single specimen of the well-groomed Highland cattle, nor a grouse nor a birch tree nor a glimpse of the English Channel was to be seen there, nor a portrait of any chairman of City Companies, but it might be questioned if, with this extinguishing of the smoky wick of banal Victorian convention, there had not been kindled another flame which might become just as conventional as the other. For whether these new types were statuesque or diaphanous, whether they were well nourished or highly anæmic, they all wore an air of remote inhuman melancholy, and whether they had clad themselves in pearls and purple, or in dim draped muslins, they wore inscrutable masks. No gleam of intelligence, no spark of humour, no hint of joy or healthy animalism ever lit those brooding or downcast countenances: they seemed completely taken up with the task of being beautiful and sad, each sundered from her companions (for there were very few men among them) in a cell of her own, where she fed on her own world-weariness and perfect features. An anticyclone of mournfulness lay heavy on them, and it was not as if "the soul with all its maladies" had passed into them, but as if the soul with all its qualities had passed out.

But the school, with Ruskin for its indefatigable prophet became a sort of religion to the highly cultured: they quite agreed that since Raphael no artist worthy of the name had arisen, and some were not so sure about Raphael. Then, as Oscar Wilde remarked, Nature elbowed her way into the charmed circle of Art, and began reproducing the types which the two most notable pre-Raphaelites had invented, and Rossetti's Junos and Burne-Jones's wan women (the latter in swiftly increasing numbers) were often seen about the London streets, especially in the neighbourhood of the New Gallery. It became fashionable in cultured circles to be pensive and willowy. Indeed the æsthetic cult of the eighties was largely derived from the pre-Raphaelites, ladies drooped and were wilted, and clad themselves in Liberty fabrics (use-

ful also for the ties of similarly minded males) and let fall
over their eyes a tangle of hair, through which they miserably
peered. *Punch*, week by week, was full of them, but
they were not an invention of the comic papers, and scarcely
an exaggeration: they actually existed in considerable numbers, until in the manner of other fashionable stunts, the glow
of the æsthetic movement as a free translation of pre-
Raphaelitism into life, began to grow as wan as its practi-
tioners. It was better to look at Burne-Jones's pictures than
to look like them, for women found that it did not really suit
them to be haggard and sad, and Englishmen seldom care
to make themselves conspicuous by outrageous breeches.

Besides the pre-Raphaelites and that sort of Brocken
spectre of æstheticism (with Oscar Wilde for its very substantial showman) which emanated from them, there was
another school of art in London, though not English in origin, which consisted of one unique and peerless master without pupils, and quite without other propaganda than that
supplied by his own pugnacious wit. This master, of course,
was James McNeill Whistler, and rich indeed was he in
masterpieces of art and entertainment. He strongly distrusted and disliked Oscar Wilde personally, as I was told by
Mr William Heinemann (one of the few friends with whom
Whistler never succeeded in quarrelling), and when he came
back from America and continued, though æstheticism had
faded away, to lecture on art and generally resume his
sacerdotal functions, Whistler lost no opportunity (rather
he made them with untiring industry) of mocking him and
his pretensions and his poems and his poses. To him, as to
most other people who expressed their views about Art,
Whistler wrote the rudest letters, communicating them to
the public press, and in his own phrase "carefully exasper-
ating" them. He ordered the poet in the most summary
manner at once to return to Nathan, the theatrical cos-
tumier, the befrogged and befurred coat in which he had
seen him walking that afternoon, and not desecrate the

streets of "his" Chelsea got up as a blend of Kossuth and Mr Mantilini. To that sort of attack no reply was necessary, for it resembled the elementary methods of small boys who chalk up on a wall "Billy is a Fool," but what was more serious and damaging was when Whistler accused him of appropriating his own theories about art, and retailing them as original reflections in his lectures. It was in vain that Oscar Wilde, in answer to such attacks, pleaded that the only original ideas he had ever heard Whistler utter were those on his own merits as an artist, and that these shrill shrieks of plagiarism from impotent lips would interest nobody, for they afforded the readers of the *World* the highest entertainment, and indeed his denial was much more impotent than the accusations, which appeared to be well founded. In fact Whistler shooed him off the premises of the House of Art by the back-door. His contention was that nobody, who was not himself an artist, had any right to pronounce on subjects of art, and though that point of view may be contested, he was perfectly right to ridicule Wilde's lectures (except such parts as were plagiarized from him) for some of them, those given in America, have since been published, and, as George IV said of Shakespeare, they are indeed sad stuff. Besides, Whistler personally disliked him, and he saw that his poison fangs were fully charged, when he engaged with him. Not even Wilde's appreciation of his wit (which usually softened him) had any effect here, and when Wilde applauded some swift repartee of his with an admiring, "I wish I had said that," Whistler immediately answered, "You will, Oscar, you will." And he probably did.

It is strange that both these men whose brush and whose pen earned, before many years were out, such very large sums for those who possessed the pictures of the one, and the copyrights of the other, should both have passed through the bankruptcy court. Whistler extracted a drop of very characteristic glee from his experience, for when proceedings were imminent, he hurriedly painted and left in his

studio for public auction, an appalling canvas called "The
Gold Scab." It was an unmistakable portrait, as far as the
head was concerned of the amiable Mr Naylor-Leyland for
whom he had decorated the celebrated peacock-room, and
who, he thought, should have paid him a far higher sum than
that for which he had contracted to do it.　So by one of
those "dainty" revenges of his, again reminding us of the
street boy who chalks up rude remarks, he left this ghastly
effigy to be put up for sale with the rest of his belongings.
There poor putty-coloured Mr Leyland sat, monstrous and
leering and playing on his piano.　His face was human
and easily recognizable, but his arms and legs were thin
and scaly like the legs of birds, and out of the interstices
between the scales oozed golden sovereigns.　That would
teach him !　Unfortunately for the success of the dainty re-
venge, the picture attracted no attention at all at the sale;
instead of completely withering Mr Leyland it found its way
into a dusky corner of some inconspicuous curiosity shop in
Chelsea.　There, several years afterwards, my friend Mr
G. P. Jacomb Hood, himself a distinguished artist, chanced
to see it, and recognizing the master's hand, bought it for
a few pounds, and learned the history of it from Whistler.
The sum which it eventually fetched when he sold it to an
American collector would have gone a considerable way to
avert the bankruptcy.　But then Whistler had much enjoyed the savage painting of it.

His selection of a butterfly for his emblem and his signature was an odd choice: never was there an insect so well
armoured and aggressive, and every page of the "Gentle Art
of Making Enemies" testifies to its native ferocity.　Never
did Whistler flutter idly in the sunshine and lightly sip the
honey from the flowers, or settle with spread wings on a
stone, unless he was engaged in making a lithograph on it.
He worked with the untiring passion of the inspired artist,
and in the intervals buzzed angrily in the limelight, and bit
and stung the unfortunate flowers on which he alighted.　He

could not stand a word of criticism, and anyone who ventured
to say that any etching or painting of his was not a masterpiece was instantly pilloried and pelted.   The joy of a Bil-
lingsgate battle, as well as the sacred duty of punishing all
whose views on art were so heretic, no doubt inspired him,
for Whistler never felt at peace with himself unless he was
in the middle of some acid squabble with somebody else.   It
was a game to him, and his rules were that he was allowed to
kick and scrag his opponents, but they must not retaliate, and
being, like most folk, who thoroughly enjoy hurting other
people, extremely sensitive himself, he bitterly resented any
rejoinder as being against the rules.   To Whistler's mind
this was as if a school boy, about to be chastised, plucked the
birch rod from his outraged preceptor and administered
what he had been designed to receive.   It was not always that
he got the best of these encounters, for the mere gesture of
putting out his tongue at somebody was so enjoyable that
he forgot to use it for the more articulate purpose of argument, and to criticize a man's top coat is not really a logical
refutation of his depreciation of one's artistic abilities.   He
published the cream of these correspondences in that "dainty"
book "The Gentle Art of Making Enemies" and never did
he paint a more masterly portrait than that which he there
executes of himself, for never did a style better express the
writer of it.   He stings, he bites, he is absolutely convinced
that he has made an end for ever of his victims, and all the
time he figures himself as the heedless butterfly that flutters
over the margin of his pages, though he draws it with fingers
trembling with passion.   But too much of the writing which
he thought so dainty is a mere cocking of snooks, and a far
more pleasing and paying device was to print, by way of advertisement, in the catalogue of one of his exhibitions of
etchings, all the foolish things which the critics said about
him, and leave it at that, for they really dug their own graves
better than he could.   In fact he never dug their graves at
all, so busy was he kicking what he believed to be the corpses

of those whom his wit had slain.   And printing their rubbish
was good business too (never had there been in the whole
history of entomology so business-like a butterfly), for all
sorts of people who cared nothing whatever for etchings, but
liked these pea-shooting contests, flocked to the exhibition in
order to get the catalogues which contained the butterfly's
"latests," and thus they paid for exhibition and catalogue
too, since the catalogue was only on sale inside the turnstiles.

Though a most serious artist, Whistler like Wilde culled
honey not in the sunlight but in the limelight, and he was
full of devices to secure for himself its utmost effulgence.
This habit of his led to the inference that whatever he did was
inspired by these motives, which was not always the case, for
the butterfly could be in deadly earnest, even when he was
construed as being most farcical.   Nothing was further
from his intention than farce when, in consequence of highly
acrimonious happenings, he challenged Mr George Moore
to a duel, sending his seconds in due and classic ritual to convey to him the bloody invitation.   What led up to this dangerous proposal was the affair known as "The Baronet and
the Butterfly," the baronet being Sir William Eden.   It was
a case of a picture and a payment, such as before now had
occurred with the Butterfly, and the climax had been when
Whistler was ordered by a French court to deliver the picture of Lady Eden which he had already destroyed, and
to pay a fine.   Mr George Moore had concerned himself
with the whole business in a manner that seemed unfriendly
to Whistler, and in reply to a very unpleasant letter from
the Butterfly, had published his answer in the *Pall Mall Gazette*, twitting Whistler with his age.   This must be considered as a personal insult, and Whistler's challenge to a
duel at once followed.

The crisis was truly interesting and indeed it was not
farcical, for surely these were two firebrands, each burning
to scorch up the other.   Mr George Moore had vividly described his own sanguinary temperament in his "Confessions

of a Young Man," and told his readers how a "beautiful
young lord" had been impertinent to him. There had been
an argument, and the beautiful young lord had struck Mr
Moore's face with his finger-tips, and Mr Moore had hit him
on the head with a champagne bottle, and had left this party
in Curzon Street with the determination to fight him. He
was a marvellous shot too, he had constantly broken dozens
of plates consecutively with his unerring revolver; besides,
as Mr Moore frankly tells us, a duel, for which he was so
perfectly equipped, would get him a great notoriety. So
he scoured the place for seconds, and met with grievous dis-
appointments for one of his friends was going abroad and
another was in the country, and a third had to bury his father. Eventually the bereaved son came to England, but
he and Mr Moore talked art instead and so the challenge was
never sent out at all, since Mr Moore so rightly preferred
Art to bloodshed. But now the situation was far more dangerous, for there was Whistler in deadly earnest, and, more
fortunate than Mr Moore, he had found his seconds, and delivered through them his message. What would have happened if Mr Moore had accepted the challenge we cannot
tell: probably friends would have intervened, but Whistler
was no *farceur* in matters of honour and he would certainly
have appeared on the scene of carnage. But Mr Moore's
common sense prevented matters coming to extremes, for
he so rightly saw that a serious writer and a serious artist
cannot in any state of reasonable civilization go about shooting at each other, for they have to do their work. So he
treated this sanguinary proposal with silence, and went on
with his book.

But through all his vindictive gaieties and bitter jests
which the public generally at that time appreciated far
more than his pictures, Whistler the Butterfly was capable of
deep personal devotion. He loved his mother and his wife
and his Art. Years before he had proved that in the famous
action which he had brought against Ruskin for libel in 1878.

At the very first exhibition at the Grosvenor Gallery which was devoted to the work of rebels from the Royal Academy, and in particular of the pre-Raphaelites, there had appeared his "Nocturne in Black and Gold" and in the trial his sense of the dignity of the artist quite outshone his wit. Ruskin in his criticism of the pictures in the Grosvenor Gallery had pounced on this wonderful canvas and had accused Whistler of being an impudent coxcomb who had had the effrontery to fling a pot of paint in the eye of the public, and ask £200 for the mess. With just the same sincerity and dispatch with which he challenged Mr George Moore to a duel, Whistler brought a libel action against Ruskin, and the account of it (which should be read with Whistler's marginal comments) seems to us now like some sheer parody of judicial administration, comparable only to the Bardell trial in Pickwick. Ruskin was unwell when the case came on, and did not appear in person, and his chief expert witnesses, to support his plea of justification, were Mr Burne-Jones (who hated the whole thing and only appeared out of loyal affection for Ruskin) Mr Tom Taylor, art-critic and editor of *Punch*, and Mr Frith, who had painted "The Derby Day." Whistler was asked by the Attorney-General how long it took him to "knock off" that Nocturne; his picture of Battersea Bridge, now in the Tate Gallery, was brought into court and Mr Justice Starleigh (I think the pseudonym by which he was known to the world was Huddleston) asked him which part of the picture was the bridge, and whether the things on the bridge were intended for people, and whether that was a barge below the bridge. Whistler professed himself much encouraged that the judge recognized these objects, though what the point of the questions was, except to impress on the jury that the judge did not think much of Whistler's work, is difficult to understand. Then the Attorney General asked Whistler if he could make him see the beauty of the Nocturne, and Whistler looked at his face and then at the Nocturne and back again and said he was afraid it was quite impossible. So in his address to the jury the foiled Attorney-General went back to the picture of Battersea Bridge and asked whether the bridge was a telescope or a fire-escape, and, if those were horses and people on it, how on earth were they to get off again ? He said he had looked out the word "coxcomb" which was part of the so-called libellous matter, and found that it meant a man who made jests professionally. So Whistler could not complain of that, since his pictures had afforded such unrivalled amusement to the public. But when he asked him whether he thought he was justified in asking £200 for a picture which had taken him, as he had confessed, only a day and a half to execute, Whistler jested no more, but, with the utmost dignity, said that he asked that not for a few hours' work, but for the experience of a lifetime.

Farce, one would have thought, could hardly have been made to go further, but the witnesses for the defence duly accomplished this difficult feat. Burne-Jones who, it must be repeated, hated to appear at all, was true to the doctrines of the pre-Raphaelites and said that though the Nocturne was pleasant in colour, it lacked the detail and finish which were essential to every serious work of art. It was therefore not a serious work of art, but only one of the numerous failures to paint night, and considering how much careful work by British artists was priced much lower, it was definitely not worth £200. Apparently it made no difference who painted a picture, or what magical inspiration lay behind it; two days' work, whoever did it, could only result in a "sketch." So then a Titian, with more jokes from the judge, was brought into court and Burne-Jones pointed out what finish meant.

He was succeeded by Mr Frith who had painted "The Derby Day" and who, almost necessarily, could see nothing whatever in either the "Nocturne" or "Battersea Bridge," and finally Mr Taylor the third of the expert witnesses said that these pictures of Whistler's "only came one step nearer pictures than a delicately tinted wall-paper." Farce then could go no further, and the jury brought in a verdict for Whistler with one farthing damages: this farthing he wore ever after on his watch chain. Technically he had been libelled but actually he had suffered no damage, for his picture was worthless. Yet if anyone had bought that Nocturne of which Mr Frith and Mr Justice Starleigh thought so poorly, at the price the coxcomb (though Mr Ruskin should not have said so) had asked for it, and sold it not many years later, he could have enjoyed from the safe investment of the proceeds of his sale as large an annual income as the capital he had expended on it. But tastes and values are always varying, and we must remember *per contra*, that many of the works of the most admired Victorian artists would not today fetch the annual dividend which their purchase price, if similarly invested, would bring in.

Whistler then, like the pre-Raphaelites, was in rebellion against the official school of English art, and in both there was such deadly singleness of aim that they could not really recognize any merit in the contemporary work of others. But the pre-Raphaelites, unlike him, had no taste for public polemics on the subject of art, nor did they desire to attack and scarify any critic who did not agree with them: all they wanted was passionately to pursue their heart's desire in the creation of beautiful things, and they cared nothing what anybody thought about their work, provided Ruskin and the Brothers approved. No touch of jealousy ever marred their concord; Burne-Jones believed that Rossetti was the greatest genius of the age, Rossetti introduced Burne-Jones into the artistic world of Holland House as being the same, and Holman Hunt knew that they all were. Topsy in his suit of butcher's blue with his hands deeply stained from the vats of vegetable dyes, declaimed the last instalment of the "Earthly Paradise" (which was the greatest poem in the world) while Burne-Jones on the top of his studio ladder was busy with the beard of King Cophetua. On Sunday morn-

ing there was breakfast at the Grange, and others of the like-
minded dropped in. One said he was late because he had
been to see a most magnificent picture by Sir Joshua Reynolds which a friend had acquired. "Sir Sploshua" said
Burne-Jones, and that was the end of Sir Sploshua. Or
when work was over, they would go round to Gabriel's house
on the Chelsea Embankment and admire the new wombat in
the back garden. Perhaps Rossetti would be writing a son-
net, or perhaps Mrs William Morris would be sitting to him,
but whether at the Grange, or at Chelsea, or at Kelmscott,
there was always the same boyish enthusiasm as in the old days
at Red Lion Square, and the same conviction sincerely held
by each and openly expressed, that the work of the others
was of the supremest merit. Burne-Jones's pencil when not
seriously employed was as humorous as Edward Lear's, and
on half sheets of paper he drew "Pleasures of the Plain," or
Rossetti's wombat, or caricatured Morris holding up a brim-
ming glass of wine, as a design for a stained-glass window.
The two were for some years in partnership, Burne-Jones
making designs for windows and tapestries, which Morris
executed. The accounts of the firm were kept by Morris,
who was the business partner as regards production, and on
the margin of the account-books Burne-Jones would comment on the fact that gentlemen in the liberal professions
were usually paid not in pounds but guineas. A delicious
joyousness in life generally and its inimitable humours possessed them in the intervals when they were not at their easels
and looms. Just as Whistler put into his work all the tenderness, as in the portrait of his mother and of Carlyle, of
which his nature was capable, and excluded from it his entire
store of waspishness and irritability, so Burne-Jones put
into his pictures all his seriousness and sense of the sacredness
of beauty, and reserved for his friends his romping sense of
fun, Puck-like sometimes, but lambent and living. Art
was to him a secret garden peopled with figures in whom the
pulses of life were quite arrested, and a picture was to him

as he fashioned it, the presentment of some dream of romance seen in a light that never shone on sea or land and wholly visionary. Herein lay his weakness and his strength; his weakness in that he shut off from art any leakage of human stuff, whether gay or tragic, that came from the stock-pot into which the woes and raptures of humanity are shredded, and so to many eyes his work is no more than friezes of sexless maidens with here or there a youth wholly epicene; his strength that he pursued with the unswerving purpose of the true artist and with unerring hand his own vision of the beautiful. Always he sought the stillness of the valley of Avilion, unvexed by the loud winds of life and its snow and its hail, and basking in a sunshine so subdued that it never casts any sharpness of shadow, while those who dwell therein are more remote than the moon from all the frets and the glories of living folk. Once only on that incomparable canvas "In the Depths of the Sea" did he aim at emotional action. There we see an undeniable woman, though a mermaid, who is triumphantly bearing down to a subaqueous bridal the body of a man. Otherwise he always eschews anything like drama in his pictures; they represent moments of what he called "lyrical quiet" and it was for this reason, as he himself stated, that he would not paint the awakening of the Princess in his "Briar Rose." It would have been dramatic, and therefore discordant with the quiet of the rest of the series.

THESE pictorial rebels had been joined by artists who worked in other mediums, and who were also in revolt against Victorian convention. George Meredith was one of these, and he had a room at Rossetti's Tudor House, where also Swinburne lived, off and on, for a couple of years. This association had its drawbacks, for however purely burns the flame of art, it is not very wise for such highly strung folk to live together, since they are certain to grate on each other's sensibilities, and though they all, in the true pre-Raphaelite fashion, believed in each other's genius, that was not sufficient

to secure domestic serenity. Indeed it matters very little
on the score of harmony whether you appreciate the genius
of the man who morning by morning sits opposite to you
at breakfast, provided he does not fidget and sips his tea
in a becoming manner. But as Rossetti told Edmund Gosse
"Swinburne used to get on my nerves by dancing all over
the studio like a wild cat," and Meredith on a highly critical occasion vowed that he would certainly have kicked Swinburne downstairs had he not foreseen what a clatter his
horrid little bottom would have made as it bounced from step
to step. So disagreeable a forecast surely betokens a very
rich incompatibility, and a further and final quarrel took
place at the Garrick Club, where they were brought together
for purposes of reconciliation. Meredith was in temporary
charge of the *Fortnightly Review,* and Swinburne asked
him why he had been sent only £10 for a poem which had appeared there. Meredith replied that this was what he himself got for his own poems. Upon which Swinburne, deeply
insulted, slapped his face, and that was the end of all things.

But Swinburne's friendship with Burne-Jones, to whom
he dedicated "Poems and Ballads," was heated by no such
friction, and their intimacy was close and unbroken throughout these unedifying and lyrical days, when Swinburne's
frail fingers were plucking such music from the lyre of English speech as had never been heard before, and will never be
heard again till another master of "beautiful things made
new" comes over the hills of the dawn. He was only a man
by pseudonym: some Greek Bacchanal or inspired spirit
born of the Ægean Sea and nourished on the honey of Hymet-
tan bees had wrapped itself, as with a cloak, in human form,
and found it difficult to adapt itself to the modes of the civilization later. He would drive down in a hansom to Burne-
Jones's house at Hammersmith, with a newly written poem of
portentous length in his pocket, and his arrival was often
made known by shrill screams and cries, for he had a conviction which nothing would shake that the correct fare from

any one place in London to any other was a shilling, neither more nor less, and so there was trouble with the cabman. My great friend Sir Philip Burne-Jones has often described to me his own boyish memories of Swinburne's epiphany at his father's house, how he was sent bundling downstairs with some more shillings for the indignant charioteer, and how his mother came down with soothings and consolations, as for a child that has seen a naughty bogie. Here it is pleasant to explode the notion that Swinburne was a heavy drinker and boozed all day. He drank very little, but he had epileptic tendencies, which he entirely outgrew in later life, and on occasion, especially when the excitement and frenzy of poesy possessed him, a single glass of claret was sufficient to intoxicate him. Of course he would have been better without it, but the real cause of these highly intemperate scenes was not (so Sir Edward Burne-Jones was sure) heavy drinking, but a sudden and apparently fortuitous inability to stand any alcohol at all. He would be completely and absolutely sober one moment, and the next a couple of sips of some light wine would fuddle and excite him. This was also the belief of Edmund Gosse, and they both, who at this time knew Swinburne better than anybody, were equally certain that the indications of moral aberration which it is perfectly easy to find in "Poems and Ballads" were quite foundationless as regards Swinburne's personal character and conduct. They were the lyrical utterances of a poet describing the moods and passions of other minds, and were as objective as the utterances of Robert Browning's "Men and Women." Swinburne kept up a lively correspondence with this friend of his for whom he had so warm an affection, but his letters, alas, have perished: Burne-Jones thought it was prudent to destroy them, and on one sad morning he burned them all.

Then there dawned that most fateful day when Destiny in the disguise of the admirable Mr Theodore Watts-Dunton (né Watts) came knocking at the door of Swinburne's rooms. A country lawyer by profession, he was a fervent admirer of the pre-Raphaelites, and coming up to London had made the acquaintance of several of the group, including Rossetti, from whom he obtained a letter of introduction to Swinburne, and he went to Swinburne's rooms to present this in person. His tappings at the door met with no response, and he entered to find an empty sitting-room. But from the bedroom (presumably) beyond there were sounds of stirring, and after having again tried to procure admission to penetrate further, he opened the door. He found Swinburne stark naked with his aureole of red hair flying round his head, performing a Dionysiac dance, all by himself in front of a large looking-glass. Swinburne perceived the intruder, he rushed at him, and before Mr Watts-Dunton could offer any explanation or deliver his letter of introduction he was flying in panic helter-skelter down the stairs, and was driven by the enraged Corybant off the premises.

Such, so Edmund Gosse told me, was the true account of this first meeting, and it cannot be called auspicious; none could have expected that out of it would spring a lifelong and devoted friendship. But Mr Watts-Dunton was not to be put off by a little misunderstanding of that kind, and he most generously overlooked the incident and the acquaintanceship was formed. Swiftly it ripened into intimacy; Watts-Dunton took Swinburne's financial affairs in hand (for he had as little notion of the symbolical forms of money, like cheques and bank notes, as Shelley), straightened them out for him, attended to his business letters which always goaded Swinburne into a frenzy of rage before he had ascertained whether they were pleasant or the reverse, and gradually made himself indispensable. Swinburne still retained what Plato in a different connection called "inward liberty," but in 1879 Watts-Dunton took charge of him altogether, and interned him (there is no other word to use) in a villa at Putney for the rest of his life, a period of over thirty years.

This event constitutes a psychological puzzle of the most

baffling sort. Doubtless, Watts-Dunton (as he said of himself) was possessed of a dominating quality, which from boyhood had always asserted itself, doubtless also, he had the power of inspiring trust and affection. Moreover, he had a passionate love of literature, and that was a bond between them: he was a critic of some standing on whose judgment Swinburne implicitly relied, and he wrote sonnets and poems and stories which Swinburne admired. But in spite of all this it is hopeless to attempt to understand how Swinburne, arch-rebel as he was against all forms of authority, could have so given up into the hands of his friend all independence, and subjected himself, his choice of associates, his occupation, his diet, his daily round to the ordering of another. There was a strain in him, as in Shelley, of the imperishable child, and Watts-Dunton somehow became to him an omnipotent but kindly nurse who to the child-like mind figures as Fate, and when Nurse said "Now be a good Algernon, and come along to Putney," it never occurred to him, either then or afterwards, to question these decrees. At the time he went to Putney he was too ill to resist, but very soon his health began to improve, and under that beneficent regime he became far more robust than he had ever been. But the very desire for liberty seems to have left him, there was no more dancing before mirrors, or of screaming at cabmen, but, alas, there was no more poetry. There was verse, plenty of it, huge stories in verse like "Tristram of Lyonesse"; there was a novel, there was a torrent of prose, appreciations of Charles Dickens, of Charlotte Brontë and denunciations of Mr Robert Buchanan and Dr Furnivall. In all these there was the glow of the coal from the altar, they teem with rage and energy and frenzy, but all this fire was out of place in the furnace of the engine which it now drove. Swinburne poured the molten stream of lyrical inspiration into a mould which would not hold it without losing its due soberness of colour and its severer lines, and the greater part of this amazing prose, though containing magnificent pas-

sages, is bombastic and exaggerated, with pages of unquali-
fied purple.   The frenzy without which all lyrical utterance
is lukewarm, causes prose to boil over, for prose, except when
delivered with the passion of the spoken voice, does not admit
of frenzy, and critical prose, such as Swinburne was composing loses all force and dignity if fashioned thus.   He loaded
it with alliteration gone lunatic, he heaped phrase upon
phrase, whether for the eulogy of Dickens or the damnation
of Dr Furnivall, and instead of using his astounding vocabulary to convey his message, let his meaning vanish in order
to employ his vocabulary.   Yet, all the time, we feel that
the fire which causes his prose to boil over and become turgid,
was exactly that which made his lyrics lambent.   But he was
now a caged bird, voluntarily it is true, because there was
nothing to prevent his leaving the Pines, and like the caged
bird he could not sing, and his energy found its outlet in
seizures of violent pecking, though never at his nurse's hand.
Poetry perhaps is a symptom of some divine disease; if so,
Putney and the devoted doctorings of Watts-Dunton rendered him tragically immune.

There was no more "Swinburne," if by "Swinburne" we
mean as we must that ecstatic Bacchanal who plucked from
his lyre, "Atalanta in Caledon" and "Poems and Ballads."
He took a walk in the morning, going very briskly and regardless of weather up Putney Hill and across Wimbledon
Common.   He often made small purchases of books at a
stall in Wimbledon, and stowed them in the pockets of his
Inverness cape.   If he got his feet wet, he took off his socks
on his return home, and put them to dry on the fender.   A
visitor arrived for lunch one morning while they were steam-
ing there: Swinburne shook hands with great cordiality
across the table, but kept dodging round it, keeping it always
between them, so as to conceal the fact that his feet were bare.
After some few moments of this mystic dance, the visitor
advanced towards the fireplace and perceived the socks.
Perhaps the poet thought he had some design on them, for

he exclaimed very earnestly, "Hold ! They are drying."

After an excellent plain lunch with a glass of beer, he went up to his bedroom and rested, lying obediently on his bed, and then, refreshed, he read or he wrote. All companionship that was likely to make the old splendours flame up again was denied him, all those who were poets at heart and who thus might be infectious were cut off from him. Burne-Jones and Rossetti were never permitted to penetrate into the Pines, and Edmund Gosse but seldom. And the worst of it was that Swinburne soon got not to miss these brothers of his mind. Edmund Gosse was his intellectual peer, and Burne-Jones the companion of the house of his dreams out of which had come "Poems and Ballads." They understood each other completely, knowing that their art for both of them was a visionary faculty that dwelt apart, and that it was in dreams that that the one looked on the "Golden Stairs," and the other on the slaying of Itylus, and the comprehension that these two, so utterly different in the conduct of life, had of each other, was based on the citizenship of the house not made with hands. But now these blood brotherhoods must cease, for all such influences (God help him !) were bad: the "old familiar glamour" might excite him, and give rise to those cerebral storms which had so nearly wrecked him physically, though out of the foam and fog of them had come the voice of the inimitable singer. "Much better," said Mr Watts-Dunton, "to have no such songs and no excitement, to have excellent health and unbroken nights with no disturbing dreams, to walk to Wimbledon, to change the socks, if wet, to rest afterwards, and then to read Dickens aloud." Swinburne had the greatest admiration for Dickens and enjoyed these readings very much: he appears also to have enjoyed hearing his friend reading aloud to him his novel "Aylwin." His mind as well as his body was subjected to this health-giving, this wise and deadly guardianship and it became a ward in Watts-Dunton's Chancery.

Watts-Dunton, for instance, shared Ruskin's and Frith's

"ALGERNON SWINBURNE TAKING HIS GREAT NEW
FRIEND GOSSE TO SEE GABRIEL ROSSETTI"

Reprinted from Bohun Lynch's "Max Beerbohm in Perspective"

low opinion about Whistler's art, and perhaps a little
personal feeling came in too, for when Watts changed his
name to Watts-Dunton, Whistler wrote him a memorable
note, which ran "Dear Theodore, What's Dunton?" This
seemed to savour of badinage. In any case, What's-Dunton
thought Whistler "a bit of a charlatan" and though in bygone days Swinburne had nobly testified in "Poems and
Ballads" to his admiration of the painter, his director now
persuaded him to write a bitter and abominable attack on
Whistler in the *Fortnightly Review*. There was no sort of
reason for it, except that Watts-Dunton wanted to get his
knife into Whistler, and so used one that was sharper than
his own, and under this suasion Swinburne produced one of
the very worst pieces of his most violent and monstrous prose.

Whistler replied to this with a characteristic letter in
which he said he had lost a *confrère*, but gained an acquaintance "one Algernon Swinburne — outsider, Putney," but
as the rest of his letter showed, he was very deeply hurt.
The "outsider, Putney" rejoined with the following lines:

To James McNeill Whistler

Fly, little butterfly, back to Japan,
Tempt not a pinch at the hand of a man,
And strive not to sting as you die away;
So pert and so painted, so proud and so pretty,
To brush the bright down from your wings were a pity.
Fly away, butterfly, fly away.

It is ludicrous and laughable that two grown men should
behave like this, it is also tragic that friendships should thus
perish. But it was Watts-Dunton who set these cantan-
kerous bantams cock-fighting.

It was the same with Walt Whitman: Swinburne had
thought very highly of "Leaves of Grass," but Watts-
Dunton could not bear the work of the American poet, and

encouraged Swinburne to write the most savage of on-
slaughts on him, a tornado of alliterative abuse. His resent-
ment against personal criticism was as bitter as Whistler's,
and because in a volume of Matthew Arnold's letters he
found a sentence describing their meeting and an allusion to
himself as a sort of "pseudo-Shelley" he retorted in his essay
on Dickens by describing Matthew Arnold as a man "whose
main achievement was to make himself by painful painstaking into a sort of pseudo-Wordsworth" and all his old admiration for him went by the board, and thereafter he could
see nothing in his poetry except chill pedantry. In all these
attacks there still burned the fire that should have been
luminous in lyrical work; instead it spurted and spat and
smouldered among damp leaves.

Possibly his days of lyrical utterance were over, but could
even Pindar have sung at the Pines ? The "hounds of
spring" slept in their baskets by the snug fireside, and instead of his heart thrilling to see how "blossom by blossom the
spring begins," he looked at the gas-lamps being kindled into
flowers of flame up Putney Hill, till Watts-Dunton was ready
to continue his reading from "Aylwin" where he had stopped
yesterday evening. It was about gipsies. No-one can
question that Watts-Dunton was inspired by the worthiest
and most moral motives, but all must lament the tragic com-
pleteness of his success. Algernon, if care and devotion
could compass it, should live to be a healthy old gentleman,
but in order to do that he must forget about Fragoletta.
And so it was; the wild bird could not sing in that suburban
cage, nor yet when Watts-Dunton took it for a holiday
to Southwold, and it no longer "filled the heart of the night
with fire." The most splendid of all the Victorian rebels
had long been dead before Swinburne ceased to walk briskly
up Putney Hill and across Wimbledon common, whatever
the weather.

CHAPTER XII

IN EVERY age and society there are women to whose houses there gravitate those who are cutting noticeable figures in the world of letters or art or politics.   Sometimes this movement is due less to their natural gravitation than to a strong and steady hauling on the part of the hostess, and her success in the capture of them is the just reward of her efforts and her infinite schemings.   Such a one must be made of stern and indefatigable stuff, and she attains the fulfilment of her innocent desires by the exercise of a ruthless hospitality.

Curious and cunning are her traps for the eminent. If, for instance, there are two great fish, who are friends of each other and who have not yet been gaffed and landed by her—she will invite them both to dinner on such and such a day, saying that each will meet the other.   This is a very pleasing device, and it often meets with the success that its ingenuity deserves, though it is liable to be detected if the two, before taking the lure, happen to confer and are astonished to find that each of them is engaged to dine with her before he has promised to do anything of the kind.   Or we may figure her as the lion-hunter who in more crude and primitive fashion goes out, an Artemis of social ambition, with her cross-bow and her arrows winged with welcome, and either from cover, or from out in the open proceeds to discharge these hospitable bolts literally at the throat of her quarry.

When shooting from cover she gets herself asked to meet her prey at the house of a friend and reminds him of the non-existent occasion of their previous meeting: when from the open she merely writes to him and gives him a plenteous choice of dates for dining.   Sometimes it takes quiverfuls to disable him, but she goes on till eventually the great wild creature drags himself for the sake of peace and quietness to the gate of her Zoo, and crawls in, a prodigal lion, so to speak, for whom the fatted calf is always ready. Probably he enjoys himself and comes again, and very soon finds that she habitually alludes to him by his Christian name. Sometimes she makes a little mistake over this, and speaks of him as "Harry," in order to convey the sense of intimacy, whereas those who know him best never call him anything but "Henry." This type of lion-hunter, who appears in fiction as well as life from the early days of Charles Dickens onwards, is sometimes an object of derision to the world in general, and in especial to those who feel themselves to be lions, but have not received the distinction of being singled out by her for the chase. They call her a snob and a climber, and very likely she has a touch of that bright tar. But it is merely platitudinous to point out that interesting people are more interesting than uninteresting people, and like every person with brains she prefers the former to talk at her table; if this is snobbishness, it is a very sensible and intelligent quality. She has really little in common with the old crusted Victorian snob who rated merit by precedence and preferred the presence of any Duchess however dreary to that of any Marchioness however amusing.

Lady Jeune, afterwards Lady St Helier, a very catholic and distinguished hostess of the nineties and the succeeding decade, had nothing whatever in common with these ruthless Dianas, nor with the coronet-hunters so pleasantly portrayed by Du Maurier in *Punch* of the period, nor with that amiable class of hostess, chiefly American in origin, whose self-imposed mission is to introduce eminent English persons to each other. The lions in Lady St Helier's case eagerly sought her threshold and purred loudly on admittance. Certainly she liked entertaining them, because an interesting dinner-party was the result, but she never felt that she had scored by getting them, nor murmured fragments of "Nunc

Dimittis" between the courses, nor made pot-shots at their Christian names. Still less was she proud of not being proud of seeing them at her table. That sounds a complicated state of mind, but it was perfectly achieved by the late Mr James Knowles, editor of the *Nineteenth Century*, who once in bidding a friend of mine to dinner wrote, "No party, I only expect the Duke of Argyll and Mr Gladstone." The great antiques came to her house, Tennyson and Huxley and the like, but her particular *flair* was not so much for those who were already monuments, but for those of whom the world was beginning to talk, and who might be described as monuments in the making. She knew all about her guests, too, however undistinguished, and once whispered to a man whom she was about to present to the woman he was taking down to dinner, "Don't allude to railway accidents: her aunt was cut to ribands on the underground." Rarely, but very rarely, was she not quite up to date, for once she leaned across the table to Mr Galsworthy who was sitting isolated between two divergent conversations and said, "We've been talking about plays, Mr Galsworthy. Why don't you write a play? I'm sure you could." It was quite true that he could for the "Silver Box," had come out a week or two before, and we thought that he had already proved it.

Every species of lion, barbarous or tame, flocked to her, cabinet ministers and channel-swimmers, poets and pugilists. Her very maid, she told me, had once sat in the dentist's chair of Dr Crippen, the notorious murderer. He was not a murderer then, but became one soon afterwards: he was a monument in the making. Naturally I was thrilled by the news, and she gave me leave to present myself at the back door and ask for first-hand information about that interesting experience. I much regret the diffidence that deterred me from doing so. Indeed it was said (in illustration of her catholicity) that a certain notable explorer, who had often been a guest of hers, was once making a journey through the territory of a cannibal tribe in Africa, and had the misfortune to be captured by those inhuman folk. They tied him up to a tree, while a message was sent to the cannibal king that there was a juicy young English traveller ready for the royal larder. The King was hungry, and he arrived with all speed to superintend the preparations for the banquet. But the moment he set eyes on the captive, the bright radiance of the gourmet faded out of his face. "Surely we met at Lady St Helier's," he exclaimed in excellent English, "I owe you a thousand apologies for the inconvenience you have suffered. You and I will dine together on the wretch who tied you up. Kill him at once. How is her ladyship ?"

Trovato though the story no doubt is, it is very *ben*, and thus, by means of fiction, conveys fact. She had a real and living interest in the deeds of all sorts and conditions of men, and wanted to know all about them, not from those who could tell her about them, but from themselves. She did not found a salon (that French brand of sociality which, like some native wine, cannot travel and retain its aroma) nor did she attempt to do anything of the sort, for she knew very well that a salon is a specialized form of entertainment, which requires that the circle should consist of homogeneous minds knit together by common interests; it requires also that the hostess should direct and control it. But she preferred a macedoine of many flavours and did not desire to exercise any control. Keen and tremendously alive, she had to a most exceptional degree that quality of a hostess without which all other gifts are nothing worth, namely that she immensely enjoyed her own parties. In that, as in all else, she differed from the lion-hunter, whose feasts while they last are to her matters of the acutest anxiety, and whose questing eye, like the lantern of a conscientious policeman on his rounds, is constantly directed into obscure corners to see that all is well. The lion-hunter, in fact, mostly enjoys her achievement afterwards when she licks her chops. Lady St Helier was more like a guest in her own house, having a most delightful evening.

A hostess of less extensive range whose personality was of a most individual kind was Lady Dorothy Nevill. She was born in the middle twenties, and though of great age in the nineties, retained the most lively memory of an era that seemed even then unutterably antique and aristocratic, an age of post horses and the Grand Tour, before the crinoline came in, when no lady would go to the pit of a theatre (which we now call the stalls), or, if young, be allowed in the streets of London without suitable male escort to protect her against the libertines who were eager to pounce on her. Of these ancient proprieties Lady Dorothy spoke with a demure respect, as if she deplored the laxness of the present day, but all the time she had a little twinkle in her eye, which made her listener wonder whether in her own youth they had appeared quite so sacred to her. Always up to the time of her death, when she was well over eighty years of age, she preserved an indomitable vitality and the keenest interest in current affairs, and always she had little sharp comments on the age she now lived in and so immensely enjoyed, delivered with a directness that surely pre-dated the Victorian conventions as to how young ladies should express themselves, and with a notable absence of final g's and initial h's which was the fashion in the fifties. "Look at the girls nowadays" she would say, "playin' golf in their thumpin' boots with never a veil or a pair of gloves till their skin's like a bit of mahogany veneer. I should think the young men would as soon think of kissin' a kipper. And to make it worse they are beginnin' to dab themselves with lip-salve and muck. I never saw a mess." Her own habit was most consistent with such views, for no-one ever looked less like a kipper or a "mess" than she. She was the daintiest and most exquisite little figure imaginable, never did she stir out of doors without layers of veil to protect her from the kippering effects of sun and wind, and she preserved untouched by unguents or "mess" the complexion of a girl, smooth and soft and unwrinkled. She wore a slightly undulated auburn wig which marvellously

became her, and was like some delicious Kate Greenaway
enchantress who had grown old without ageing. She dressed
in some manner of her own, which it would be idle to try to
identify with that of any epoch: it was very neat and smart,
and somehow coquettish and Quakerish together, and en-
riched with innumerable adornments of amber and amulets
and Egyptian beads. Her Victorianism protested against
the restless way in which so many people left London for the
week-end; there wasn't time for them to unpack their trunks,
she said, before they were off again goodness knew where.
This protest took the practical form of her giving the most
delightful little lunch-parties on Sunday for those of her
friends who shared her views. She lived for ever in Charles
Street, Berkeley Square, and the house was full of ornamental
relics that vastly pre-dated the pincushion to which I have
before referred. Many of these were the work of her hands,
little boxes encrusted with shells, little landscapes constructed,
with incredible patience, from snippets and spirals of coloured
paper, peep shows and kaleidoscopes and examples of that
lost art skeletonized leaves. "You pick your leaves," she
explained, "vine leaves or what not, and put them to soak
in some chemical muck that eats off the green part, but it
can't tackle with ribs and fibres. Then you wash them with a
bit of fixin' in the water, and dry them and set them up in
bouquets. . . Very pretty they used to be reckoned, and
keep a girl out of mischief," she added with a little secret
smile all to herself. . . Then there were ancient sketches
and cartoons of a topical nature, one of which pictured herself young and bewitching sitting lightly on the curve of a
crescent moon. Then was a rope let down to earth from this
lunar throne, and up it were swarming three or four men
in peers' coronets, Disraeli being conspicuous among them
and out-distancing the rest. Then came the secret smile
again. "Some saucy young man drew it and sent it me,"
she said, and one wondered which of those coroneted climbers
was the artist.

Mixed with this Kate Greenaway daintiness, was a dash of a quality that can only be called "gamin." Often it appeared quite unexpectedly and was truly surprising. She told me once how she used to make experiments in food. There were a great many things that made good victuals which were sadly neglected. "Guinea-pig," she said, "there's a tasty dish for you, but it was always a job to make your cook do it. They want bakin' same as the gipsies serve the hedgehogs. I tried eatin' donkey too, but I had to stop that, for it made me stink. . ." Or, again, I had been lunching with her, and had to drive straight from her house to the station to catch my train to Overstand, where I was to stay with Lord Battersea : Lady Dorothy was coming to the same house later in the week. "Give them my love," she said, "and say I'll be down by lunch-time on Thursday, and I shall want a good blow-out of Cromer crab !" I gave the message, and when she appeared there was a dressed crab for her and she duly blew herself out with it. In spite of her principles about week-ends, she often did violence to them, and she and I were once guests together in Helen, Lady Radnor's riverside house at Cookham. Lady Dorothy spent all Sunday afternoon in our hostess's gondola, plying slowly up and down the reach of the river above Boulter's Lock, deeply interested in the intimate relations rapidly ripening between the couples in punts below the trees of the Clieveden woods, and occasionally saying to Lady Radnor who was some twenty years her junior, "When we get to our age, my dear, we mustn't be shocked at anything." On Monday morning the carriage was ordered to take her to the station, but she would have none of it. "There'll have to be a cab as well for my maid and my luggage," she explained, "and I shall have to tip the coachman and then go searchin' for my maid. Pop into your cab with your maid and your luggage, I say, and have done with it !" Though kippered faces and the restless modern ways of Londoners provoked her scorn, she thoroughly approved of modern conveniences, and when motors came in, liked nothing better than a drive in one as fast as the car would go. With the arts, save those of paper landscapes and skeletonized leaves, she had little sympathy, and with music none at all. One evening at that same house on the Norfolk coast, where she had her blow-out of crab, there came to dine with us that very excellent violinist Lady Speyer, who had an exotic villa close by, and she played divinely to us afterwards. Lady Dorothy found the noise rather distracting: she could not give her full attention to her game of Patience while it was going on, and when Bach's "Chaconne" or something of the same monumental sort was over, she said to me in a discreet aside, "My dear, I 'ate that scratchin' sound." Walpole by birth and Nevill by marriage (and rather enjoying these distinguished ties) there was not about her the smallest trait of the Victorian great lady. But Puck, with all his charm and something of his mischief, must surely have been amongst her ancestors, and no-one could have been surprised if, looking out at night onto a moonlit lawn, he had seen Lady Dorothy daintily footing a fairy ring to the admiration of the surrounding fays.

Romance is a bird that will not sing in every bush, and love-affairs, however devoted the sentiments that inspire them, are often so business-like in the prudence with which they are conducted that romance is reduced to a mere croaking or a disgusted silence. But some of these Victorian ladies could make it sing surprising (though most regrettable) melodies. There were, for instance, in the nineties a man and woman whose history contained some very tuneful passages. He was a prominent public servant of his country, had been abroad on a difficult mission and conducted it with so gay and impudent a success that his chief, on its conclusion, telegraphed to him the message, "England thanks you." He came home soon after, and instead of going to his wife's house, went straight, by arrangement, to that of his lady. She had filled her husband's house with a large party to welcome him, but the boat-train was very late, he missed his connection in London, and the party sat down to dinner, where his vacant place, next hers, awaited him. She had given instructions to her butler to tell her and her alone, when his carriage was seen approaching, and in the middle of dinner he said something quietly to her and she got up. Without a word to anyone she radiantly passed out through the door of the dining-room and locked it behind her, so that the butler who attempted to follow and receive the late-comer was, like the rest of the party, confined to the dining-room. So, alone, and without the possibility of interruption, she welcomed her lover on the threshold. Then when the first rapture of their meeting was over, she led him back, unlocked the dining-room door, and entered with him. He had much to tell them all, and the hot summer night was dark before dinner was done. Long windows opened on to the terrace outside, and now she said that they would all have their coffee there. They seated themselves, and she clapped her hands, and above the lawn in huge letters out-lined in rows of electric lights, there flamed out the words, "England thanks you."

AMONG the vanished and irrecoverable figures of the Victorian age, there were none who more thoroughly enjoyed and contributed to the sunshine of that social pageantry which (momentarily clouded by the South African war) lasted up to its fatal and final eclipse in 1914, than Mr Harry Chaplin, created Viscount Chaplin, and his sister Helen, Countess of Radnor. He was of a type that has never existed anywhere except in England, and will never exist there again, and he might have sat, body and mind alike, for a national statue of John Bull. His father, rector of a parish near Stamford in Lincolnshire, died while he was a boy not yet in his teens, and he was brought up at Blankney, the family place, by his uncle, his father's elder brother. The "old Squire" died childless, when Harry Chaplin was still at Oxford, and he then inherited a very large property, chiefly of wheat-bearing acres, and the tradition of the English country Squire, in whose veins ran the robust yeoman blood. Many decades of wholesome rural life, of suitable substantial marriages, and of uncomplicated mental processes had gone to the making of the type, and some of its representatives had grown to be large and very wealthy landowners, exercising in their own territories a benevolent but unquestioned autocracy; Tom Coke of Norfolk, whose descendants are Earls of Leicester, was, in an earlier generation, of that vanished breed.

Many of them had never crossed the Channel and were quite sure that no foreigner could ever be trusted, and that outside England there was nothing fit to eat. They were the aristocracy of the class which Queen Victoria had so early recognized to be the new ruling class in England. They controlled the local Parliamentary elections, of course in the Tory interest, and their tenants as a matter of course voted according to the Squire's views; the prosperity of their leased farms was their personal concern, farming their business, and their diversions manly and rural. Hunting, horses and hounds, and all that horse-breeding stood for, were their occupations in the winter, when the land was asleep, and in the autumn, when the harvest was gathered, shooting over the high stubbles not yet cropped close by American machinery, where the big coveys of partridges could be walked up. Rural districts were then rural indeed, the railway was still far from Blankney, much of the land fenny and undrained, and Lady Radnor, who, when quite a young girl, kept house for her brother when he came of age and opened Blankney again, has often told me of those days. To the ornithological mind nothing will convey their remoteness better than her story of how, when there was no shooting going on from the Hall, the keeper would come in of a morning to see if there was any particular bird she would like for the Squire's table. She thought perhaps that half a dozen ruffs and reeves would make a pleasant course, for there was abundance of them on the marshy meadows, and the Squire was fond of a fat ruff.

But the young Squire, who, on coming of age, found himself the owner of so fine an inheritance, was not content with the old order under which his forefathers had prospered. He had been the contemporary and friend of the Prince of Wales at Oxford, he had lived there in the best style of Ouida's young guardsmen, so numerous had been the hunters he kept, so benevolent his neutrality towards the authorities of the University, and he had no notion of settling down at Blankney in the manner of the older generation. Besides, he was personally of the type known seventy-five years ago as a "magnifico." Young and handsome and rich, with an unrivalled appetite for splendid pleasures, and with a host of friends, not country neighbours alone, but the smart young people of Clubland and Mayfair, he sought to combine the rôle of country Squire with that of the big landowner on more modern lines. He entertained great parties at Blankney, he had his coach and four, he had his own two packs of hounds, so that he and his friends could hunt six days in the week; he took a house in Lincoln in order to be nearer the centre of the Burton country, and while thus more than maintaining the fox-hunting tradition of the Squire, he started a racing stud as well, and by way of making a good beginning he bought a couple of three-year-olds for the sum, absolutely unheard of in those days, of eleven thousand guineas. A deer forest in Scotland was of course a necessity to a magnifico, and though he still often resided at Blankney, it became a modern country house filled, when he was there, with troops of his friends from outside, for whom he provided sport and hunting, but it was empty for long months together while the Squire was in London or in Scotland, or at the race meetings he so sedulously attended. He never dreamed of stinting himself of any pleasure which money could procure and his purse was equally wide-mouthed for the entertainment of those with similar tastes.

He had fallen in love at the age of twenty-four with Lady Florence Paget, known as the "Pocket Venus" and had become engaged to her. The date for the marriage had been fixed and was imminent, presents had poured in, Blankney was ready for the reception of the bride. A few days before the appointed date, Lady Florence went out one morning to do some shopping. She went into Marshall and Snelgrove's by a minor entrance, passed through the shop and came out at the Oxford Street door, where the Marquis of Hastings was waiting for her with a cab and a license, and they were married. She had come to the conclusion at the very last moment that she could not face the fulfilment of her promise and the experience must have been horribly humiliating for Mr Chaplin. The lady made a very poor exchange, for Lord Hastings did not afford her much happiness, while Mr Chaplin made, some ten years later, one of the happiest marriages it is possible to conceive, with Lady Florence Leveson-Gower. It was entirely characteristic of him that not only did he subsequently befriend the woman who had treated him thus, but also behaved with extraordinary kindness to Lord Hastings himself. The story concerns one of the most exciting episodes in the history of the turf.

Mr Chaplin and Lord Hastings had already been in rivalry over racing, when this business occurred, and Lord Hastings now consistently ran horses and betted against those of Mr Chaplin's stable. His conduct was an instance of that well-established piece of psychology, that there is a strong tendency in human nature to hate those whom we have injured. In 1865 Mr Chaplin had brought a colt called Hermit, and had entered him for the Derby of 1867. It was sufficient for Lord Hastings that the horse belonged to Mr Chaplin, and he bet heavily against him. A fortnight before the race Hermit, in his training quarters at Newmarket, was given a "Derby trial," that is to say a full gallop over a course of that length, and had a severe hæmorrhage apparently from the lungs. It thus seemed quite impossible that he could run in the Derby at all, but it was decided not to scratch him. During the next week it became clear that there was nothing very wrong with the horse after all: there was no recurrence of the hæmorrhage, and it looked as if it had come merely from some blood-vessel in the throat. Hermit had a few fast canters and seemed fit. Accordingly he was sent down to Epsom and put in some good work there. The news of his mishap, of course, had become known, and the betting against him on the day of the race was 66 to 1. Mr Chaplin believed in the horse and in his trainer's opinion about him and continued to back him: Lord Hastings continued to bet against him. There came a cold spell of weather that year in the last fortnight of May, and Derby Day was an affair of furs and thick coats. Hermit had a thick coat too, for he had not been clipped and the small interest he excited in the Paddock was chiefly derisive. After the horses had gone down to the post, a storm of snow and sleet swept across the course, obscuring any distant view from the stands. After a long delay they came streaming up the course, and it was seen that Hermit and Marksman were desperately racing for the first place. Hermit won by a neck, his owner cleared somewhere about £140,000 and Lord Hastings had lost £120,000; £80,000 of this was due to Mr Chaplin who might of course have insisted on immediate payment. Instead of pressing him he waited for several months and eventually the debt was discharged.

Derby Day 1867 must have been the greatest day of Mr Chaplin's life; he had won the Blue Riband at the age of twenty-six: he was young, he was rich, he was popular and he had an absolutely unique power of enjoying himself. He raced, he shot, he hunted, he warmed both hands at the numerous fires of life, and from them both he scattered money as if Pactolus flowed through the park at Blankney, for where was the use of money except to secure a good time for himself and his friends? He entered Parliament, he made an exceedingly happy marriage, and if the value of agricultural land and the price of home-grown wheat went down, it would surely go up again: something would happen. Something unfortunately did happen, his rents dwindled, his expenditure remained firm and steady, and Blankney already burdened by mortgage passed into other hands. Never again, it is safe to prophesy, can the conditions in which Mr Chaplin entered his inheritance at Blankney be revived. In his own instance, he broke it himself, for never before had the Squire of Blankney attempted to play the double rôle of Squire and man of the world. If we come to think of it, the two are in their very nature incompatible, for the essence of Squirearchy, as he received it, was rural life (with gaieties no doubt at the county town, hunt balls and what not, and a few weeks in London) and continuous sojourn on the estate, identification of himself with the interests and concerns of his tenants in all matters of sport and agriculture, and for reward a local and ancestral autocracy. The great popular figure that Mr Chaplin cut in London and at race-meetings, even if an unlimited purse had been his, could not have been played by one of the old Squires, for it entailed too long absences from his local kingdom, and implied too prolonged immersions in affairs outside it. Wealth and land inherited from a long succession of ancestors are not in themselves enough to constitute it, and though the great nobleman with half a dozen inherited houses and political duties in London for half the year, may be an admirable landlord and a pillar of national stability, he is no more a Squire than is the brewer who buys his great places from him and reads the lessons in church of a Sunday morning. In fact Mr Harry (as he was universally called) had ceased to be Squire of Blankney in the real sense of the word long before Blankney ceased to be his. All over England in the sixties the same thing was going on. The spread of railways provided swifter and cheaper locomotion than posting, dwellers in the country began to move about more, and life generally to be centralized in towns. The break-up of Squirearchy must be considered part of the general break-up of Victorian traditions.

BUT none of the blows of fate, the elopement of Lady Florence Paget, the death of his wife to whom he was devotedly attached, the loss of money, the loss of Blankney, the acquisition of gout, ever dimmed Mr Harry's zest for life which made him so remarkable a personage. There were a number of very pleasant things left and vastly he enjoyed them all. His wife had been the sister of the Duke of Sutherland, and now when Blankney was no more, and he a widower, Stafford House and Dunrobin and Lillieshall became home for himself and his children. His sister was now Countess of Radnor, his daughter was soon to marry Lord Castlereagh, and such relations and all his innumerable friends were warm in hospitality to him who had so bounteously dispensed it. Racing, though there were no more Hermits, nor purchasings of colts at six thousand guineas, was every atom as fine a sport as he had found it before, so too was hunting, though not with his own packs of hounds, and every day he took the very keenest interest in his dinner, combining, which is rather rare, the capacity of the *gourmand* with the trained appreciation of the *gourmet*. He placed high among the pleasures of the table, as every true *gourmet* does, victuals of plain perfection. Lady Radnor and he and I were once strolling after lunch on Sunday in her kitchen-garden at Cookham, and he observed a fine row of broad beans. "My dear," he said to her, "those look excellent beans. Do tell your gardener to send some into the house and let us have beans and bacon for dinner. There's nothing in the world so good." The gardener was off duty, as it was Sunday afternoon, but she said that if he cared to pick them and bring them to the house, he should have his dish. So off came his hat, and we filled it with the bean-pods, and carried it in triumph to the cook, and Mr Harry said he would have beans and bacon for dinner, and nothing else whatever; he

could not imagine a more delicious dinner. But then the
gourmet had a word to say to that, for when dinner-time
came, he first refused soup, but then discovered that it had
the most attractive aroma, and said he would just have "a
spoonful of soup," which meant an ordinary helping for a
grown man. Some fish was then placed before him, and he
ate his fish in an absent-minded manner, almost mournfully
in fact, for it was salmon, and it reminded him of a heavy
fish he had lost on the Brora. Then, so suitably for this
hot evening, there was some cold pressed beef (for he remembered how excellent his sister's pressed beef always was)
and a mouthful of chicken. Then naturally he must eat the
beans and bacon which had been provided specially for him,
and so he had two helpings of them and said he had never
tasted such excellent beans and the bacon was very good too.
Where did she get it ? . . . A very pleasant custom of his, if
the dish was remarkable and he made a second attack on it,
was to put a sovereign on the edge of it, to be given, with his
compliments to the cook. Dinner was a serious matter demanding his entire attention: his neighbour in the middle
of that function, alluding to the famous *boiseries* of the
dining-room where they were sitting once said to him, "What
beautiful carving !" And naturally he replied, "Yes, the
service is always very good in this house."

Now anyone who thinks that a vivid appreciation of the
exquisite flavours of wine and food implies greed, is the
victim of confused thinking. Taste is one of the five senses,
and the man who tells us with priggish pride that he does
not care what he eats is merely boasting of his sad deficiency:
he might as well be proud of being deaf or blind, or, owing
to a perpetual cold in the head, of being devoid of the sense
of smell. There is no reason to suppose that taste is in
any way a lower sense than the other four; a fine palate is
as much a gift as an eye that discerns beauty or an ear
that appreciates and enjoys subtle harmonies of sound, and
we are quite right to value the pleasures that all our senses

give us and educate their perceptions. The greedy man is he who habitually eats too much, knowing that he is injuring his bodily health thereby, and this is a vice to which not the *gourmet* but the *gourmand* is a slave. But Mr Harry, though he undoubtedly was a *gourmand* also, and ate prodigious quantities of food, could not, so admirable was his digestion, and so well large masses of solid food suited him, be called greedy at all. He had a noble and healthy appetite *le foie du charbonnier*, and as he once observed with a very proper satisfaction, "I should like to see my stomach disagree with anything I choose to give it." Indeed his confidence in that superb organ was well founded, for never was a man more faithfully served. He was anxious also that others to the best of their punier capacities should enjoy like delights: he observed, for instance, when he and I were both dining one night at a highly gastronomic table, that I was not partaking of some particular dish, and held up an admonitory finger to me. "You oughtn't to pass that," he said, "they do it very well here."

Over seventy at the outbreak of the European war and enormously corpulent, he thought that he could still do a day in the saddle, and wondered whether he might not be able to manage the duties of a dispatch-bearer at the front. But those days were over for him, and, as if he knew that the old order was over also, he accepted a Viscountcy which he might have had if he had wanted it sixteen years before in 1900. He had sat in Parliament for close on fifty years and had twice been in the Cabinet as Minister for Agriculture and as President of the Local Government Board. These were high distinctions, but it is not they which make him so memorable a figure, nor yet that no man ever more solidly earned his peerage, but because he was among the last of a type that will never be seen again.

When raised to the peerage he had to choose supporters for his coat of arms, and instantly he thought of his racing days, and said that he would have Hermit. In due time the design came back from the Heralds' College for his approval, and there was the conventional heraldic quadruped, something between a dragon and a dachshund, instead of a striking portrait of his Derby winner. "But it's not an atom like the horse," he indignantly exclaimed, and routed out an old picture of Hermit to show them how they had mishandled him.

His sister, Lady Radnor, passed her girlhood in the same tradition of field-sports and Squirearchy, and covered, with a zest equal to his, a far greater range of interests. She was really musical in the sense that music was to her not merely a pleasure but a need; she had a soprano voice of remarkable beauty and power, which she preserved, owing to the excellent training which it had received, till late in life, and it was of a quality, when it was at its prime, which would undoubtedly have placed her high in the ranks of professional singers. Her voice and her real gift for music she put to far wider uses than Victorian performances at the piano after dinner, and, breaking through the conventions of the day, she appeared on such platforms as the St James's Hall and the Albert Hall in aid of charities. Then too, she organized a string band of girls, daughters chiefly of friends and relations, to which she added a chorus of women's voices, and from 1881 for fifteen years, first as Lady Folkestone and then as Lady Radnor, she gave annual public concerts in St James's Hall, training her band and voices herself, and herself conducting. The scheme with all the work and organization it implied was completely her own, and in the early eighties it was, for a woman in her position, revolutionary of the current Victorian conventions to a degree which it is now almost impossible to grasp, and for any woman at any time a remarkable achievement. The performers were all of her own class of life, the women appeared in their best gowns and jewels, and the concerts were of high artistic merit. For one of the last of the series, when her singers had grown into a choir of a hundred and twenty voices and

her band numbered over eighty instruments, Sir Hubert
Parry wrote his suite for strings in F major, one of the most
English and melodious of all his compositions, which con-
firms his direct musical descent from Purcell; and he, Arthur
Sullivan and Barnby, who from time to time assisted her,
treated her not as an amateur of the fashionable world with
a hobby, but as a serious musician. She neither possessed
nor professed profound technical knowledge, and never attempted music which she did not thoroughly understand, but
she had immense enthusiasm, a wonderful voice, and, as a
conductor, that particular imagination which makes the performers realize the tone and the quality wanted from them.
Musically she was never a pioneer: she did not quickly grasp
new ideas, and she came out, as she told me, from the concert
at the Albert Hall at which Wagner, on his visit to England
in 1877, conducted his own work, with the registered resolve
that if this was the new music, the old was better. But in
course of time Wagner ceased to be the new music, and a
visit to Baireuth made her quite suddenly the most fervent
of converts. Strauss she never arrived at, nor yet Debussy;
the one to her way of thinking dealt in unpleasant crashes of
noise, the other in tinklings. But knowing that she did not
appreciate, she was aware that this might be because she did
not understand, and never in musical matters did she fall
into such abysses as some of the most enlightened critics
have tripped into. One of these, and he the most authoritative of his time, described in an astonishing article how,
wounded and outraged from his first hearing of Strauss's
"Salome," he hurried home with acute oral indigestion, and,
in order to get these monstrous dissonances out of his system,
he stretched his hands to the uttermost, and, with the loud
pedal of his piano firmly trodden on, played the completest
chord of C Major that his fingers could compass. It seemed
that the great man had failed to notice that the last chord
in the dissonant affair, proclaimed by the entire band, was
precisely that for which he had hurried home. . . Lady Rad-

nor never indulged in such ludicrous Jeremiads; instead, with a wiser sincerity, she enjoyed all that was to her mind, said she did not understand the rest, and retained a perfectly frank admiration for the Lost-Chord-music of Victorian taste and for melodies that gave rise to tears.

Horses and sport and material splendour as well as music were in her blood: she was a great rider to hounds, and when her riding days were passing, she had a marvellous pair of high-stepping ponies which Mr Harry had given her, which she drove herself in London. Behind her was seated the smallest "tiger" ever seen, and she always gloried in the fact that her turn-out was just a shade smarter than that of anybody else. So, too, when her husband succeeded, she rejoiced in the magnificence of Longford Castle, its gardens, its chapel, and most of all in its wealth of incomparable pictures finer, before the American millionaire began to buy, than any collection outside royal or public galleries. Of these she compiled a very noble catalogue, tracing the history of them, invoking professional aid for the identification of doubtful ascriptions and from rummaging among ancient account-books of the estate, finding the prices that were paid in the purchase of now priceless masterpieces. The unequalled "Erasmus" by Holbein, for instance, was bought about the year 1750, for £110, and "Egidius" by the same painter for £95. Three of these pictures were sold to the nation soon after her husband succeeded to the Earldom, and now are in the National Gallery: "Il Homo" by Morelli, the "Admiral" by Velasquez, and the "Ambassadors" by Holbein. One of the Ambassadors in this picture, it may be remembered, holds in his hand a small scroll of music. It is upside down from the observer's point of view, and before it left Longford, Lady Radnor had the picture turned about and identified the notes with a sixteenth-century melody. In the centre of the foreground is a strange slanting object, difficult to recognize, and yet evidently an important feature in the picture. But if looked at from below and close to

the canvas, the foreshortening makes it clear that it repre-
sents a skull. The inference that it is to be construed
into a canting signature of the painter ("Hohle Beine," or
hollow bone) has much to recommend it. For these three
pictures in 1890 the National Gallery paid £55,000 which
was then reckoned a large price. Today, in the open market,
not one of these would be purchasable at that figure.

But far more fundamental in Lady Radnor than all these
tastes and decorations, was her profound religious sense,
which was truly childlike in its gay, unquestioning simplicity.
Among the avenues of approach to the eternal mysteries of
life and death, spiritualism to her mind, ran open and
broad and straight. One of her greatest friends was Miss
Katie Wingfield, who was certainly possessed of remarkable mediumistic powers, and, with her as medium, frequent
séances were held at Longford, and very curious manifestations seem to have taken place, levitations, direct voice, correct answers given by the medium in automatic script to
questions of which she could have had no normal knowledge.
Men like Sir Oliver Lodge, eminent in the world of science
and physics, and Societies like the Psychical Research have
since then devoted their study to occult phenomena, and
much which thirty years ago was believed by spiritualists
to be supernatural and by sensible men (with no nonsense
about them) to be the result of trickery on the part of the
medium and credulity on the part of the sitters, has been
thoroughly tested, and has been brought into the domain of
obscure but well ascertained laws: it is no longer possible even
for men with no nonsense about them to deride telepathy and
all the dim unspoken commerce between the minds of living
folk, as charlatanry and credulity. But, on the other hand,
those who have studied these phenomena believe, and indeed
have proved, that most of them are not due to the inter-
vention of discarnate intelligences, but are in accordance
with natural laws. Thus the limits of what used to be thought
supernatural have been narrowed, and the sphere of natural

law extended, though the most thoroughly scientific investigators affirm that phenomena do occur for which no explanation can be found except that of the agency of spirits now no longer on the plane of material things. At the same time they have rightly insisted on a very strict control of the medium before these manifestations can be accepted as genuine. Such tests and such investigations, in order to see whether some at least of these phenomena were not more rightly to be classed among the now known workings of natural though obscure laws, were not made at these Longford séances: the circle was that of a party of friends experimenting among themselves, and all were disposed to accept a supernatural source for these manifestations, rather than to reject such if a natural law (such as telepathy) could account for them. The manifestations in fact, were not produced under test conditions, nor were there skilled independent observers watching. The circle as a whole believed that supernatural powers, guides and personal protectors were present, and the phenomena were accepted as proof of it. But Miss Katie Wingfield was certainly possessed of those abnormal powers which we call mediumistic, and doubtless produced phenomena for which no explanations of natural law, as then known, would account. Under test conditions these séances might have been of real scientific value.

These guides in whose active aid in the affairs of every day Lady Radnor firmly believed, were not by any means wholly solemn spirits bent on edification, or superior to the minor trials of human life, nor did the sitters regard them as other than personal friends, who lived on a plane of existence different from theirs but closely connected with it. On one occasion, so she told me with gusts of laughter, a member of the circle was suffering from internal bodily aches in the usual region, and was extremely uncomfortable during the séance. That night the direct voice of some control was being heard, and the manner of procedure was that each member of the circle in turn wrote down (with due precautions so that none present could see the inquiry) a question to which, it was hoped, the direct voice of the control would give an answer: the piece of paper on which this question was written was folded up and placed securely under a candlestick in the middle of the table. When it came to the sufferer's turn, he, full of material woes, and not feeling on at all a high plane, wrote down: "What shall I do to get rid of my stomach-ache?" After a pause the direct voice from a corner of the room (quite away from the medium) answered in deeply impressive tones, "Put some flannel round your stomach." This most sensible suggestion on the part of the disembodied spirit caused the circle to laugh itself into dissolution.

THIS intense, wholly natural and uncritical belief of Lady Radnor's that close round her were intelligences, kind and beneficent, active to protect and eager to bestow, combined with her equally intense enjoyment of the beautiful and jolly things of the world, made up a personality of wonderful quality; never have I known one so beaming with general sunshine. Admirable as were to her the pleasures of this life, they were nothing compared to those that were coming, but in the interval it was her business richly to enjoy. Quite deliberately, though in no way from lack of tenderness, she turned away from things painful and distressing, for she knew that powers wise and gracious were looking after her personally, and it was very ungrateful not to respond by being happy. She made it her duty to be happy, and strenuously performed it, banishing from her mind all that stood in its way, her own worries included. She had no great intellectual grip: ethical problems and abstract speculations necessitating close argument set no machinery at work in her mind. She judged genially and broadly, by feeling far more than by logic, and was a Tory of the most convinced school; in her heart I am sure that she knew that God was a Tory, too. She had all the vitality of Mr Harry, and when on the death of her husband, to whom she was utterly devoted, Longford and its spaciousness passed from her, she built up for herself a new life different in scale and scope, with no diminution of her sunlight. She took the *piano nobile* in the Palazzo da Mula in Venice, and spent some six months of the year there. Her past activities, though now less exuberant, blossomed again there like autumn roses, and, just as before she had organized and carried through those concerts at St James's Hall, so now she took in hand the music of the English Church in Venice: she compiled a hymn-book for use there, she formed a glee-club that met weekly at her house; just as before her high-stepping ponies were the smartest things in London, so here her gondola was the best turned out on the Grand Canal. She bought a plot of land on the Giudecca, and out of a dust heap of shards made a Paradise of blossom and fragrance. Her life thus repeated in its diminished scale the old hospitalities and dignities and to it she brought undimmed the enthusiasms and eagernesses of her earlier days.

Physical infirmities increased: she could no longer manage the journeys to Venice, and the year before the outbreak of the European War, she gave up also her house in London and that on the Thames at Cookham, and settled down for the rest of her life near Ascot. Grandchildren and great grandchildren multiplied, and though her visits to London and to the houses of relations grew fewer and fewer, she never lost touch with the doings of the world in which she no longer took any part. But though she was still keen and alive to all the interests of her friends, she began herself to live much more in memories, and to those who loved to spend quiet days with her she talked of hunting-fields and royal visits, and séances and her days of song. Many years before, her husband had been the first president of the Anglo-Israelitish Association, and from that time onwards, and increasingly so as her activities grew more and more limited, she studied the books and pamphlets on the subject of the identification of the Anglo-Saxon races with the Lost Tribes of Israel. She took a busy part in the work, serving on its committees, and writing leaflets and pamphlets for its propagation. Then one day when I was in London I received a message from her that she had come up and would like to see me. She was cheerful and quite herself as we talked for a while, and then she said, "Now, my dear, I've got bad news," and she told me how she had been to see her doctor and that the most terrible of all physical sentences had been passed on her. They did not advise an operation but there was other treatment which she would go through. And then with all her old interest she said: "That's all: now tell me what you've been doing. And when will you come down to Ascot for a week-end ?"

Movement on her feet which had long been painful and difficult became impossible, and she descended in the lift from her bedroom, and was wheeled to the side of the big armchair in the window of her sitting-room, where she could see the tits swinging in the split cocoanuts hung outside, or sometimes she would be wheeled out on to the stoep overlooking her garden. With her table in front of her, she wrote letters in her beautiful firm hand, she read the paper, she read new books that were recommended to her, and above all she searched her Bible for more evidence on the subject that so occupied her. She loved long quiet talks with friends and relations and laughter and tales of amusing and absurd happenings, and to be with her was to sit in the sun.

CHAPTER XIII

THE MOVEMENT OF THE NINETIES

THERE has lately been a considerable amount of interest exhibited in what is known as "the literary movement" of the nineties, and it was indeed time that the contemptuous neglect into which it had fallen should be mended. But its chroniclers have found themselves much beset by the temptation to classify, and seem to have swept together into a group certain poets, artists and prose-writers who had really very little in common with each other as regards either aims or method. This habit of classification certainly makes for neatness, and is a favourite device of the writer who passes a period in review. He sets up a frame-work or skeleton which he calls "Underlying Purpose" and proceeds to plaster on to it in the manner of a sculptor building up his clay model with masses of sinew and muscle, a quantity of contemporary names of literary and artistic folk. But the result is not always happy when he essays to breathe the spirit of life into his image. Its movements lack an internal controlling mind and co-ordinated impulses, and it is really more like a marionette with limbs imperfectly obedient to the strings which the accomplished gentleman behind the scenes is pulling.

This particular "literary movement" of the nineties is an example of marionette-making and the desire to classify and define has proved a snare to the industrious chronicler rather than a guide to his students. He bids us ("Observe, ladies and gentlemen !") notice the symptoms of revolt against Victorian conventions; but under his efforts to make his figures dance, one arm jerks galvanically, the head turns, but the lips remain cataleptic. There is neither unity nor inherent life in his image, for, as a matter of fact, the revolt against Victorian conventions and reticences which is supposed to animate it had already taken place and had long ago been completely successful.

Miss Rhoda Broughton was well aware of that. She told me once that for nearly fifty years she had been busily writing exactly the same sort of novel. When she began writing, her books were deemed to be very risky, she was thought to be of the breed of Zola, and no well brought-up girl was allowed to read them. But now, though her novels were just the same as they had always been, she was considered of the breed of Miss Yonge, and well brought-up girls were strongly urged to read them by their mammas, because they were so thoroughly nice. But the girls thought so too, and could not get far in them. (Upon which, in parenthesis Howard Sturgis observed, "When she was young she was Zola, and now she's Zola [older] she's Yonge.")

Before the dawn even of the nineties, the old idols had been quite toppled over, and the attempt to demonstrate that there was now marching out of the premises of the Bodley Head under the flying flag of *The Yellow Book* a band of April-eyed young brothers singing revolutionary ditties and bent on iconoclasm is disastrous to any clear conception of what was actually going on. Aubrey Beardsley, we are told, the greatest of them all, was the artist of the corps of rebels, Oscar Wilde was its dramatist, Arthur Symons, Ernest Dowson, Lionel Johnson, Richard Le Gallienne its poets, Max Beerbohm and Hubert Crackenthorpe its prose writers. Arthur Symons was also its critic and Aubrey Beardsley was not only its typical and supreme artist, but poet and prose-writer in the same ranks. The banner of *The Yellow Book* went on before.

Now the confusions and misconceptions resulting from such a classified arrangement are numerous and profound. For, to begin with, if these rebels (of a rising already successfully accomplished) were marching under the flag of *The*

Yellow Book, they marched under false colours, for *The Yellow Book,* an interesting illustrated quarterly the first number of which appeared in April 1894, so far from being a revolutionary gazette was a respectable, almost high-brow organ, and its contributors (leaving Aubrey Beardsley aside for the moment) were for the most part persons of recognized standing and were no more rebels against Victorian conventions than the Queen herself. In the first four numbers, which, as we shall see, were the only ones which counted, there were pictures by Walter Crane, Wilson Steer, John Sargent, Charles Furse, Joseph Pennell, and above all, Sir Frederick Leighton, President of the Royal Academy, who, incidentally, had the greatest admiration for Beardsley's work. In the letter-press there were two most substantial stories by Henry James, namely "The Death of the Lion," which opened the first number, and "The Coxon Fund," while Miss Hepworth Dixon, Dr Richard Garnett, George Saintsbury, John Oliver Hobbes (with George Moore as her collaborator) contributed stories, articles, and dramatic sketches, José Maria de Heredia (of the French Academy), Edmund Gosse, William Watson, Theo Marzials, dear to the heart of all true Victorians by reason of his song "The Summer Shower," were among its bards; but as for Oscar Wilde who has been gazetted as the official dramatist of the group, it is sufficient to state that he never published a single line of verse or prose in *The Yellow Book* at all, nor was he in any sense a revolutionary dramatist, but of the Sheridan school. Apart from a poem by Arthur Symons called "Stella Maris," which Mr Philip Hamerton found very grievous and profane, it is really impossible to find in these first four numbers of the magazine a single piece that could possibly shock the moral or artistic susceptibilities of that or any other day, or a single sign that these distinguished contributors intended to do so. Max Beerbohm, it is true, wrote in the first number "A Defence of Cosmetics" which earned him some startling maledictions, but he explained in the second number that it was not meant to be taken seriously and pointed out the joke. Most of these authors had wit and graceful diction, but there was not one bubble of revolutionary ferment among them all.

But then there was Aubrey Beardsley, and his work remains to this day as individual and apart from that of all subsequent artists as it was then from those of his period. Instead of being the principal figure in a group of the like-minded, he was unallied to any of the contributors to *The Yellow Book*, and, after four numbers of it had appeared, the editor and publisher showed how little they were prepared to risk for the one feature of the magazine which indeed was startlingly novel. The editor was Henry Harland, best known as the author of an excellently written romantic sentimentality called "The Cardinal's Snuff-box," and the publisher was John Lane, whose enterprise on behalf of new and startling talent was tempered with sound business instincts: he had no objection, that is to say, to thin ice, provided he felt reasonably sure that it would not let him through. William Watson, one of *The Yellow Book* bards, and of high reputation in the nineties, now sent these two an ultimatum, and told them that his poems should not appear between the same covers as those which carried and contained Beardsley's designs. It was up to them to choose, and after consultation they chose Watson and safety. The fifth number of *The Yellow Book* containing more of Beardsley's work was already in the press, but it was withdrawn and Beardsley's connection with it was severed. Arthur Symons left it also, and in the next year he started a new magazine called *The Savoy* of which eight numbers were issued. He himself, Ernest Dowson, George Moore, and Bernard Shaw were among those who contributed to it, and these are very distinguished names. But as regards *The Savoy*, none of them really counted at all, in spite of the excellence of their work. *The Savoy* was admittedly Beardsley's organ.

Admirable stuff appeared in it, for Symons had a very fine critical taste, and *The Savoy* represented a definite point of

view which was his, whereas *The Yellow Book* had no point of
view at all.   But it was only significant because of Beardsley's work, and the public subscribed to it (though very
meagrely as soon appeared) for that reason.   There were
published in it not only his drawings, but poems by him and
two long and wholly amazing instalments of a story from his
pen called "Under the Hill" which he also illustrated.   Of
this it may be said that no prose-writer of that day or perhaps
of any other could have written a letter-press to which the
drawings were so completely appropriate and no artist but
he could have illustrated the story.   Picture and press echo
each other like the voices of a fugue, and both reek of that
fascinating and evil suggestiveness of which the nineties considered him so skilled an exponent.   He wrote further chap-
ters of it, but his health was already far gone in its final
decline, and for that reason, as well as perhaps for others, no
further instalment of it appeared in the six subsequent issues
of *The Savoy* which from that time was published monthly
and then, from want of support, expired.   His poems with
accompanying illustrations by him were "The Three Musi-
cians" (only to be described as "naughty") and "The Ballad
of the Barber": there was also a masterly translation of
Catullus's ode "*Ave atque vale.*"   Without seeking to de-
preciate in any degree the value of the rest of the contents of
The Savoy, of which the last number was entirely written by
Arthur Symons and entirely illustrated by Beardsley, there
was nothing very distinctive about them.   In this last
number the editor promised a future revival of the magazine,
but nothing further appeared, for Beardsley died, and the
sap of it was gone.   He had been the *clou* of *The Yellow
Book*, for after he ceased to draw for it, it turned grey, as was
remarked at the time, in a single night, though it lingered
on, feeble and quite respectable, for nine issues more, and
The Savoy died with him.   In a word he had been the life of
them both.

These two magazines have since then been taken as having

constituted the organs of the "literary movement" of the nineties, but for the foregoing reasons I think this is an entirely mistaken view. Moreover, their contents disclose no evidence of the existence of any kind of concerted movement, like that of the pre-Raphaelites, nor were those who are now classed as a school, bound together, as the pre-Raphaelites were, by the common aim of revolt against convention. Those painters, with affiliated members of identical aims in other arts, like William Morris and Swinburne, were consciously fighting conventions as definitely stated in their creed, but this literary movement had no such foes to contend against, for Victorianism was already dead and buried, and nobody was concerned to meddle with what was already decaying so nicely. The movement had neither crusading aspirations nor an inspiring aim, and at the time nobody thought of it as a school or even a movement. The interest in the two magazines (and that a very limited one) was due to the fact that Beardsley's drawings appeared in them.

It is, however, perfectly true that in this period there were published a remarkable number of poems which now, after the lapse of more than thirty years retain the freshness of true classics. There was Lionel Johnson's poem "A friend" which appeared, I think, first in an Oxford undergraduate magazine called *The Spirit Lamp*, there was Ernest Dowson's "Cynara," there were sonnets by Lord Alfred Douglas, and the "Anthology of the Nineties," lately collected by Mr A. J. A. Symons, proves how remarkable in that decade was the output of poetry which is undated by any mannerisms or artificiality. Lionel Johnson's work in particular might have been that of some Elizabethan singer, for the sheer direct simplicity of it. Lovers of poetry owe a real debt to Mr Symons for having made accessible once more so surprising a store of lyrical beauty. But what strikes one most about these poets collectively is not their underlying unity but their diversity of aims and technique.

THE nineties for the purpose of a short literary survey cannot, of course, be limited to the strict decade. No sharp line of any sort separated them from the later eighties or from the earlier years of the next century, and these sixteen years or thereabouts during which I traversed the period of my own twenties were surely an era of justifiable excitement to one who had been brought up in a very literary home, where books of all sorts were regarded by the thirsty as a perpetual well-spring of pleasure. Not one atom of pedantry was permitted in that household, none of its members wanted to be learned or to improve their minds, they all read omnivorously because it afforded them the greatest pleasure to do so, and they all criticized with untempered frankness; they were all mad keen to write themselves and most of them were already hard at it. I cannot think of any epoch in the last hundred years and more of English literature in which there was appearing so much diverse and first-rate work which, to judge by its vitality today, is as likely to live as anything we know. Sufficient time has elapsed since then to have proved corrosive of the corruptible, and it is astonishing to find how secure so much of the output of those years appears to be. Or, to apply another test, time acts on sound work much as it does on the vintages of the grape, maturing and bringing out, if the juice be noble, the fuller savour of the sunshine in which the berries ripened, while if it is thin by nature, time only reveals its weakness and age its acidity. Though it sounds a paradoxical notion to suggest that a book once written can possibly change, there is a certain truth in it, for a book does change in relation to its age, and what was harsh when it was new, and what was hot and fiery with ideas to which the age was unaccustomed, mellows with time; there comes to it a ripening and a crudeness vanishes. Much of that vintage of the nineties has thus mellowed, and the harshness which some of the most experienced critics of the day detected then, has passed away, leaving a wine which everyone acknowledges to be great. There was

Thomas Hardy, for instance, who during the strict decade was producing some of his finest work. "Tess of the D'Urbervilles" came out then and "Jude the Obscure," but the reception the press gave to the latter was such that he resolved to write no more novels. True and ardent lovers of literature had been put off by the harshness of Tess when it came out, and failed to appreciate its stoic tenderness. Henry James for instance, found it "vile" and wondered at "good little Thomas Hardy." But anyone today who would refuse to his work the rank of *premier cru* merely shows that he has no palate for literature, for the time comes when an author almost ceases to be subject to the judgment of critics, and his work becomes a criterion of them. The critic who does not perceive that the Wessex novels are great literature (though they may not be of the type with which he is personally most in sympathy) demonstrates his own deficiency, and his belittling today of such a book as "Tess" merely belittles his own critical powers. He may not like the book, but that is hardly the point: he has to be able to recognize its qualities.

Though there was no-one else quite of the now-accepted stature of Hardy there were some very tall men. R. L. Stevenson was hard at work up to the day of his death in 1894, and to judge by the estimate of the thirty-five years that have followed, he must be placed at least on the threshold of the house of the immortals. But does he (so we asked ourselves then, and so we ask ourselves still) partake of the ageless quality which is part of immortality or of that bleak imperviousness to the vagaries of critical weather? There is, in all that he wrote, youth and the romance of youth which in life rendered him the most attractive of human beings and cast over his friends a glamour which they confess entirely dazzled them, but when it comes to the solemn business of canonization, the *advocatus diaboli* must always be given an impartial hearing, and he suggests that this sunny and courageous writer has too much of Mark Tapley in him to

join the band of those who, while realizing the bitter trage-
dies and sufferings which seem inseparable from human
existence, still turn eyes tender and unflinching on the grim
concert of woe and rapture and death. He fought his own
disabilities and won his way through them by dint of his
determination to disregard them and to continue, while an
ounce of strength remained in that frail body, absorbing himself in the work he loved. He would have no truck with his
tormentors, he would not do other than despise them, but
while rendering our utmost tribute to that admirable valour,
we feel somehow (says the devil's advocate) that he is like a
boy, who in spite of a severe toothache continues to bat in
some cricket match with unabated vigour and gaiety. Life
to him was a sea sown with Treasure Islands, and the joy of
adventure gilded the bleakness of every driving squall. He
had nothing but the breeziest contempt for his own infirmities, and would not suffer them to tarnish his brightness,
and thus it came about that he lacks that deep stark tenderness for the sorrows of the world which, without a touch of
sentimentality, runs vibrant through the work of the greatest.
That tragic chronicle had nothing to do with him; he turned
his back on it, lacking the ultimate courage of admitting
and facing it, and blew on his penny whistle. But then (so
we answer the devil's advocate) there came out after his
death that wonderful unfinished fragment "Weir of Hermis-
ton," and those who had seen in Stevenson only a charming
essayist of chased and hammered style, and a writer of books
of rollicking and brave adventure, wondered whether his
death had not robbed the world of a masterpiece of true
humanity greater by far than all that the gaiety of his life had
given them. He seemed to step within the house of the immortals.

Then there was Rudyard Kipling, with the gorgeous East
and the British Empire rattling like loose change in his
trouser pockets. He took out a coin and spun it, and with a
conjurer's patter he caught it and covered it up with a dish-

cloth, and when he raised the dishcloth the night of full moon in the jungle among questing beasts spread round us. Nothing the least like it had ever been seen before, and the critics, whose business it was to preserve the public from being taken in by flashing flummery, warned them that this young man from a newspaper office in India was nothing more than a journalist with no sense of style. One serious writer compared him to a potman in shirt sleeves serving out mugs of beer over the counter of a public-house, and Oscar Wilde said that he revealed life by superb flashes of vulgarity. But the public was far too busy swilling the heady stuff and looking at the life he so vulgarly manifested to care whether they ought to enjoy it or not. The critics speedily came into line, and those who had the dignity of English letters so much at heart perceived that if a writer conveyed with matchless economy precisely the impressions which he desired, there was something to be said for beer. . . Then there was Conrad, "full of blown sand and foam," and Meredith was writing right up to the end of our epoch, and Barrie, and George Moore, who attained that unique literary distinction of his not through decorated phrase and jewelled device but through the entire absence of such. Bernard Shaw had begun to send up those rockets of distress to call attention to his own unnoticed talents, and these were the first discharges of that unending pyrotechnical display which dazzles us still, and presently, before the epoch was over, he had come to the rescue of the English stage and taught theatre-goers that plays were not meant to amuse them but to make them think. H. G. Wells, to our infinite enjoyment, was coining romance out of science; and Henry James, over whose name I affectionately linger, was applying scientific methods to romance.

Hopefully but sometimes ruefully did this family of young literary aspirants try to follow him into his new manner, for there were no more fervent worshippers than they of his earlier work, "Roderick Hudson," "The Portrait of a Lady" and such clear gems of story-telling. He had been speaking to my mother about this change. "All my earlier work was subaqueous, subaqueous," he said, "Now I have got my head, such as it is, above the water, such as it was." One evening when he was staying with us at Addington, he and my father lingered, talking together after tea, while we all drifted away to our various occupations, and though we heard no mention of the contents of that conversation at the time, there came of in an odd and interesting sequel. For, years later, Henry James wrote to my brother, on the eve of the publication of the volume containing "The Turn of the Screw," to the effect that the story had been told him on that occasion by my father. It is among the grimmest stories of the world, and, as has been noticed by more accomplished critics of his work than I, it has a singular directness and clarity which are not characteristic of Henry James at that period: the development and growing grip of the two spectres which pervade it are singularly simple and uninvolved. Indeed the structure of it, apart from the actual style of the writing, is not like him, but if the bones and the blood of it were thus given him, the difference is easily accounted for: he followed definite lines. But the odd thing is that to all of us the story was absolutely new, and neither my mother nor my brother nor I had the faintest recollection of any tale of my father's which resembled it. The contents of the family story-box are usually fairly well known to the members of the circle, and it seems very improbable that we should all have forgotten so arresting a tale, if it was ever told us. The whole incident is difficult to unravel, but Henry James was quite definite that my father told him this story, though in outline only, as having been one which he had been told in his youth, and he repeats the history of it in the preface he wrote to it, when it was republished in his collected edition. It is possible, of course, that my father merely gave him the barest hint for the story, saying what a shocking tale could be fashioned on the plot of two low and evil intelligences of the dead possessing themselves of the minds of two innocent children. That may have been enough to wind up Henry James's subconscious mind and set it ticking away, so that all but the barest basic idea was his. But in view of the simplicity of the narration, I am inclined to think that the gradual and gruesome approach of Peter Quint, from the time when he was first seen at the top of the tower down to his final assault and the tragic rescue of the boy's soul, was given him also.

I did not know him personally in the pellucid "subaqueous" days of his early work, before he got his head above that crystal clearness and (to my mind) emerged into a fog. Enormously admiring, as I do, the beautiful direct simplicity of such a book as "Roderick Hudson," it is only natural that I should find his later methods dim and nebulous. But whether or not in the early days his speech had a directness corresponding to his work, I cannot imagine anything more fascinating or more wholly individual than the manner of his talk in the later days, which certainly had much in common with the processes though not the finished product of his later style. Nothing would be further from the truth than to say that he talked like a book, but most emphatically he talked like a book of his own in the making, just as he used to dictate it, with endless erasures of speech, till he got the exact and final form of his sentences. Just so in his talk he tried word after word to express the precise shade he required; he avoided, just as he avoided in his writing, any definite and final statement, if what he meant to say could be conveyed in a picturesque and allusive periphrasis. The most trivial incident thus became something rich and sumptuous with the hints of this cumulative treatment. I remember, as the simplest instance, how he described a call he paid at dusk on some neighbours at Rye, how he rang the bell and nothing happened, how he rang again and again waited, how at the end there came steps in the passage and the door was slowly opened, and there appeared in advance on the threshold, "something black, something canine." To have said a black dog, would not have done at all: he eschewed all such bald statements in these entrancing narrations, during which he involved himself in enormous and complicated sentences, all rolling and sonorous to the ear, as if he was composing aloud.

I was staying with him once at Lamb House in Rye in the quite early days of his ownership; a book of his was in progress, so every morning after breakfast he sequestered himself in the garden-room, and till lunch time perambulated between window and fireplace, dictating it to his typist in an intermittent rumble. Hour after hour on those hot June mornings, as one sat in the garden outside, the sound of his voice as he composed, punctuated by the clack of the type-writer came rolling out through the tassels of wistaria which overhung the open window. Then came a morning when he emerged some half hour before his usual time, and he took me by the arm and walked me up and down the lawn.

"An event has occurred today," he said, exactly as if he was still dictating, "which no doubt to you, fresh from your loud, your reverberating London, with its mosaic of multifarious movements and intensive interests, might seem justly and reasonably enough to be scarcely perceptible in all that hum and hurry and hubbub, but to me here in little Rye, tranquil and isolated little Rye, a silted up Cinque-port but now far from the sea and more readily accessible to bicyclists and pedestrians than to sea captains and smugglers; Rye, where, at the present moment, so happily, so blessedly I hold you trapped in my little corner, my angulus terrae — " On and on went the rich interminable sentence, shaped and modelled under his handling and piled with picturesque phrases which I can no longer recapture; and then I suppose (not having a typist to read it over to him) he despaired of ever struggling free of the python-coils of subordinate clauses and allusive parentheses, for he broke off short and said, "In point of fact, my dear Fred Benson,

I have finished my book." It took a long time to arrive at that succinct statement, but the progress towards it, though abandoned, was like some adventure in a gorgeous jungle, a tropical forest of interlaced verbiage. All other talk, when he was of the company, seemed thin and jejune by this elaborate discourse, to which one listened entranced by its humours and its decorations.

I must tell too, not only for the sake of his decorative speech, but on account of the catastrophic sequel in which I was miserably involved, the story of the two nimble and fashionable dames who had a thirst for the capture of celebrities. Both longed to add Henry James to their collections, and having ascertained that he was at Rye, they travelled down from London, rang the bell at Lamb House, and sent in their cards. He did not much relish these ruthless methods but, after all, they were in earnest, for they had come far in pursuit, and with much courtesy he showed them his house, refreshed them with tea, and took them for a stroll through the picturesque little town, guiding them to the church and the gun-garden, and the Ypres tower and the Elizabethan inn. The appearance of these two brilliant strangers in his company naturally aroused a deal of pleasant interest among his friends in Rye, and next day one of them called on him, bursting with laudable curiosity to know who these dazzling creatures were. She made an arch and pointed allusion to the two pretty ladies with whom she had seen him yesterday.

"Yes," he said, "I believe, indeed I noticed, that there were some faint traces of bygone beauty on the face of one of the two poor wantons. . . "

At least a couple of years afterwards this story was told me exactly as I have recounted it, without the names of the wantons, and one day, lunching at the house of one of the most enterprising hostesses in London, I recounted this little tale to her, for she was a friend of Henry James's and delighted in his rich speech. I noticed a slightly glazed expres-

sion in her eyes, as my artless narrative proceeded, and she
was not as much amused as I had hoped; in fact, as soon as
she had a chance, she changed the subject with strange
abruptness.   After lunch a friend of mine who had been sitting on the other side of her, came up to me and said, "What
on earth possessed you to tell her that ?   Don't you know
that she was one of them ?" . . .

Only once in my life, so I optimistically believe, have I
made a more desperate gaffe.   On that dismal occasion, my
intention, again of the most harmless kind, was to go to a
dance to which I had been bidden, at a house in Portman
Square.   I gave the right direction to my driver (this was
in the dark days of hansoms) and in due course drew up at
a door from which over the pavement there was spread a red
carpet.   My hostess, I had been told, was indisposed, and her
daughter whom I had never seen, was to take her place, and
upstairs I went.   Dances used to begin early in those days,
and it was about ten o'clock.   The door into the rooms on
the first floor was open, and by it was standing a young
woman (who of course was my hostess) with whom I cor-
dially shook hands and passed within.   Close inside was
standing Queen Alexandra, then Princess of Wales, but still
I felt no qualm, for why should she not be there ?   Probably
she had dined there.   I had just come from Greece, where
she had been also, and she asked me a few questions and we
had a pleasant little talk.   But by degrees this pleasant
little talk began to wear the aspect of a nightmare, for looking round the room I perceived that I was the only person
in it who was not of Royal birth.   There was a galaxy of
princes and princesses but not even an earl or a marquis to
bridge the bottomless gulf which lay between them and me.
In fact the house to which I had so gaily come was that of the
Duchess of Fife who had a big family party.   She had asked
a few people to come in afterwards, and that was why I was
passed upstairs as one of her guests.   But she had not asked
me. . . Let us get back to less appalling experiences.

ONCE in a letter to me Henry James described himself as being "ferociously literary." He could not have hit on an apter adverb, and this genial ferocity directed every sentence that came to his tongue, whether it was addressed to his typing secretary for transcription or to the tea-table. In the same letter he urged on me the paramount importance of acquiring a style: "It is by style we are saved," he wrote, and to this creed he was fanatically faithful, for (whether we like it or not) his later style is wholly individual. Nobody ever wrote like that before and though certain admirers of his have tried to do so since, the sad hash they have made of it proves how intensely individual it is. Yet, when all is said and done, style must still be regarded as the coach in which the story sits, and the wheels on which it rolls along. Its mission is to convey what the author has to tell us, and though more than shadow it is less than substance. Perhaps his style (that of his later manner) was the best, even as it was for him the only vehicle, that could carry the intricate mental processes of his characters, their subtleties and psychological finesse, their excursions into torturous labyrinths of thought, which it was his business to record, and these processes perhaps cannot be simply stated, since they are extremely complicated. But where was there ever a richer tapestry than that which he himself in earlier days had woven in his picture of Christina Light ? By it he managed to convey great complexities of motive with a triumphant lucidity, and we cannot help wondering whether so fine an artist gained anything by these enigmas and conundrums of his later work. His earlier stories before he found the later manner are conveyed in a style of admirable clarity, but though he was already master of that instrument he sought for a new literary quality in elaboration and allusiveness. Stevenson, in a somewhat similar way, who had, as his letters witness, a natural style full of grace and vivid simplicity, forged for himself with infinite pains one that was picturesque but artificial and highly decorated, finding in it the literary quality for which he and Henry James so eagerly sought.

All these masters, young and old, Hardy and Stevenson, Meredith and Kipling and Wells and James were writing in the early years of the nineties, and it is because of them that the epoch is so remarkable. Some were already past-masters of their craft, and had worked on through years of neglect and contempt, others were in the flush of their youthful vigour, but all were then producing first-rate and individual work, and all seem now to us to have won a secure seat in the serenity that reigns high above the gabble of the market-place, where the hawkers daily proclaim the fresh immortalities, frail as egg-shell and often addled, which they have detected over-night, and the money changers are loud in the courts of the temple. Books are, and have always been, subject to the whims of fashion, like a taste in millinery or earrings, but by degrees from among the mutable forms and popular fancies there emerges the incorruptible, even as when on southern beaches the dredged oysters rot away, and there glimmer the few rare pearls which are the ransom of a king.

It was in this epoch, for which "the nineties" is a convenient expression, that the long retarded spring burst into fullest summer and never has there been a more diverse flowering. Reaction against the old conventions had already done its work, and out of it there came the new force which reaction generates. It had its fakes and its hoaxes, ever so many of them, but spurious reputations are won in every decade and quietly lost in the next, and time has dealt with them as it will no doubt deal with those of today, whose possessors now broadcast each other's praises through groves of loud-speakers. Many volumes of prose and poetry held by the nineties to be pearls of great price have long ago crumbled into dust, and certain critics now point derision at the nineties because they thought that such were real. Such a method is unsound, for no age has ever been able to judge of its own output, since fashion and the whim of the moment invariably selects much that takes its fancy and ascribes to it immortality, but now we are far enough off from the nineties to be able to judge with some approach to true perspective, and those authors, whom I have named, seem to me to be just as admirable today as they did when with the enthusiasm of youth I hailed each new volume as containing some supreme and ultimate revelation of art. I confess that I was then tipsy with the joy of life and the horns of Elfland were continually blowing, but the ferment still stirs in me and the horns still blow with undiminished magic when I read "Tess of the D'Urbervilles" or the "Jungle Book."

It was not only because in those years I was of an age ripe but still fresh to enjoy the flowering of fine literature, that I account myself fortunate, but because these same years saw, glimmering from the darkness of the unknown, such manifestations of scientific marvels as no other short period can point to. Motor-cars and moving pictures, telephones and electric lighting, X-rays and other ultra-spectrum potencies, flying and submarines and the beginnings of wireless were all then in process of discovery and adaption to human uses. Today these have passed into the categories of conveniences which we take for granted, but then they were amazing and scarcely credible. Motoring was an adventure: well do I remember staying at a country house some ten miles from the nearest station, whose owner had one of those new-fangled spit-fires, a hoarse tremulous monster of most uncertain gait. Some half dozen guests of whom I was one were leaving at the end of our stay, and the ritual was as follows. A cart with our luggage started an hour and a half before the time of our train. Twenty minutes later the motor set off with those who were daring enough to trust themselves to it, and, a quarter of an hour after the motor had gone, a brake with a pair of fast horses, so that if the motor had broken down or become intractable it would pick up the derelicts and convey them to the station. On this occasion the motor behaved surprisingly well. In spite of its having to stop whenever a horse-drawn vehicle appeared on the road, while the terrified animal was led past it, it came within sight of the luggage-cart half a mile from the station, and arrived there a quarter of an hour before the brake. So those great strong horses had not gained on us at all !

Motors were then built with high wheels and engines much higher from the ground, and a very remarkable incident occurred in a motor-race from London to Brighton. Stoppages for engine-trouble, as well as for those due to approaching horse-drawn vehicles (whether from in front or from behind) were of course frequent, and the driver of one of these racers had gone round to the front of his car to tinker it up, for at present it was unable to go any further. He had forgotten to push back the starting lever, and so successful was his tinkering, that his car suddenly moved on again with a jerk, knocked him down and proceeded on its way. He was quite unhurt, for the blow had not been a severe one (more in the nature of a push) and he had passed in safety between the wheels. He picked himself up, spurted after his car, caught it up and sprang in, and so finished his course with joy. I wish I could add that he was an easy winner, but I am rather afraid that he only came in second.

Then there were very uneasy apprehensions concerning the X-ray, when it was known that it would penetrate solid substances, and timorous folk greatly feared that privacy was at an end (so like the general trend of the age !) if an unscrupulous scientist could direct his baleful ray on to the walls of your seeming-solid house and discover you in your bathroom. Again with what excitement we hurried down to Sandown race-course to see the French airman Louis Paulhan make, or attempt, his perilous ascent. Some would not go because they knew he would not leave the ground, others because they knew he would be killed. But even those most sceptical about the possibility of flying were much impressed by the ease with which his machine mounted, and described a wide circle above our heads amid the indignant protests of a rookery. But how they pooh-poohed the notion that perhaps some day an aeroplane would cross the English Channel without falling into the sea ! . . . A possible future in store for moving pictures was faintly adumbrated by the exhibition of the scene outside St Paul's Cathedral when Queen Victoria celebrated her Diamond Jubilee in the year 1897. It was certainly the west front of St Paul's that appeared on the screen, and, sure enough, visible through a blizzard of flashes and winks and large black dots, there did drive up an open landau with the Queen, easily recognizable, sitting on the back seat, with the Princess of Wales opposite her. They had parasols up, so the glimpse was only momentary. It was all very trying for the eyes, but it was worth a frontal headache to have beheld such a marvel.

The Queen was old now and her anxiety about the Boer War which broke out two years afterwards swiftly aged her. She thought from the beginning that neither her ministers nor the War Office sufficiently appreciated the seriousness of it, and she wanted a larger force to be dispatched, and the direction of it to be entrusted to other hands. Therein she showed once more that supreme soundness of judgment that had characterized her for the last sixty years. In December 1899 there occurred a very black week, when three disasters to the English arms at Stormberg, Magersfontein and Colenso proved how right she had been. She was very blind now of a morning until she had had her dose of belladonna in her eyes, and early on the day when the news of the third disaster arrived, dispatches had been brought up to her before she had her treatment. She dimly deciphered them, but, by some tragic mischance of her infirmity, as she peered at them, she entirely misread their import and thought that here was the tidings of an English victory. Down she went in high spirits and to her daughter who was breakfasting with her she told the good news, and said how rejoiced she was: this would make an excellent impression after the two previous disasters. But by this time the daily papers had come in and the Princess had to tell her that what she had

believed to be a victory was a third disaster, far more serious
than the others. She received that in silence: then after a
moment she said, "Now perhaps they will take my advice,
and send out Lord Roberts and Lord Kitchener, as I urged
them to do from the first." This time her ministers did take,
her advice, and she lived to see the relief of Ladysmith and
Mafeking.

THE dawn-bells of the new century had been a muffled peal by
reason of the war, but the death of Queen Victoria in Janu-
ary 1901 renewed in an intensified form the general sense of
instability. For the war was now practically over and
security returning, but the death of the Queen was a thing
which no-one could at once realize: the pillars of the house
were shaken. Only the aged could remember, as children,
the days before she had come to the throne; to everybody
else she was a cosmic institution and it was as if an essential wheel from the machine of the Empire and indeed of
the world, had slipped from its spindle. No-one could figure
the national existence without her. And then it quickly
became apparent that the reins, which she had so jealously
held, had passed into hands far more capable of masterly
coachmanship, and for the first time we had a sovereign
who knew Europe, and especially France, not through the
reports of ministers alone, or from the visits of foreign
monarchs to Windsor or from short polite conversations with
the President of the French Republic in the saloon of the
royal train as it took the Queen to the Riviera or to Florence,
but through the King's very sagacious personal observation. In these last years of her reign England was at the
very zenith of her unpopularity on the Continent: there
was scarcely a European nation which would not have rejoiced to see her in such difficulties as they all hoped might
have arisen out of the Boer War, and the Queen's illness and
death had been a welcome subject for ribald cartoons in the
foreign press. Though statesmen alluded majestically to

England's "splendid isolation" the isolation was far more apparent than the splendour. Something had to be done, and, largely on the initiative of King Edward and through his skilled handling there came about the grouping of Anglo-Russo-French interests. The King loved his Paris, he had the profoundest distrust of his nephew, the Emperor of Germany, and it seemed as if with these checks on the aggressive policies of the Central Powers, an era of peace and prosperity was assured. Cordialities abounded: there was a review of the French fleet by the young Czar on a very rough day off Brest, and the fact that he and the President of the Republic were exceedingly unwell together seemed a pledge of mutual sympathy in case of troubled times. The resources of Russia were held to be unlimited, her units of man power beyond the capacity of any census to compute, and though when she went forth to chastise Japan she resembled a tipsy moujik badly stung, hastily retreating from a nest of hornets, it was supposed, without a shred of evidence to support so satisfactory a theory, that she had pulled herself together and was busy with reforms and effective organization. She figured in the popular imagination as a Colossus of the East, in case the Central Empires attempted to break through the iron ring of battalions and ships of war which so conveniently enclosed them, just as in the early days of the European war she figured as the steam roller which would presently flatten out a road to Berlin. Metaphors failed to express the potential might of Russia, and England, no longer isolated but attached by ties of the strongest mutual interests to her and France, settled down to enjoy for a decade more a splendour of material prosperity which had never yet been equalled. Germany settled down too, to a decade of ship-building and militarism.

The nine years of King Edward's reign must thus be reckoned as the epilogue to the chronicles of the Victorian era. The death of the Queen and the Boer War had made a certain break between then and the nineties, but that was soon mended again, and all the movements of the nineties, the romance of its huge scientific progress, its literary splendours, its pageantries now glittering more brightly than ever, swept on again with an added momentum. The King was a king indeed, rejoicing in his sovereignty, revelling in the skilful discharge of the work to which he brought an unrivalled cosmopolitan experience, and possessing an enormous personal influence which he used to the utmost. He made his royal visits to foreign courts and at home his own blazed out again after the widowed quiescence of forty years. No longer was the monarch a craped sequestered presence, with a great prestige which nobody quite grasped, but a power apparent everywhere. The national prosperity was reflected in social brilliance, the fairy tales of science were fast crystallizing into sober facts of commerce and convenience, and throughout his reign no cloud of menace appeared above the glittering horizon of an empire which reached to the ends of the earth. Kings counted in those days, crowns were not being blown about like withered leaves in Vallombrosa, and one neice of his was Empress of all the Russias, another was the Queen of Spain, his daughter was Queen of Norway, his brothers-in-law were Kings of Denmark and of Greece. And his nephew was the German Emperor.

The year after King Edward's death there arose a cloud out of the sea at a place called Agadir, of which most people had never heard. It proved to be on the coast of Morocco. Thunder muttered out of the cloud, and there was a glimpse of the German Emperor clad in shining armour. Responsible level-headed people, ministers and diplomats, were believed to be very much disturbed at the incident, but most of our easy-going countrymen were only amused or irritated at this royal buffoon: he was a mere figure of fun, a preposterous Valentine, a Valkyrie with a fierce moustache. The Editor of a very well-known comic paper announced that a rough copy of a telegram had been brought to him, which had evidently been sent by King George to the Emperor: the King gave him a breezy warning that if this sort of thing occurred again he would jolly well blow all his ships out of the water. That reflected the general view: that was the stuff to give him, and it seemed to be justified, for no more was heard of this prank of the Emperor's. Was there any real danger lurking behind this tomfoolery ? Certainly not: it was one of his megalomaniac gestures, an imperial pirouette, and now he was immersed again in musical composition. A hymn to Aegir, wasn't it ? Aegir interested him far more than Agadir. So the whole affair was forgotten. It was one of those hoaxes, those false alarms with which the timorous scare themselves and of which astute stockbrokers take advantage.

THREE years passed in peace and plenty, and I was spending the month of June 1914 at Capri, that island of lotus-eating enchantment, on which all thought of what is going on outside its shores fades into a dream of things blurred and remote. Long mornings of swimming through translucent waters interspersed with baskings in the sun, siestas, fresh figs, walks up to the top of Monte Solaro, home-comings in the growing twilight, dinner under a vine pergola, games of piquet in the café, strollings on to the piazza at night to look at the lights of Naples lying like a string of diamonds along the main with the sultry glow of Vesuvius behind, fitted, to the exclusion of all exterior interests, the hours of the day. Sometimes a post brought in letters that must be answered, sometimes the daily paper contained topics from outside that claimed a momentary attention, but these were no more than the faintest jerks and twitches of reminder that one was still attached to the world that lay beyond the sea.

For several years I had been out here for some weeks of the summer, sharing the quarters of a friend of mine resident on the island, but now we had taken between us the lease of the Villa Cercola, and my footing in Capri was on a more permanent basis. The house stood a little above the town, white-

walled and cool and covered with morning glory and plum-
bago. A garden in terraces lay below it with a pergola above
the water cisterns, and a great stone pine whispered with the
noise of a far-off sea whenever there was the faintest breeze
astir.

I had been very busy (for Capri) with furnishings, for
the house was much bigger than Brooks's last habitation. I
had cupboards and tables and chairs carpentered for me out
of chestnut-wood, cushions must be stuffed, rugs laid down,
and linen and crockery and cutlery had been arriving from
Naples. I purposed, now that our joint occupation of the
Villa was accomplished, to spend three or four months of the
summer here every year, but during this June I began to
think I would go back to England early in July and return
again before the end of August, coming out by sea to Naples
and bringing with me an assortment of possessions from home.
My small house in London was more than replete, this Villa
Cercola needed far more furnishing, and I would make this
transformation of superfluities into necessities without delay.
I wanted more books and bookcases here, more tables and
chairs, a complete supply of summer clothes, pictures and a
piano, for now Italy was to be my home as well as England,
on my journeys to and fro I should be going ὄικοθεν ὄικαδε, and
thus at either end I should have that fine luxury of familiar
things about me. Besides, what an infinite saving of bag-
gage and bother and registration to start from one home
for sojourns of months at the other with no more impediment
than a suitcase for the journey. How immensely important
it all seemed !

We talked it over, Brooks and I, one morning on the beach
between bathes. He urged me not to break into the summer
by returning to England now. I could dispatch my cases
of effects from there when I went back in the autumn. He
said I could get along very well for the present with what
I had, and he promised to go across to Naples to receive them
and bestow them, so that when I arrived again next spring

they would all be in place. But there were other considerations as well, for the jerks and twitches which showed that I was in connection with the world outside the island had lately been tugging at me. I wanted to spend a week with my mother. I wanted to see certain people, who, I knew, would be in London during July. I wanted to visit one or two extremely pleasant houses where I had been bidden for week-ends, I wanted to play golf, and most particularly did I want to go to Baireuth for the second cycle of the festival, for which a ticket was waiting for me. It would be something of a rush (but how agreeable a one), and before the end of August I with my packing-cases would be back again for two more months in Capri before the summer was over. . . But it was time now to take to the sea again, for the tourist boat with trippers for the Blue Grotto had already passed, and that showed, in the absence of watches, that it was round about noon. Just one swim more then, kicking lazily through the tepid water: so clear was it and so steeped with sunshine that the white pebbles at the bottom gleamed like jewels seen through the faintest tinge of blue.

We dressed, and strolled slowly up the stony path between vineyards in the sunspeckled shade of the olives. Lizards basked on the walls, orange trees were in flower and fruit together, the berries of the red grapes were already flushed with colour and growing tight. The yards of the few cottages that we passed were gay with carnations grown in petroleum-tins, and there were friendly greetings for us as we went by. Almost I repented of my resolve to leave here next week (for already June was nearly over, today was the 29th) so foolish it seemed to break into the sequence of these summer days in the land which I loved. A couple of the days that I might spend thus would be passed in the baking heat of trains, the nights in a grimy little berth jolting along and shrieking through the midnight stations, and at the end I should arrive across a grey and sullen sea in the loud town by the Thames. After that the next six weeks would be mere scurry, though among people I loved and pursuits that I enjoyed, but why start scurrying when so blissful a quietude was mine now, burned brown from head to foot by baskings in the sun, blessed with so intelligent and sympathetic a house-mate and surrounded by all the loveliness of the enchanted island ? But, having talked of all the things I wanted to do, I felt the magnet pulling from the north, and when Brooks asked me finally, was it any use talking or did I really mean to go, I said that I did.

A little jingling victoria, its horse gay with a pheasant's feather stuck between its ears, was waiting for us when we emerged from the cobbled path between the vineyards on to the road, and it set us down at the piazza. The boat from Naples bringing papers and letters had already been in some time, and when we went into the post office the mail was sorted. There were a few letters and a copy of *The Times* for me, and we went on to the Villa Cercola on foot, stopping to buy an Italian paper. Brooks unfolded it as we sat at lunch, and skimmed the news.

"Hullo," he said, "An Archduke was assassinated yesterday. Franz Ferdinand."

"What an awful thing !" said I. "Who is he ? And where did it happen ?"

"He's the Emperor of Austria's heir," he said. "He was attending manœuvres at Serajevo."

"Never heard of it . . . I want to go up Monte Solaro after tea. Do come. Those tawny lilies should be in flower."

"Too hot," said he. "Besides, I must water the garden."

We separated after lunch for the usual siesta, and I found him poring over a big Atlas when I came yawning in for an early tea.

"Serajevo is the capital of Bosnia," he said.

"Serajevo ?" I asked. "Oh, yes, I remember. Bosnia is it ? I'm nearly as ignorant as I was before."

That was all: we did not allude to it again.

I GOT back to London during the first week of July. Apparently some folk, who had seen danger in the affair at Agadir three years before, had been apprehensive again as to what this murder of the Archduke might lead to. Austria had tried to prove the complicity of the Serbian government, and having failed to do that, had made some sort of appeal to Germany. But there the matter had stayed, and London did not much concern itself. Any disturbance of peace that might arise would be localized, and the last few weeks of the season were on. Since boyhood I had been native to that environment, and took it for granted, as part of the eternal order of things, that there should always be round me this sense of stability, of well-ordered and comfortable existence, which took no thought for the morrow except to make pleasant plans. So permanent a consciousness was scarcely analysible, for almost everything I knew was part of it. Work at my own profession, and music, and August in Scotland (or in this particular year at Baireuth), games and winter in the high Alps, and now for the future, summer in Capri were ingredients in it. Some friends had big houses in the country, others had small flats in London where was to be found frugality and affection and kindred interests. I had my house there, and my mother the home of her widowhood in Sussex, dear and dignified and always welcoming. It was of mellow red brick, seventeenth century, and was encompassed with garden and orchard and fields that sloped down to the stream that burrowed among the copses of the valley. . . But life was no affair of aimless drifting, there was keenness to work and to enjoy, and behind it all lay this conviction of complete and life-long security. That was quite outside conscious thought, even as, when sitting in a familiar room, we do not trouble ourselves about the foundations on which the house is built. Of course they can be trusted.

There was trouble in Ireland during that month of July, and there were threats of serious strikes. But Ireland was always giving trouble, and there had been strikes before now.

Who cared ? There were able and sensible men who looked after such sporadic frictions, and the duty of the reasonable citizen was to behave as usual. So I worked and played with immense enjoyment, and put little adhesive paper stars on the furniture I should soon take out to Capri, and spent week-ends in the country, and looked forward to Baireuth. There was a choice of routes: via Ostend and Cologne was one, but how about the Orient express to Munich ?

Up till the last week in July which I spent at my mother's house, this sense of security remained firm. Then came the first tremors of the solid earth, faint, but felt in the foundations of the house. Austria sent Serbia an ultimatum in which no free State could acquiesce, demanding her acceptance of it within forty-eight hours. It was followed by Russian preparations to mobilize and remonstrances from Berlin. Backwards and forwards flew the shuttle, weaving catastrophe, and at every passage of it the web of war grew on the clashing loom. Early in August the shirt of fire in which Europe was to burn for four years, was ready for the wearing, and the old order of secure prosperity, of which I have been speaking, smouldered into ash, and England will know it no more.

INDEX

ABERDEEN, Countess of, 86
Abergeldie Castle, 47
Acropolis, the, 30, 133
Aegina Marbles, 135
Aeroplanes, 285, 287
Aestheticism, 204, 223, 224
Agadir, 290-291, 295
Ailsa, Marchioness of, 86
Albert Hall, the, 106, 260, 261
Albert Memorial, 28
Albert, Prince Consort: character-
    istics, 4, 28, 87; as musician, 6,
    30, 105; family life, 31, 33, 77,
    87-88; and Wellington College,
    3, 4, 5, 7, 60; and the Peerage,
    27; and Balmoral, 30; the
    Queen's reliance on, 7, 28, 30, 32-
    33, 87; death, 4, 6, 7, 28, 32-33,
    86, 105
    Alfred Austin's poem, 168
    Mentioned, 14, 27, 47, 158
Albert Victor of Wales, Prince, 191
Alexander, George, 193, 194
Alexandra Feodorovna, Czarina,
    290
Alexandra, Queen, 136, 282; as
    Princess of Wales, 89, 90, 104,
    106, 140, 160-161, 287
America:
    Lady Henry Somerset's lecture
    tour in cause of Temperance, 82
    Oscar Wilde's lecture tour, 204,
    224, 225
Anglo-Israelitish Association, 266
Anglo-Russian-French entente, 288-
    289
Archaeology, 132, et seq.
Argyll, Duke of, 245
Arnold, Matthew, 241
Art, 29-30, 215 et seq.

Arthur, Prince (Duke of Con-
    naught), 7
Ashley, Lady Harriet, 80
Asquith, H. H., 163, 196
Athens, 132, 135 et seq.
    Athleticism in, 143-144
    Marathon race, 144
    National spirit in, 135, 142-143
    Olympic Games, the, 143
    See also Greece
Atholl, Duke of, 47
Austin, Alfred, 102, 166-170, 171
Austria:
    Archduke Franz Ferdinand, as-
    sassination of, 294-295
    Empress of, 113, 140-141
Aviation, 285, 286

BACCARAT scandal. See Tranby Croft
    affair
Baker, Miss Harriet, 40
Baker, Sir Thomas, 40, 49
Balliol Chapel, 129
Balmoral, 30
Balzac, Contes Drolatiques, 218
Barnby, 261
Barrett, Wilson, 219
Barrie, Sir James, 277
Battersea, Lord, 249
Beaconsfield, Lord, 63, 96, 102, 248;
    dictum on Queen Victoria, 24
Beardsley, Aubrey, 269-270, 271-273
Beaufort, Duchess of, 78-79
Beaufort, Duke of, 78-79
Bedford, Adeline Duchess of, 85
Bedford, Duke of, 84-85
Beerbohm, Max, 269, 270
Belgians, Leopold King of the, 31,
    87

297